Change and Promise

Change and Promise

Bilingual Deaf Education and Deaf Culture in Latin America

Barbara Gerner de García

Lodenir Becker Karnopp

Editors

Gallaudet University Press
Washington, DC

Gallaudet University Press
Washington, DC 20002

http://gupress.gallaudet.edu

Printed in the United States of America

Library of Congress Cataloging-in-Publication Data

Names: Gerner de García, Barbara, editor. | Karnopp, Lodenir Becker, editor.

Title: Change and promise: bilingual deaf education and deaf culture in Latin America / Barbara
   Gerner de García and Lodenir Becker Karnopp, editors.
Description: Washington, DC : Gallaudet University Press, [2016] | Includes index.
Identifiers: LCCN 2016026253 | ISBN 9781563686740 (hardcover : alk. paper)
Subjects: LCSH: Deaf–Latin America. | Deaf–Education–Latin America. | Education,
   Bilingual–Latin America.
Classification: LCC HV2580.5 .C43 2016 | DDC 371.91 / 2098–dc23
LC record available at https://lccn.loc.gov/2016026253

∞ This paper meets the requirements of ANSI/NISO Z39.48-1992 (Permanence of Paper).

Contents

Contributors

Verónica de la Paz Calderón
Instituto de la Sordera
Santiago, Chile

Fabiola Otárola Cornejo
Pontificia Universidad Católica
  de Valparaíso
Valparaíso, Chile

Miroslava Cruz-Aldrete
Universidad Autónoma del Estado
  de Morelos
Cuernavaca, Mexico

Barbara Gerner de García
Gallaudet University
Washington, DC

Ana María Morales García
Universidad Pedagógica Experimental
  Libertador
Instituto Pedagógico de Caracas
Caracas, Venezuela

José Ednilson Gomes de Souza, Jr.
Federal University of Santa Catarina
Florianopolis, SC, Brazil

Yolanda Mercedes Pérez Hernández
Universidad Pedagógica Experimental
  Libertador

Instituto Pedagógico de Caracas
Caracas, Venezuela

Lodenir Becker Karnopp
Department of Special Studies and
  Graduate Program in Education
Federal University of Rio Grande
  do Sul (UFRGS)
Porto Alegre, RS, Brazil

Madalena Klein
Department of Educational
  Foundations and Graduate Program in
  Education
Federal University of Pelotas
Pelotas, RS, Brazil

Cristina B. F. Lacerda
Federal University of São Carlos
Graduate Program in Special Education
São Carlos, S.P., Brazil

Juan Andrés Larrinaga
University of the Republic
Montevideo, Uruguay

Elizabeth M. Lockwood
CBM International Representative
  at the United Nations
New York, New York

Márcia Lise Lunardi-Lazzarin
Department of Special Education and
  Graduate Program in Education
Federal University of Santa Maria
Santa Maria, RS, Brazil

Mariana Martins
Portuguese Association of the Deaf
Lisbon, Portugal

Boris Fridman-Mintz
National School of Anthropology
  and History
Mexico City, Mexico

Maribel González Moraga
University of Bristol
Bristol, United Kingdom

Marta Morgado
CED Jacob Rodrigues Pereira,
Casa Pia de Lisboa
Lisbon, Portugal

Alex Giovanny Barreto Muñoz
Open and Distance National University
  (UNAD)
Bogotá, Colombia

Leonardo Peluso
University of the Republic
Montevideo, Uruguay

Gladis Perlin
Federal University of Santa Catarina
Florianopolis, SC, Brazil

Patrícia Luiza Ferreira Rezende
National Institute of the Deaf (INES)
Rio de Janeiro, Brazil

Carlos Skliar
Facultad Latinoamericana de Ciencias
  Sociales
Buenos Aires, Argentina

Miguel Ángel Villa-Rodríguez
Facultad de Estudios Superiores
  Zaragoza
Universidad Nacional Autónoma
  de México
Mexico City, Mexico

Silvana Veinberg
Founder and Director
Canales, Creciendo en Señas
Buenos Aires, Argentina

Preface

Carlos Skliar

This significant book offers us a map of the situation of bilingual education for deaf children in Latin America over the last 30 years, as well as an analysis of its ethical strengths, linguistic and educational purposes, and political ambiguities. What is presented in this book is a question that has been constantly reiterated to the point of becoming redundant but which contains the entire dilemma of our world. That is, the political, economic, social, media, and technological dilemmas that, despite universal proclamations of equality, equity, and quality, keep producing more inequalities, inequities, and educational reforms of dubious significance. The following two questions, which may seem unchanging, were, are, and will remain as palpable as they are profound.

Is there still room for an education aimed at specific individuals (and their needs) that is not simply based on a theoretical or generic idea of a person? And what are the specific, unique features that make deaf education a controversial issue whose processes and outcomes involve claims and denials back and forth to the extent that it has created a discontinuity, a disruption, a break, a chasm between Deaf children, the education community, public policies, educational institutions and the Deaf community? To state it in a straightforward way: What is it that keeps deaf education from producing absolutely, for the length and breadth of the continent, a defined identity in public policy that leads to a genuine difference in the meaning and organization of educational structures? And furthermore: Is there room to think about bilingual education for Deaf children without the irrational pressure to "normalize" within a stagnant and stale debate that opposes the language of "the other" (recognizing difference) and proposes the language of "we," in the context of legal discourse in a push towards educational inclusion?

A number of years have passed in Latin American countries since the first models of bilingual deaf education were made concrete in the 1980s, particularly in Venezuela and Uruguay. It seems incredible that there are continued demands that ask nothing more than to transform deaf education, which in Latin America exists as a kind of dispersed geography. While there are intense illuminated nuclei (Venezuela,

Uruguay, and others), there are also arid desert landscapes where bilingual deaf education remains elusive.

One may note the contrast between advocacy of the need for early access to their (sign) language and the tremendous problems of access for the youngest Deaf children to the appropriate language environment. On the one hand, we see awareness of the need for comprehensive education, and, on the other hand, the immense difficulties in implementing an education that includes, at a minimum, wide-ranging materials and exemplars. We see the belief in the transcendental role played by Deaf adults in the education of Deaf children and the insufficient development of training programs to prepare them for this role. Lastly, we hear all the rhetoric about providing a comprehensive educational path for Deaf individuals, yet we know an insignificant number of Deaf students attend secondary schools and an even lower number attend higher education programs.

It should be clear, judging by all that has been accomplished to date and the richness and depth of the research and theoretical chapters in this book, that deaf education cannot be reduced to a quandary of optimism or pessimism. I would propose that it is a matter of public policy or, rather, the public nature of a policy whose tendency towards medicalization and pathologizing of childhood and of universal inclusion (in schools) in recent decades has resulted in nothing less than the total fragmentation or "atomization" of Deaf people, as if they were individuals who can cope in isolation or be left to their families, neighborhoods, cities, regions, and so on.

Precisely therein lies the essential nature of the public, of the ordinary, what it is for everyone is also for each and every one. No one remains a prisoner of his own fate. That fate depends on how we are born, the family we have, the schools available, the governments in place, and what the law provides or does not provide for the special situations of certain people. It is well known that this kind of "naturalization" of education, the idea that continues to insist on a "natural order of life and of things," has produced more marginalization of the already marginalized, more impoverishment of the impoverished, more exclusion of the excluded, and more violence in already violent contexts. Public policy must be aimed at those twisting paths that are not spontaneous or natural but are a kind of social, economic, and political artifice.

Therefore, read this book through the lens of the public and not the political, where everything has been aimed with respect to the need to change the course of those individuals who come into the world under conditions that, even today, are unanticipated and considered imperfect. Indeed, all those societies that still vacillate between modernity and modernism, which have not yet gone beyond the excess of legal reason, insist on confusing charity and essential public policy with public welfare and supervision. They maintain an image of certain people as fragile or ill, an "otherness" that should be redirected onto the path of normality, for only then can they become (hypothetical) full citizens.

On the whole, this promise of redemption has not been fulfilled and perhaps is impossible to realize, beyond the supposed arguments of progress that govern an educational idea. The promise is unenforceable because it exists within a vision of achieving a utopia of equality, at the end of the educational process, while beginning with and continuing inequality, consciously or not. And equality cannot be achieved in the education of deaf children for the very simple reason that it entails a huge philosophical dilemma. For infants, for any infant, for children, for any child, any postponement of exposure to language is always too late.

Let's consider the issue of delaying, that is, of putting off, the acquisition and use of a language. This is not only dangerous it is criminal, if I may take the substantial risk of using such a strong term. It is criminal because it kills or anesthetizes the individual's existence, transforming it into a kind of impediment, not only to the possession of language but also for all that language contributes to human life—that is, invention, creativity, storytelling, fiction, community life, exposure to the world, writing, and reading—in short, what makes a person a human.

This postponement of access to language shows how the controversies of cochlear implants and inclusive education have changed the state of the art. They have opened a Manichaean discussion about the language acquisition of deaf children beyond what have been the effects and results of this dual interpretation of public policy. At least four phenomena that have been unidentified and deemed inconceivable until recently must be evaluated thoroughly in the coming years. These are: (1) fewer deaf children are using sign language around the world; (2) fewer Deaf adults participate in the Deaf community; (3) there are fewer cultural and educational encounters between deaf children and Deaf adults; and (4) a majority of residential and special schools for deaf students have been closed or redesigned as shared education facilities.

If we measure these consequences as "natural," we obscure or hide an essential discussion: what about those vast numbers of deaf children who are cut off from these two "trends": cochlear implants and inclusive education? But additionally, what happens to those deaf children and youth who still access this form of politics, who get cochlear implants without the required follow-up or documentation of their language development, and who don't thrive in inclusive educational programs and public schools? Is there a deaf population whose inexorable destiny it is to be educationally impoverished and another, on the contrary, to be "normalized" into the hearing world?

The questions are obvious and their essential radicalism and tension should be sustained. This is not merely a technical discussion but principally the reflection of a way of understanding the position and ethical exposition of education. That is, we have a responsibility to provide answers now; we cannot and should not delay any further.

And this is where bilingual deaf education persists with all its richness and impact. This proposal for bilingual deaf education has never been restrictive at its core but, on the contrary, emerges as a serious effort to broaden and enrich the context of accessible language. It goes beyond the customary disputes between the use of sign language or the oral modalities and considers a comprehensive educational approach. When the "public" becomes political, the "bad luck" (being different) becomes good luck, offering thousands of deaf children the opportunity to enter the world and stay in it, with their uniqueness, without the need to be told by specialists that they are incapable, sick, weak, or disabled.

Let us continue, then, with a second point: the unfolding of the unfulfilled or unenforceable promise. All education takes the form of a conversation about what to do with the world and what to do with us and with others in the world. In other words, all pedagogy is a conversation, and clearly no pedagogy is possible without conversation. We can say that the entire book presented here reveals the issue in a clear, raw way, either its affirmation or its negation. Despite efforts realized in order to open up spaces for discussion, there is much that has been left undone. Indeed, one of the most exasperating indications in deaf education, since time immemorial, has been the absolute lack of discussion in educational spaces, particularly, about the impossibility of teaching deaf children if they had not first mastered a language. The result has been a view that deaf children are defective. Bilingual education arose to put an end to this unacceptable situation and created the bridges necessary to reverse it. It was understood that educating teachers to be fluent in sign language was a prerequisite, as were programs designed to train interpreters for the classroom and the significantly increased presence of Deaf adults (although sometimes merely as assistants and other times as educators). Thus, deaf schools that abandoned the clinical mode and its insistence on the exclusive use of the oral language were discovering that behind the debate about languages was the urgent need for educating deaf students.

There is no doubt that this book is a serious invitation, in capital letters, to consider everything that has been done so far. It is also a profound study that helps reflect on the changes suffered in deaf education with the passage of time together with changes in the world. However, the question as to the fate of bilingual deaf education remains tense, unalterable, and ethically concerned with the history of a linguistic community and its presence and the realization that certain individuals cannot and should not be abandoned to their own fate.

Change and Promise

1

A Panoramic View of Bilingual Deaf Education in Latin America

Barbara Gerner de García and
Lodenir Becker Karnopp

The themes of bilingual deaf education, sign language, and Deaf movements are entwined and interrelated throughout Deaf history. Historically, Deaf schools have been the incubators for national sign languages and Deaf culture. These schools have served as the springboards for Deaf communities and the development of Deaf leaders. The first Deaf public school in the world was the Paris institution established by Abbé de l'Epée in 1754, now known as the Institut National de Jeunes Sourds de Paris. Laurent Clerc, a pupil and later teacher at the Paris school, changed the history of the American Deaf community when he accompanied Thomas Gallaudet to Hartford, Connecticut, to found the American School for the Deaf in 1817 (Lane, 1984).

The Escuela Anne Sullivan, founded in Chile in 1852 and directed by an Italian, Eliseo Schieroni, was the first Deaf school in Latin America. In Spanish-speaking countries, deaf education was heavily influenced by oral education methods used in Spain, and Spanish religious orders (primarily nuns) ran many of these institutions. Deaf education in Latin America continued to emphasize oral methods into the 1970s (General Secretariat, 2008).

A French Deaf educator, Eduard Huet, initiated the establishment of the first Deaf school in Brazil, the second in South America. He presented a report to Emperor Dom Pedro II of Brazil, which resulted in Law 839 in 1857. This law established the Institute Imperial dos Sordos-Mudos (IISM, Imperial Institute of the Deaf and Dumb) in Rio de Janeiro. The school offered basic literacy instruction and vocational education for boys aged 7–14 (Soares, 1999). The purpose of the IISM was to provide Deaf boys with training that would result in gainful employment. The institute was founded at a time when the royal court was extending education throughout Brazil in order to unify the national language (Portuguese), propagate the Catholic faith, and teach reading and writing (Pinto, 2007).

In too many Latin American countries, education of Deaf children was not a priority for many years. In the Dominican Republic, before the establishment of a national school in 1967, Deaf children and adults were scattered across neighborhoods of the capital city of Santo Domingo and over the entire country (Gerner de García, 1990, 2001). In the 1980s, a Deaf community began to emerge in the capital. The national school brought together Deaf children who, by the 1980s, were forming the first generation of Deaf leaders.

While the histories of de l'Epée and Clerc are well documented, the histories of the development of deaf education, sign language, and Deaf culture in Latin America are not as accessible. To a great extent, this is due to the fact that much of the material, which is only available in Spanish and Portuguese, has not been collected to create a coherent history of the region. There are some publications in English concerning Latin American deaf education, culture, and language in academic journals and books. These are primarily focused on sign linguistics and research on Deaf children's language and literacy development. Few Latin American scholarly and Deaf community publications are available in English. The result is that an erroneous stereotype of deaf education and Deaf communities in Latin America as hopelessly backward is widespread in the English-speaking world. Mistakenly, too few educators and academics in the United States, Canada, and Europe consider that Latin America has anything to teach us. In this chapter, we will describe the growth of bilingual deaf education through three case studies—Brazil, Columbia, and Chile. Each country has followed a different path, with lessons learned and important milestones made. They provide a panorama of the development of bilingual deaf education in Latin America.

THE CHANGING LANDSCAPE OF DEAF EDUCATION

In the past three decades, the education of Deaf children, and the lives of Deaf people worldwide have changed considerably. The United Nations Educational, Scientific and Cultural Organization (UNESCO) Salamanca Statement of 1994 propelled the inclusion of all children with disabilities in general education, asserting their right to attend neighborhood schools (Centre for Studies on Inclusive Education, 2013). These policies have transformed the education of Deaf children, who now are more likely to be educated in classrooms alongside hearing children than in Deaf schools.

In the 1980s, bilingual deaf education was in very preliminary stages in the United States (Strong, 1988). Although bilingual education for Deaf children has been widely discussed for three decades, it is still not widespread in the United States. Currently, approximately 75% of Deaf and hard of hearing children in the United States are in general education settings, mainstreamed full or part-time, or in a self-contained classroom. The remaining Deaf students, about 24% in 2009–2010, are found in residential or state Deaf schools, Deaf day schools, and center programs (Gallaudet Research Institute, 2011). There are teacher preparation programs in the United States focused on preparing teachers for bilingual deaf education, including Gallaudet University in Washington, DC, Lamar University in Beaumont, Texas, University of California San Diego, and McDaniel College in Westminster, Maryland. Other teacher preparation programs address bilingual deaf education among other models.

The beginning of discussions and implementation of bilingual deaf education in the United States in the 1980s coincided with the first pediatric cochlear implants. The House Institute in California pioneered implants in the United States beginning in 1980. By 1986, centers in the United States and Australia began clinical trials of pediatric implants (Christiansen & Leigh, 2002; Eisenberg & Johnson, 2008). Implementation of implantation of children two years and older was approved in the United States by the FDA in 1989, and as of 2002, profoundly Deaf children as young as 12 months may be implanted. In certain cases, children younger than 12 months are eligible (NIH Fact Sheets, 2013; Papsin & Gordon, 2007).

Thus, deaf education looks very different in the twenty-first century due to the policies of inclusion and the growing number of children with cochlear implants. Many residential Deaf schools in the United States and other countries have closed. Internationally, the increase in the use of cochlear implants has led to a sharp drop in the use of sign language by Deaf children in many countries (e.g., Australia; see Johnston, 2006). In some countries (e.g., New Zealand, Ireland, Brazil), cochlear implants are paid for by governments, most likely in the hope this will reduce future costs of education and rehabilitation (Irish Health, 2015; Lodi, 2013; Sampaio, Araújo, & Oliveira, 2011). In the United States, the widespread use of cochlear implants and the shrinking number of residential schools have had a significant impact on the use of American Sign Language (ASL) and have limited the implementation of bilingual deaf education.

These developments have also had an impact in Latin America. Some countries, such as Costa Rica, provide cochlear implants under the national health insurance at no cost to families (Ureña Garcia, 2013). In Brazil, cochlear implants are extensively used, and as a result, there are fewer Deaf children using sign language. There are many Deaf children and adults in Latin America marginalized by poverty who live in poor urban areas or rural areas far from schools, hospitals, and clinics. These Deaf children are less likely to go to a Deaf school or have cochlear implants. For example, in Guatemala, implanting Deaf children may not be an option if the child has limited or no access to the follow-up services required after implantation. Many Deaf children in Guatemala live far from hospitals and clinics in the capital Guatemala City, and/or their families cannot afford the follow-up services needed (P. Castellaños, personal communication, August 2006).

Bilingual Deaf Education as a Political Issue

Internationally, the right to bilingual education was already under discussion in the 1950s. A 1951 UNESCO conference guaranteed the right to bilingual education by recognizing the right of children who use a language other than the dominant language to be educated in their native language (Swadesh, 1951). Extending this concept of the right to be educated in one's own language, it becomes clear that bilingual deaf education substantiates the political recognition of Deafness as a difference and that bilingual deaf education is not just a decision of methodology and pedagogy but also one that must be politically constructed as sociolinguistically justified (Skliar, 1999a).

In calling for bilingual education, it is critical to go beyond merely considering pedagogical approaches when providing education in two languages. It is necessary to also focus on the larger context of the politics of bilingual education. Bilingual education is not simply bilingual schooling—that is, the use of two languages of instruction. Bilingual education includes the historic, cultural, and political contexts of providing education using the primary language of the children being taught, while giving them access to, and teaching them the majority language. Thus in the implementation of bilingual deaf education, it is important to consider how the concept of Deafness is being constructed within projects (Skliar, 1999a).

What are the different historical and cultural contexts that should be considered? Bilingual deaf education challenges the status quo by elevating sign language to the same level as the spoken/written language used in schools. Bilingual deaf education requires educators who are fluent in the sign languages used by the Deaf community. This is turn requires the incorporation of fluent signers, primarily Deaf adults, and consideration of the status of those Deaf adults. Will they be teachers? Assistants? Are there legal or educational barriers that limit the use of Deaf teachers, and how do we work to overcome these? In the case studies included in this chapter, these and other questions will be considered.

Bilingual Deaf Education in Latin America

Latin America has been a stronghold of oral deaf education for decades, even longer than oral education dominated the schooling of Deaf children in the United States. Because of the shared language, as well as history, Latin American Deaf schools turned to Spain for support. Spain remained under the "oral decree" of the 1880 Congress of Milan until 1970, when a new law required that all children with special needs, except the most severely disabled, be educated in regular schools. In 1982 in Spain, the Law for the Social Integration of the Handicapped (Ley de Integración Social del Minusválido, LISMI) resulted in the inclusion of virtually all Deaf children (European Agency for Special Needs and Inclusive Education, 2009). The law was implemented in 1985, and as a result, many Deaf schools closed over the next eight years. It wasn't until 1995, when the use of sign language and training of teachers in sign language was revived, that Deaf children in Spain had access to bilingual education (Fernández-Viader & Fuentes, 2004). Spain was late to make the shift to the incorporation of sign language in deaf education.

Gallaudet University had some influence in deaf education in Latin America through its PROGRESO center established in 1981 in Costa Rica (Novitsky & Eastman, 1991). The PROGRESO center focused primarily on countries in Central America, and Americans influenced the sign language. James Woodward (1991) describes the existence of an indigenous Costa Rican sign language and a new one, which was heavily influenced by ASL. However, while Total Communication had some influence in Central America, it did not really make inroads into South America.

In the late 1980s, the Universidad de los Andes (ULA) in Merida, Venezuela, became a center for sign language research. The Venezuelan Ministry of Education realized the need for research on Venezuelan Sign Language (LSV) in order to realize their goals for providing bilingual education for Deaf children (Perez, 2005). Two linguists in ULA's Department of Linguistics, Alejandro Oviedo and Lourdes Pietrosemoli, became active in documenting the sign language. There were also linguists and proponents of bilingual deaf education working in Colombia, Uruguay, Argentina, and Brazil.

At this time in the early 1990s, an ad hoc group of researchers, academics, and educators began a biennial conference, the Congreso Latinoamericano de Educación Bilingüe para Sordos (Latin American Congress on Bilingual Education of the Deaf). The congress is held about every two years in a different Latin American country. Although there is an organizing committee as well as a scientific committee to develop the program, there is neither a central repository of conference proceedings nor a permanent website. Congresses have been held in Argentina (1992), Brazil (1994, 1999), Chile (2001, 2010), Colombia (1997), Costa Rica (2008), Cuba (2005), Mexico (2003, 2015), Peru (2012), and Venezuela (1996) (Personal communication, A. Lodi, December 14, 2015). The most recent congress, the twelfth, was held in October 2015 in Monterrey, Mexico (Instituto para el Desarollo Integral del Sordo, 2015). These congresses have been a positive force in promoting discussion, sharing research, and disseminating information on bilingual deaf education in Latin America.

The 1990s saw the emergence of publications in Latin America investigating the theme of bilingual deaf education. The fifth congress in Porto Alegre, Brazil, in April 1999 was by far the largest and most successful of the congresses. It resulted in a two-volume collection *Atualidade da Educação Bilíngüe para Surdos* (The Current Situation of Bilingual Education for the Deaf) (Skliar, 1999a, 1999b). At the congress, the Brazilian Deaf community released a document titled *Que educação nós surdos queremos* (Deaf Education: What We Deaf Want) (FENEIS, 1999). The tone of the discussion during the 1999 congress in Porto Alegre was a proposal for bilingual education based on opposition to oralist educational practices and hege-monic discourses. This congress marked the political recognition of Deafness as a difference, causing an epistemological shift in Latin America as to how Deaf people were treated and narrated, shifting from "Deaf as handicapped" to Deaf people as a linguistic minority (Skliar, 1999a, 1999b).

As noted earlier, bilingual deaf education occupies a political space that includes broader educational policy. Policy must address political topics, including the repre-sentations of Deaf people and sign language, visibility of Deaf culture, connections between schools and the Deaf community, the control mechanisms that silence those who are different, the denial of multiple Deaf identities, and the diversity of the Deaf community. Equally important is the need to train teachers, sign language interpret-ers, and other professionals for these bilingual schools (Skliar, 1999a, 1999b).

The Case of Brazil: A History of Deaf Education

In 1957, the Imperial Institute of Deaf Mutes (IISM) changed its name to the National Institute of the Deaf (Instituto Nacional de Educação de Surdos, INES). In 2012, INES celebrated 155 years of providing deaf education (Instituto Nacional de Educação de Surdos, 2014). The Concordia Special School in Porto Alegre, Brazil, in 1985 was the first Deaf school in Brazil, and possibly all of Latin America, to provide full secondary education for Deaf students. The private Lutheran school was founded in 1966 by Dr. Carlos Martim Warth and his wife, Naomi Warth, who stud-ied at the Central Institute for the Deaf in St. Louis, Missouri. The school embraced signing and Total Communication in 1980 (after Naomi Warth visited Gallaudet University in 1976–1977), but it is currently a bilingual school. For years, it served as a model school for teachers of Deaf students who came from all over Latin America for training. Since 1996, the school has been administered by the Lutheran University of Brazil (ULBRA) (Colégio Especial Concórdia, n.d.; Raymann, n.d.).

Brazil is the largest country in South America with numerous Deaf schools. Since the 1990s, the national Ministry of Education has strongly pushed for the inclusion of Deaf children in regular education (Ministry of Education, 2008). Many of the existing Deaf schools are in urban areas, leaving rural children with limited choices. In cities such as São Paulo, one of the most populous cities in the world, there are large Deaf schools, but it is common knowledge that there are many more Deaf chil-dren who are not being educated. Currently, in a push back against a national policy of inclusion, there are calls for São Paulo educational policy to establish bilingual deaf education, rather than continue the relentless push towards inclusion (Lacerda, Albres, & Drago, 2013).

Since the 1980s, in Brazil, the primary issues discussed have been: (a) to gain legal recognition of Brazilian Sign Language (Libras), (b) to ensure access of Deaf children to sign language in primary and secondary education (ages 4–17), and (c) to foster epistemological change that recognizes Deaf people as a linguistic minority. Thanks to the political mobilization of the Deaf community, the legal recognition of Libras has been secured. Organizations such as the Federação Nacional de Educação e Integração dos Surdos (National Federation of Education and Integration of the Deaf [FENEIS]) have worked to strengthen the Deaf community. Their efforts have focused on the recognition of Libras, the ongoing provision of sign language courses, and the training of sign language instructors, interpreters, and bilingual teachers. Additionally these organizations have produced various publications, as well as videos in Libras, which give visibility to the political agenda of the Deaf community, present ways of being Deaf and mark milestones of the Deaf community (Lodi, 2013; Thoma & Lopes, 2005).

In Brazil, deaf education was long dominated by clinical practices that resulted in generations of Deaf people without access to a sign language, who failed to progress educationally, with low social expectations and fragmented knowledge. These practices have resulted in an educational gap between general education and deaf education. The Brazilian Deaf community has mobilized to confront these dismal outcomes, building an agenda that transforms societal views of Deaf people and sign language and demonstrating their strong opposition to the colonizing discourses of oralism. They have debated the pedagogical implications of acting as an educational interpreter, methodologies for teaching Portuguese to Deaf people, assessment and curriculum, how to best reshape linguistically appropriate educational spaces, and how to enhance learning and the use of sign language in school.

In recent years following official recognition of Libras, institutions of higher education have expanded the training of bilingual educators and sign language interpreters. The Federal University of Santa Catarina (UFSC/MEC) has pioneered undergraduate courses in Libras since 2006 through online education and increased the training of teachers and sign language interpreters. Bilingual deaf education has steadily gained support in Brazil. Work in the 1990s laid the ground for official recognition of Libras, and the 2005 decree for action on bilingual deaf education, as well as the publication and dissemination of research on sign language and deaf education, advanced the conversation. Another factor that has given more visibility to Libras and the struggles of the Brazilian Deaf movement is cultural production in Libras of narratives, stories, and poems. These are disseminated via VHS, CD/DVDs, and the Internet (e.g., YouTube), creating representations and a literature by and about Deaf people (Karnopp, Klein, & Lunardi-Lazzarin, 2011).

Political recognition of linguistic and cultural difference of Deaf communities allowed debates on bilingual education policy beyond the linguistic dimension, giving rise to complications concerning curriculum and the language of instruction. Consequently, publications began to emerge focused on curriculum, assessment, literacy, Deaf participation in policy decisions, as well as Portuguese language texts considering the experiences of Deaf people with usage of sign language and school practices related to literacy in Portuguese (Karnopp & Klein, 2007; Lacerda & Lodi, 2008; Pereira, 2005; Skliar, 1999a; Souza, 1998; Thoma & Lopes, 2005).

Beginning in the 1990s, Deaf students began attending Brazilian universities with the support of interpreters, seeking higher education opportunities. Some universities began to provide interpreters for the university entrance tests (vestibular) and in classrooms. This mobilized the Deaf community and universities to increase the supply and accessibility of interpreters for Deaf people and services for people with disabilities. Admission of Deaf students into graduate programs also began in the 1990s, and Gladis Perlin was the first Deaf person to complete a master's degree in Education in 1998 and the first Brazilian Deaf woman to earn a doctorate in 2003 (Perlin, 1998, 2003). The Federal University of Rio Grande do Sul (UFRGS) and UFSC, among others, are active in producing Deaf graduates with doctorates.

With a growing group of Deaf people with doctorates working in universities and the strong social profile of Deaf movements and organizations, Brazil is a model for mobilizing to change laws, advocating for the needs of Deaf children, and building a strong social movement to improve life for Deaf children and Deaf adults in the country.

Deaf Education in Colombia

Like other Latin America countries, Colombia has shifted its understanding of Deafness from following oralism to considering bilingual education models since the late 1980s. Colombia is a country with regions that have different political histories and parties as well as cultural differences. These differences may explain the diversity of sign language and the marked differences between the development of educational models in each of the regions (M. B. Rios, personal communication, November 18, 2015).

Colombia preceded its neighbor Venezuela in opening its first Deaf school in 1923 (Ramírez & Castañeda, 2003) preceding Venezuela's opening of the Instituto Venezolano de Ciegos y Sordomudos (the Venezuelan Institute for the Blind and Deaf) in 1936 in Caracas (Oviedo, 2003). The first Deaf institutions in Colombia were established by religious orders, including the congregation of the Sacred Heart communities. The first institution for Deaf children and youth was the Instituto Francisco Luis Hernández in Medellín (Antioquia), which also educated blind children. In the following year, 1924, the Instituto Nuestra Señora de la Sabiduría (Institute of Our Lady of Wisdom) opened in Bogotá (Pardo, 2000; Ramírez & Castañeda, 2003; Vicente, 2011). These institutions used the oralist methodology promoted in France and Spain, the countries of origin of the religious orders involved in deaf education (Ramírez & Castañeda, 2003). Despite the educational emphasis on spoken language, sign language flourished wherever Deaf people gathered.

The 1970s saw the creation of the Division of Special Education within the national Ministry of Education. At that time, Instituto Nacional de Sordos (National Institute for the Deaf [INSOR]) and Instituto Nacional de Ciegos (National Institute for the Blind [INCI]) were moved from the Ministry of Health to the Ministry of Education. Oral education continued to dominate deaf education. A minority of Deaf students made it through the oral system, while the majority barely finished primary education or received no education at all (Pardo, 2000).

With the formation of the National Federation of the Deaf of Colombia (FENASCOL) in 1984, the Deaf community claimed Colombian Sign Language (LSC) and demanded greater quality in deaf education (Moneada, 2005; Vicente, 2011). It was at this time that Total Communication methodologies were beginning to be introduced, and a breach in the wall of pure oralism was made (Ramírez & Castaneda, 2003).

The new national constitution in 1991 recognized the ethnic and cultural diversity of the country. Acknowledgment of the linguistic diversity in the country lead to consideration of bilingual education. This in turn paved the way for the adoption of Law 324, which states that the LSC is the natural language of Deaf people in the country. Following this recognition of LSC in 1996, bilingual deaf education and interpreting services were subsequently regulated by Decree 2369 of 1997.

The major political changes of the 1990s had consequences in the field of deaf education, when the first proposals for bilingual deaf education emerged (Moneada, 2005; Ramírez & Castañeda, 2003). Sweden, and other Scandinavian countries, and Venezuela were the models of bilingual deaf education that they emulated (Ramírez & Castañeda, 2003). The first school to use LSC was Colegio Nuevo Mundo, which opened in 1992. In 1994, INSOR began its bilingual education project focused on Deaf children under age five (Ramírez, 1998).

These legal developments of the 1990s were related to the demands promoted by FENASCOL research and the creation and development of INSOR under the Ministry of Education. Among its responsibilities, INSOR is responsible for providing guidelines for the implementation of the bilingual model for Deaf people in the organization country.

Proposals for bilingual education and projects have been described by a number of researchers and practitioners, including Paulina Ramírez (1998), Lionel Tovar (1998), Eliana Moneada (2005), and INSOR (1998, 2008), among others. Currently in Colombia, bilingual education includes programs at the preschool (up to age five) and primary level (grades 1 to 5). In Basic Secondary, grades 6 to 9, students are either in a Deaf school or in a program for Deaf students within a regular (hearing) school. In rural areas with small populations, Deaf students may be in a multi-graded classroom within a regular school. Basic Secondary is followed by Middle Secondary, grades 10 and 11. Finishing grades 10 and 11 leads to a high school degree (diploma or *bachiller*) and is required for going on to post-secondary education. Students at the secondary level who have LSC as their first language, are integrated into regular classrooms with hearing students with interpreters.

INSOR

INSOR is a part of the Ministry of National Education organization, whose mission is "to promote, from the education sector, the development and implementation of public policy for the social inclusion of Deaf people" (INSOR, 2015). INSOR has broad goals that focus on the social inclusion (i.e., full citizenship) of Deaf individuals. One of their functions is the support of the diffusion of LSC by producing content, tools, and educational materials in LSC (INSOR 2016b). The INSOR website has bilingual access with information in LSC in each area. Direct access via LSC to the director, a fluent signer, is available weekly.

As of 2009, INSOR is charged with improving the lives of Deaf Colombians by conducting research (such as sociocultural studies and the collection of statistics on Deaf population demographics), developing tools and guidelines with the goal of strengthened public policy strategies of care and services nationwide. For example, INSOR has data on the percentage of school-age Deaf students not in school. This is an important category of data, which in many cities and countries (not only in Latin America) is not available. In 2009, approximately 35% of the school-aged Deaf population was not getting an education, or around 2,600 out of more than 7,400 school-aged Deaf children and youth. Another census in 2014 found that the Colombian Deaf population was 134,750 and 5.51% (7,425) were in school (INSOR, 2016a).

In conclusion, we see that Colombia has been engaged in offering bilingual deaf education for over two decades. The role of the Deaf community in gaining recognition of LSC and educational change is notable. Like its neighbors, Colombia faces many obstacles not the least of which is a long history of violent internal conflict, which impacts all citizens including Deaf people (Medina, Quisoboní, Díaz, Mosquerra, & González, 2013). Despite social unrest, progress has occurred and young Deaf Colombians are optimistic (Sordos incorporados, 2015).

A Shining Example: Bilingual Deaf Education in Chile

Chile historically has long been a country with a strongly oral education tradition for Deaf children. In the 1980s, and increasingly after the end of the Pinochet dictatorship and return to democracy in 1990, the emphasis was on the inclusion of Deaf children in regular classes (Hererra, 2010). Awareness of bilingual education and sign language began to develop in the last 1980s and 1990s. Today, there is a growing body of research conducted in Chile on Deaf children's reading and writing (e.g., Alvarado,

Puente, & Herrera, 2008; Herrera, 2013; Lissi, Salinas, Acuña, Adamo, Cabrera, & González, 2010; Puente, Alvarado & Herrera, 2006),the linguistics of Chilean Sign Language (LSCh) (e.g., Adamo, Cabrera, Acuña, & Lattapiat, 2005; Adamo, Ramírez, Navarro, & Robertson, 1999; Becerra, 2008; Ibáñez, Becerra, López, Sirlopú, & Cornejo, 2005), pedagogical approaches for bilingual deaf education (e.g., Instituto de la Sordera, 2012; Lissi, Salinas, Acuña, Adamo, Cabrera, & González, 2010; Hererra, 2013; Robertson, Adamo, Ramirez, & Lissi, 2012), and more.

In a modest neighborhood in the capital city of Santiago, the Instituto Jorge Otte is located. A tall wall conceals this marvelous school, which has been and continues to be a center for profound educational change in the education of Deaf Chilean children. In 1998, it was the first Chilean school to offer bilingual deaf education (Herrera, 2010), and it is a school that exemplifies the possibilities of bilingual education for Deaf children.

The school is part of the Instituto de la Sordera (Institute of Deafness [INDESOR]), a private non-profit corporation. It is a subsidized institution that educates poor, low-income Deaf children and youth in the capital (Herrera, 2010). INDESOR houses Escuela Dr. Jorge Otte Gabler (Dr. Jorge Otte Gabler School for the Deaf), Centro de Recursos e Investigacíon Mundo Sordo (Resource and Research Center: Deaf World), and Centro de Diagnóstico Auditivo (Center for Hearing Diagnosis) (Instituto de la Sordera, 2014). Dr. Otte Gabler founded the school in 1957 in order to provide education and vocational training in the capital city of Santiago for Deaf children and youth who were not receiving services. INDESOR became a legally recognized entity in 1959 by agreement with the National Health Service, Ministry of Education, and University of Chile. With funding from the Ministry of Labor, vocational training was established for Deaf youth to address the problem of unemployment and underemployment in the Deaf community. A hearing diagnosis center was created in the 1980s and a research center in 2004 as part of INDESOR (Herrera, 2010).

In 1997, the Universidad Metropolitana de Ciencias de la Educación, UMCE, (Metropolitan University of Education Sciences) through its Special Education Department took over the Deaf school. The relationship between Instituto Jorge Otte and UMCE supports the professional development of all teachers and staff (Instituto de la Sordera, 2014). Among the teachers, administrators, support staff, and other professionals at the school are a number of individuals with graduate degrees from prestigious universities, including Gallaudet University in Washington, DC.

In Chile, there is a dedicated and growing group of academics and practitioners who understand that the process of bilingual deaf education is not simply a question of languages of instruction. The fundamental values of the Instituto Dr. Jorge Otte Gabler are intercultural bilingual education, meaning a view that promotes interaction and cooperation between hearing and Deaf communities on an equal footing. Deaf culture and LSCh are valued as part of the landscape of Chilean life. From their earliest years of education, the goal is to develop consciousness in each student of themselves as a Deaf person, and in that way, be able to be part of the larger society. Their goal is for Deaf individuals to participate in the social and cultural life of their country while being respected for their own language and culture (de la Paz, 2014; de la Paz & Salamanca, 2014).

The theoretical framework for the school curriculum is based on humanist and constructivist education models associated with the work of Vygotsky, Dewey, Piaget, Montessori, and others. In discussions about curriculum, the school incorporates the relationship between culture and identity, and their view is that curriculum is co-constructed with Deaf people not for Deaf people. The staff is highly motivated to continue learning and developing knowledge of bilingualism and pedagogical strategies. They participate in professional development, conferences, and actively disseminate information about their institution by making presentations (de la Paz, 2014; de la Paz & Salamanca, 2014).

A critically important part of the Institute's mission is early intervention. Since 2005, Chilean hospitals have conducted hearing screening of high-risk infants, but universal hearing screening is still only available at some hospitals (Gerner de García, Gaffney, Chacon, & Gaffney, 2011). Many Deaf babies are not identified early and show up at ages three or four, when their families realize they are not developing spoken language. Families often cannot afford the needed follow-up, and early intervention programs for Deaf people are still not widespread. The Institute offers parents weekly sign language classes with a Deaf teacher. The early intervention team consists of a specialist in speech and hearing, a Deaf adult, a psychologist, and an occupational therapist. Children aged birth to two receive 10 hours a week of intervention at the school. A team of a hearing and Deaf teachers collaborate to provide fluent and natural language models and access to both oral and signed language (Otárola, 2012).

Beyond early invention, the Institute provides programs and services not commonly found in Deaf schools in Latin America. There is a program for Deaf students with disabilities. These children's parents have had difficulty finding schools that would accept a child who is Deaf with a disability. While special education schools in Chile accept children with a range of disabilities, services are designed for students with specific disabilities, not multiple disabilities. Parents of these Deaf children are welcomed as partners in their child's education in order to enable them to develop a vision of their child's potential and future (Otárola, 2014). A psychologist, fluent in LSCh and a CODA, provides support in multiple ways, including psychological (intelligence) testing. The purpose of this testing is to identify each student's strengths and weaknesses in order to support strengths and compensate for weaknesses (Salamanca, 2014). Clearly, a psychologist who is a native signer and culturally Deaf is a valuable asset in a bilingual school. Attention is also given to physical and creative development through theater, mime, and yoga classes. These programs are based on a philosophy of attention to and development of the whole child (Oyarzún & Vargas, 2014).

One of the authors of this chapter has visited this school multiple times between 1999 and 2010. Philosophies, guiding principles, and descriptions of programs on paper do not convey how special this school is. When visiting the school, one immediately notices that Deaf adults are highly visible. They are integrated into the educational teams and never peripheral. As the goal of the school is to have a completely bilingual staff, the hearing teachers are fluent in LSCh. The school works to support Deaf staff in studying towards and obtaining university degrees, which is facilitated by the close relationship with UMCE. UMCE has recently established the first interpreter training program in Chile, and three of the school's teachers are enrolled. The Escuela Jorge Otte continues to strive to better the education of Deaf children, putting the school at the forefront of Chilean deaf education.

Conclusion

The cases presented in this chapter provide three distinct examples of the struggles and progress that has been made in Latin American deaf education over approximately 25 years. They provide a counter narrative to the prevailing view in more developed countries of a continent that is waiting and eager for the intervention of American and European experts. There are lessons to be learned from these cases that teach us what works and, in some instances, what doesn't work. Above all, they present possibilities for collaboration as equals in improving outcomes in deaf education and for securing the rights of Deaf children and adults in all societies.

References

Adamo, D. A., Ramírez, I. C., Navarro, P. L., & Robertson, X. A. (1999). Verbo de concordancia en la lengua de señas Chilena. *Onomazei, 4,* 335–344.

Adamo, D., Cabrera, I., Acuña, X., & Lattapiat, P. (2005). La lengua de señas chilena, la cultura y la educación de las personas sordas en Chile [Chilean Sign Language: Culture and education of Deaf people in Chile]. *Perspectivas Educacionales, 5,* 27–33.

Alvarado, J. M., Puente, A., Herrera, V. (2008). Visual and phonological coding in working memory and orthographic skills of Deaf children using Chilean Sign Language. *American Annals of the Deaf, 152*(5), 467–479.

Becerra, C. (2008). Metáforas en lengua de señas chilena [Metaphors in Chilean Sign Language]. *Psykhe (Santiago), 17*(1), 41–57.

Centre for Studies on Inclusive Education. (2013). The UNESCO Salamanca Statement. Retrieved from http://www.csie.org.uk/inclusion/unesco-salamanca.shtml

Christiansen, J. B., & Leigh, I. W. (Eds.). (2002). *Cochlear implants in children: Ethics and choices*. Washington, DC: Gallaudet University Press.

Colégio Especial Concórdia. (n.d.) Histórico [Historic]. Retrieved from http://www.ulbra.br/especialconcordia/

de la Paz, V. (2014). La educación de los sordos desde un enfoque intercultural bilingüe [Deaf education from a bilingual intercultural approach]. In INDESOR & UMCE (Eds.), *10 años de bilingüismo en Chile: experiencias pedagógicas de la escuela intercultural y bilingüe para estudiantes sordos* (pp. 1–20). Santiago, Chile: Fondo Editorial UMCE.

de la Paz, M. V., & Salamanca, M. (2014). Elementos de la cultura sorda: una base para el curriculum intercultural [Deaf culture elements: A basis for intercultural curriculum]. In INDESOR & UMCE (Eds.), *10 años de bilingüismo en Chile: experiencias pedagógicas de la escuela Intercultural Bilingüe para estudiantes Sordos* (pp. 21–48). Santiago, Chile: Fondo Editorial UMCE.

Eisenberg, L. S., & Johnson, K. C. (2008). Audiologic contributions to pediatric cochlear implants. *The ASHA Leader*. Retrieved from http://www.asha.org/Publications/leader/2008/080325/f080325a.htm

European Agency for Special Needs and Inclusive Education. (2009). Development of inclusion: Spain. Retrieved from http://www.european-agency.org/country-information/spain/national-overview/development-of-inclusion

FENEIS – Federação Nacional de Educação e Integração dos Surdos. (1999). *A educação que nós surdos queremos* [The education we Deaf want]. Document developed in the Pre-Congress of the V Congresso Latino Americano de Educação Bilíngue para Surdos. Porto Alegre, RS, UFRGS, 1999. Digital text.

Fernández-Viader, M. P. & Fuentes, M. (2004). Education of Deaf students in Spain: Legal and educational politics developments. *Journal of Deaf Studies and Deaf Education, 9*(3), 327–332.

Gallaudet Research Institute. (April 2011). Regional and national summary report of data from the 2009–10 Annual Survey of Deaf and Hard of Hearing Children and Youth. Washington, DC: GRI, Gallaudet University.

General Secretariat. (2008). Global Survey Report. WFD Regional Secretariat for Mexico, Central America and the Caribbean. Global Education Pre-Planning Project on the Human Rights of Deaf People. Helsinki, Finland: World Federation of the Deaf and Swedish National Association of the Deaf.

Gerner de García, B. (1990). The emerging Deaf community in the Dominican Republic: An ethnographic study. In C. Lucas (Ed.), *Sign language research: Theoretical issues* (pp. 259–274). Washington, DC: Gallaudet Press.

Gerner de García, B. (2001). La comunidad sorda en desarollo en la Republica Dominicana [The Deaf community development in the Dominican Republic]. In L. M. Patiño, A. Oviedo, & B. Gerner de García (Eds.) *El estilo sordo: ensayos sobre comunidades y culturas de la personas sordas en Iberoamérica* (pp.131–137). Cali, Colombia: Universidad del Valle.

Gerner de García, B., Gaffney, C., Chacon, S., & Gaffney, M. (2011). Overview of newborn hearing screening activities in Latin America. *Rev Panam Salud Publica, 29*(3), 145–152.

Herrera, V. F. (2010). Estudio de la población sorda en Chile: evolución histórica y perspectivas lingüísticas, educativas y sociales [Study of Deaf people in Chile: Historical evolution and linguistic, educational and social perspectives]. *Revista Latinoamericana de Educación Inclusiva, 4*(1). Retrieved from http://www.oei.es/noticias/spip.php?article6988

Herrera, V. F. (2013). En busca de un modelo educativo y de lectura coherente con las necesidades educativas especiales de los estudiantes sordos [In search of an educational model and consistent reading with the special educational needs of Deaf students]. *Revista de Estudios y Experiencias en Educación, 8*(16), 11–24.

Ibáñez, A., Becerra, C., López, V., Sirlopú, D., & Cornejo, C. (2005). Iconicidad y metáfora en el lenguaje chileno de signos (LENSE): un análisis cualitativo [Iconicity and metaphor in Chilean Sign Language (LENSE): A qualitative analysis]. *Revista Electrónica de Investigación y Evaluación Educativa, 11*(1), 27–45.

INSOR. (2008). Educación bilingüe para sordos—etapa escolar: Orientaciones pedagógicas. [Bilingual education for the deaf—School stage: Pedagogical orientations]. Bogota, Colombia: Ministro de Educación Nacional.

INSOR. (2015). Misión y visión [Misson and vision]. Retrieved from http://www.insor.gov.co/mision-y-vision/

INSOR. (2016a). Estadísticas básicas población sorda colombiana [Basic statistics of the Colombian Deaf population]. Retrieved from http://www.insor.gov.co/observatorio/porcentaje-de-poblacion-sorda-en-edad-escolar-no-escolarizada-2014/

INSOR. (2016b). Ojectivos y funciones [Objectives and functions]. Retrieved from http://www.insor.gov.co/objetivos-y-funciones/

Instituto de la Sordera. (2014). Prologo. In INDESOR & UMCE (Eds.), *10 años de bilingüismo en Chile: experiencias pedagógicas de la escuela intercultural bilingüe para estudiantes sordos* [10 years of bilingualism in Chile: Pedagogial experiences in an intercultural bilingual school for deaf students]. Santiago, Chile: Fondo Editorial UMCE.

Instituto Nacional de Educação de Surdos. (2014). História do INES [History of INES]. Retrieved from http://portalines.ines.gov.br/ines_portal_novo/?page_id=1078

Instituto para el Desarollo Integral del Sordo [Institute for the Integral Development of the Deaf Individual]. (2015). XII Congreso Latinoamericano de Educación Bilingüe para Sordos. Retrieved from http://www.idis.org.mx/

Irish Health (2015). Cochlear implants. Retrieved from: http://www.irishhealth.com/article.html?con=457

Johnston, T. A. (2006). W(h)ither the Deaf community? Population, genetics, and the future of Australian Sign Language. *Sign Language Studies, 6*(2), 137–173.

Karnopp, L., & Klein, M. (2007). Narrativas de professoras sobre a(s) língua(s) na educação de surdos [Narratives of teachers on the languages in deaf education]. *Educação e Realidade, 32*(2), 63–78.

Karnopp, L., Klein, M., & Lunardi-Lazzarin, M. (2011). Produção, circulação e consumo da cultura surda Brasileira [Production, dissemination and consumption of Brazilian Deaf culture]. In L. Karnopp, M. Klein, & M. Lunardi-Lazzarin (Eds.), *Cultura surda na contemporaneidade: negociações, intercorrências e provocações* [Deaf culture in contemporary: Negotiations, events and provocations] (pp. 15–28). Canoas, Brazil: Editora ULBRA.

Lacerda, C. B. F. de, & Lodi, A. C. B. (2008). *Uma escola duas línguas: letramento em língua portuguesa e língua de sinais nas etapas iniciais de alfabetização* [One school, two languages: Literacy in English language and sign language in the early stages of literacy]. Porto Alegre, Brazil: Mediação.

Lacerda, C. B. F. de, Albres, N. A., & Drago, S. L. dos S. (2013). Política para uma educação bilíngue e inclusiva a alunos surdos no município de São Paulo [Policy for a bilingual and inclusive education for Deaf students in São Paulo]. *Educação e Pesquisa, 39*(1), 65–80. Retrieved from http://www.scielo.br/scielo.php?script=sci_pdf&pid=S1517-97022013000100005&lng=en&nrm=iso&tlng=pt

Lane, H. (1984). *When the mind hears: A history of the Deaf.* New York, NY: Random House.

Lissi, M. R., Salinas, M., Acuña, X., Adamo, D., Cabrera, I., & González, M. (2010). Using sign language to teach written language: An analysis of the strategies used by teachers of Deaf children in a bilingual context. *Educational Studies in Language and Literature, 10*(1), 57–69.

Lodi, A. C. B. (2013). Bilingual education for the Deaf and inclusion under the National Policy on Special Education and Decree 5.626/05. *Educação e Pesquisa, 39*(1), 49–63. Ministry of Health. Retrieved from http://www.health.govt.nz/your-health/conditions-and-treatments/disabilities/hearing-loss/hearing-services/cochlear-implants

Medina, Á. G., Quisoboní, E. Z., Díaz, L. G. G., Mosquera, N. A., & González, M. A. G. (2013). Las sorderas de los profesores como lenguajes del poder [The deafness of teachers as languages of power]. *Plumilla Educativa, 12,* 382–402.

Ministry of Education. (2008). Secretaria de Educação Especial. Política Nacional de Educação Especial na perspectiva da educação inclusiva [Department of Special Education. National Policy for Special Education in the perspective of inclusive education]. Brasília. Retrieved from http://www.mec.gov.br

Moneada, E. M. (2005). Representaciones y politicas de la educación sobre los sordos y la sordera en Colombia [Representations and politics of the education of the deaf and deafness in Colombia]. *Revista Educación y Pedagogía, 17*(41), 71–81.

NIH Fact Sheets: Cochlear implants. (2013). Retrieved from http://report.nih.gov/nihfactsheets/ViewFactSheet.aspx?csid=83

Novitisky, M. L., & Eastman, G. (Producers). (1991). Deaf Mosaic episode 610: Costa Rica (Television broadcast). Retrieved from http://videocatalog.gallaudet.edu/?video=1735

Otárola, F. C. (2012). Nuestro enfoque desde el inicio [Our focus from the beginning]. In INDESOR & UMCE (Eds.), *10 años de bilingüismo en Chile: experiencias pedagógicas de la escuela intercultural bilingüe para estudiantes sordos* [10 years of bilingualism in Chile: Pedagogial experiences in an intercultural bilingual school for deaf students] (pp. 232–259). Santiago, Chile: Fondo Editorial UMCE.

Otárola, F. C. (2014). Dando repuestas a los desafíos [Answering the challenges]. In INDESOR & UMCE (Eds.), *10 años de bilingüismo en Chile: experiencias pedagógicas de la escuela intercultural bilingüe para estudiantes sordos* [10 years of bilingualism in Chile: Pedagogial experiences in an intercultural bilingual school for deaf students]. (pp. 283–319). Santiago, Chile: Fondo Editorial UMCE.

Oviedo, A. (2003). La comunidad sorda venezolana y su lengua de señas [The Venezuelan Deaf communities and its sign language]. *Venezuela. Editorial Edumedia.* Retrieved from: http://www.cultura-sorda.eu.

Oyarzún, R., & Vargas, V. M. (2014). Expresar en silencio [To express in silence]. In INDESOR & UMCE (Eds.), *10 años de bilingüismo en Chile: experiencias pedagógicas de la escuela intercultural bilingüe para estudiantes sordos* [10 years of bilingualism in Chile: Pedagogial experiences in an intercultural bilingual school for deaf students]. Santiago, Chile: Fondo Editorial UMCE.

Papsin, B. C., & Gordon, K. A. (2007). Cochlear implants for children with severe-to-profound hearing loss. *New England Journal of Medicine, 357*(23), 2380–2387.

Pardo, D. S. (2000). Reflexiones y preguntas frente a la integración escolar del estudiante sordo [Reflections and questions facing the school integration of the deaf student]. Bogota, Colombia: INSOR.

Pereira, M. C. (Ed.). (2005). *Leitura, escrita e surdez* [Reading, writing and Deafness]. São Paulo, Brazil: Secretaria da Educação do Estado de São Paulo.

Pérez, Y. (2005). Fenómenos de lenguas en contacto en una intérprete de LSV en el contexto escolar [Phenomena of languages in contact in a LSV interpreter in the school context]. *Lengua y Habla, 9*(1), 45–70.

Perlin, G. (1998). Histórias de vida surda: identidades em questão [Stories of Deaf life: Identities in question]. Unpublished Masters thesis. Universidade Federal do Rio Grande do Sul, UFRGS, Porto Alegre, Brazil.

Perlin, G. (2003). O ser e o estar sendo surdo: alteridade, diferença e identidade [Being and being Deaf: Otherness, difference and identity]. Unpublished dissertation. Universidade Federal do Rio Grande do Sul, UFRGS, Porto Alegre, Brazil.

Pinto, F. B. (2007). Vendo vozes: a história da educação dos surdos no Brasil oitocentista [Seeing voices: The history of deaf education in nineteenth-century Brazil]. Retrieved from http://www.cultura-sorda.eu

Puente, A., Alvarado, J. M., & Herrera, V. (2006). Finger spelling and sign language as alternative codes for reading and writing words for Chilean Deaf signers. *American Annals of the Deaf, 151*(3), 299–310.

Ramírez, P. (1998). Modeles bilingüe de atención integral a niños sordos menores de cinco años. [Bilingual models for the integral attention for deaf children under five years]. In INSOR (Ed.), *Memorias de VII Congreso Latinoamericanos para Educación Bilingüe para Sordos* (pp. 79–82). Bogotá, Colombia: INSOR.

Raymann, B. W. (n.d.). *History of Concordia School—RS, Brazil 1966–1999: A summary.* Unpublished manuscript. Porto Alegre, Rio Grande do Sul, Brazil.

Robertson, X. A., Adamo, D., Ramirez, I. C., & Lissi, M. R. (2012). Descriptive study on narrative competence development in Chilean Sign Language. *Onomázein: Revista de Lingüística, Filología y Traducción, 26*, 193–219.

Salamanca, M. (2014). La evaluación intelectual de estudiantes sordos: recomendaciones extraídas desde una experiencia intercultural bilingüe [Intellectual assessment of Deaf students: Recommendations extracted from a bilingual intercultural experience]. In INDESOR & UMCE (Eds.), *10 años de bilingüismo en Chile: experiencias pedagógicas de la escuela intercultural bilingüe para estudiantes sordoss* [10 years of bilingualism in Chile: Pedagogial experiences in an intercultural bilingual school for deaf students]. Santiago, Chile: Fondo Editorial UMCE.

Sampaio, A. L., Araújo, M. F., & Oliveira, C. A. (2011). New criteria of indication and selection of patients to cochlear implant. *International journal of otolaryngology, 2011.* Retrieved from http://www.hindawi.com/journals/ijoto/2011/573968/

Skliar, C. (Ed.). (1999a). *Atualidade da Educação Bilíngüe para Surdos* [Today's Bilingual Education for the Deaf]. Vol. 1. Porto Alegre, Brazil: Mediação.

Skliar, C. (Ed). (1999b). *Atualidade Da Educação Bilíngüe Para Surdos* [Today's Bilingual Education for the Deaf]. Vol. 2. Porto Alegre, Brazil: Mediação.

Soares, M. A. L. (1999). *A educação do surdo no Brasil* [Deaf education in Brazil]. Campinsas, Brazil: Bragança Paulista.

Sordos incorporados al sistema educativo, manos que hablan de sueños [The deaf incorporated into the education system, hands that speak of dreams]. (2015, August 2). Vanguardia.com. Retrieved from http://www.vanguardia.com/colombia/321928 -sordos-incorporados-al-sistema-educativo-manos-que-hablan-de-suenos.

Souza, R. M. de. (1998). *Que palavra que te falta? Lingüística, educação e surdez* [What words are you missing? Linguistics, education and Deafness]. São Paulo, Brazil:

Martins Fontes.

Strong, M. (1988). A bilingual approach to the education of young Deaf children: ASL and English. In M. Strong (Ed.), *Language learning and Deafness* (pp. 99–112). New York, NY: Cambridge University Press.

Swadesh, M. (1951). The use of indigenous languages in education. Meeting of Experts on the Use of Vernacular Languages in Education. Paris. Retrieved from: unesdoc.unesco.org/images/0014/001447/144722eb.pdf

Thoma, A., & Lopes, M. (Eds.). (2005). *A Invenção da Surdez: cultura, alteridade, identidade e diferença no campo da educação* [The invention of Deafness: Culture, otherness, identity and difference in education]. Santa Cruz do Sul, Brazil: Edunisc.

Tovar, L. A. (1998). Relexiones acerca de la educación de los sordos colombianos para Siglo XXI [Reflections on the education of Deaf Colomgians for the 21st century]. *Lenguaje, 26*, 24–37.

Ureña Garcia, O. (2013). Doctor Julián Chaverri: Con el implante coclear los sordos pueden oír [Doctor Julian Chaverri: With cochlear implants the Deaf can hear]. Retrieved from http://periodico4ojos.blogspot.com/2013/01/doctor-julian -chaverri-con-el-implante.html

Vicente, V. G. (2011). Un acercamiento histórico a la comunidad sorda de Bogotá [An historical approach to the Deaf community of Bogota]. Bogotá, Colombia: FENESCOL.

Woodward, J. (1991). Sign language varieties in Costa Rica. *Sign Language Studies, 73*, 329–345.

2

Educational Projects to Create a Bilingual Scenario for Deaf Students in Argentina

Silvana Veinberg

Bilingual intercultural education (BIE) for Deaf students has been presented mainly from pedagogical and linguistic practices. It has been interpreted that BIE is the sum of methods linked one way or another to language: sign languages or oral languages. However, this educational philosophy transcends language and educational spheres, which requires designing schools for the Deaf taking into account multiple factors that are part of a new vision of the education of Deaf students.

To understand the situation of deaf education in Argentina, it is necessary to review, on the one hand, the winding route through which we have been passing from the time when Argentina was considered the referent in oralist education for Deaf students in Latin America. On the other hand, it is necessary to analyze the system in which school designs are engraved and the results that are reflected in educational practices.

The Argentine education system is composed of educational services managed by state and private management, cooperative management and social management. Basic education in Argentina includes three levels: early childhood (ages 3–5), primary (6 or 7 years depending on the jurisdiction), and secondary (5–6 years). Education is compulsory from the age of five until the end of high school (Gragnolati, Rofman, Apella, & Troiano, 2015).

The education system in Argentina is integrated. Argentina has a decentralized education system, which means that each of the 24 jurisdictions is responsible for defining the policies concerning each of their fields of action. Thus, each jurisdiction has taken different paths in relation to the implementation of actions related to deaf education, inclusive education and teacher training. In all cases, deaf education is part of a special education approach with the implications that this entails.

Like any scenario, deaf education in Argentina is not easy to describe; a variety of actors that can be viewed from many angles stand on it. Although the meaning assigned to bilingual deaf education varies across the country, in most cases it is understood that a school becomes bilingual when teachers begin to use sign language in Deaf students' formal education, often without reference to the teachers' proficiency and regardless of the many variables that make up the design of these schools.

At the national level, certain educational policies concerning the recognition of Argentine Sign Language (LSA) as the natural language of Deaf students have been established. However, educational projects remain isolated and fail to reverse the situation of educational exclusion of the student population. On the other hand, global "inclusive" policies that also echo our country, aim to turn schools into "centers for attention" (centros de atención) for those deaf students who are in regular schools, weakening the implementation of bilingual deaf education practices.

In this chapter, various reflections and proposals for the design of educational policies and practices in order to facilitate the construction of scenarios for bilingual deaf education will be presented. The first part of this work will aim to describe some of the changes that have been undertaken in deaf education in Argentina and the concepts underpinning our actions. The second part will be dedicated to explaining how Canales' practices attempt to respond to the model of bilingual and intercultural deaf education. Canales is an association founded in 2003 in which Deaf and hearing people work for an accessible and quality education for Deaf children and adolescents. It is a non-governmental organization (NGO) funded by individual donors, corporations, and foundations and doesn't receive any government funding and has no political or religious ideology. Educational projects include the following lines of action:

1. the design of educational practices to promote BIE for Deaf students;
2. the production of video materials for access to information and to promote reading in LSA; and
3. the training, awareness, and communication related to the education of Deaf people.

The Route of Deaf Education in Argentina

Deaf education in Argentina has followed a path similar to other Latin American countries influenced by European and American educational streams. However, there are some notable idiosyncrasies in Argentina; one is that it has been a leader in deaf education for many years, training professionals in neighboring countries. The oralist education in our country has been a model and has cultivated, strengthened, and spread the medical perspective of deaf education. This long-lasting model has spread to the teacher training that we struggle to reverse today (Veinberg, 1996).

Consequently, today deaf education has been inserted into a special education framework, an educational model that has historically been influenced and supported by a medical view of deafness and deaf education. Currently, some of the units of special education became sections of "inclusive education" in which the student with disabilities is seen as the subject of rehabilitation. The influence of the medical perception of deaf education is not only symbolic; the muddling of these two areas (education and health) is so extensive that medical and social services are required to cover costs of schooling for people with disabilities. This public policy is based on the belief that schools for Deaf children (or any other child included in the population of children with disabilities) must perform functions related to medicine and rehabilitation.

Today, the situation of Deaf children and youth continues to be marked by the representations that teachers have of their students. These ideas are rooted in their teacher training, which often reinforces prejudices that some teachers have at the time they chose their profession.

In this sense, the structure and the way in which deaf education is designed strengthen and feed this standpoint. Teachers are comfortable in this place because the clinical perspective on deaf education does not require them to know sign language or even have contact with Deaf issues and Deaf people if they want to work in a school for the deaf. Warning signs at school are acoustic and physical, and linguistic accessibility is designed by and for the hearing. The teaching of Spanish is still the core objective at school, and within this setting hearing teachers, not Deaf people, make the decisions (Veinberg, 2010a).

This is the result of educational approaches that hearing educators offer Deaf students and that continue to strengthen (hearing) teachers' representations about language, education, and culture of the Deaf community. It is surprising that many teachers still preserve the old concepts held by the oralist ideology about deaf education, but even more surprising is that these ideas are not archaic; they are part of the current history.

At this point, I think it would be fair to mention certain movements that promise a different destiny for the Deaf population. These include: (a) the growing visibility of the Deaf community and the work they are doing with various public and private institutions, (b) new conceptions about Deaf people that derive from the latest national and international standards, and (c) certain best practices experienced in BIE for Deaf students that are taking place in some schools for the Deaf. Inclusive education policies, training in LSA, and the use of interpreters in secondary and university education levels are starting to be reconsidered.

A number of policies have been specifically established by national laws and regulations intended to ensure quality education with equal opportunities. The International Convention on the Rights of Persons with Disabilities, which became a national law in 2008, specifically mentions the importance of including sign language and promotes the development of the linguistic identity of Deaf students. In 2006, it led to a revised National Law on Education in which it was established that the area of Special Education (SEd) becomes one of the eight sections included in the general education system. This means that the SEd area is not a parallel system; instead, it traverses all levels of education. Whether we refer to special education, inclusive education, intercultural education, or any type of education, schools for the Deaf are part of the mainstream education system. After the presidential elections of fall 2015, with possible changes in the government, some political scenarios in relation to deaf education shall be modified.

In 2011, the Federal Board of Education, including all ministries of education of the Argentine provinces, enacted Resolution 155, which included procedures to improve the quality of education for Deaf students. Guideline criteria were established for the allocation of teachers and LSA interpreters' positions, and access for Deaf students to information was assisted by the use of LSA. These new standpoints question the old paradigms that focused on a medical view of the Deaf community; they instead propose the participation of Deaf people in education, and they recuperate the centrality of education within schools, rather than placing deaf education in medical or health categories.

However, when we have not yet finished (and sometimes we haven't even started) the discussion on how we're going to shape deaf education in schools for the Deaf, we are facing homogenizing movements that respond to the integrationist policies we have mentioned. These policies question the existence of schools for the Deaf and promote the inclusion of all students in regular schools.

Inclusive Education/Educational Inclusion

The interpretation given to inclusive education in some provinces of our country has led to the closure of special schools and forced school integration of Deaf students in those jurisdictions. The Deaf student population attends regular schools sometimes supported by interpreters but most of the time without that support. This situation means they have to go to schools for the deaf in order to receive additional support for the information they could not get at the regular school. Many teachers succumb to the pressure of parents, who frequently invoke the right of their children to attend regular schools, and reject the right of their Deaf children to learn, participate, decide, and build their own linguistic and cultural identity in a school that was planned for Deaf students.

These integrationist practices (derived mostly from Spain) have not evaluated the consequences that this action has on the population of Deaf students. In an attempt to "equalize," these inclusion actions adapt some elements of the regular school in order for all to be included. Thus, the teachers accompanying the children act as interpreters and the pedagogical content is reduced.

The discussion should focus on the meaning of these inclusion concepts. Included where? Who designed the space and for whom? Equal for whom? Who works as a role model? Do inclusive schools benefit or do they result in a limitation for deaf students? Whose is the prevailing right: the parents', the student's, or the teacher's?

The educational approach we propose is incompatible with the idea of educational inclusion that is understood simply as the incorporation of Deaf students into regular schools, as it has been interpreted in Argentine schools. A school is inclusive for Deaf people when students understand what is happening around them, they participate in activities, they are able to reflect through their language and through their way of interpreting the world, and they become constructors of their own school.

Why do some think that a school for the deaf is not a regular school? The widespread idea that special education schools are within a sort of "parallel system" has led to the development of unusual practices in schools for the Deaf. One of the most common practices in some provinces is proposing that only students who attend "regular" schools will be provided with the primary level certificate. This means that, in order to complete their schooling, all Deaf students must be integrated, thus prioritizing the type of school they attend over the quality and quantity of curriculum content that students acquire (Veinberg, Carracedo, & Suchodolski, 2015).

The situation regarding school integration of Deaf students in hearing schools as a synonym for educational inclusion interferes in the process of creating inclusive schools for the Deaf. Schools for the Deaf are gradually becoming places of support and rehabilitation treatments for Deaf students attending hearing schools. How can we bring back the objectives of deaf education within schools for the Deaf if more than half of its target population is integrated in different schools? How do we create linguistically accessible and socially valuable environments in these conditions?

Bilingual Intercultural Education: The Magnitude of Its Meaning

For decades in every country in the world, the process of transforming deaf education has been traveling different paths, which in recent years has resulted in a common model: BIE for Deaf people. However, to examine these paths and imagine possible horizons, it is necessary to analyze the meaning of BIE related to deaf education. In any case, this concept should not be interpreted literally. Bilingual in this circumstance does not refer exclusively to the use of two languages.

Although languages are an essential part of this process, it is first necessary to describe in depth the significance of deaf education because its definition is based on the representations of the people who implement it, somehow defining their actions within schools for the Deaf (Veinberg, 2010b). Interculturality refers to the need of including in school various ways of understanding the world that are not limited to being deaf or being hearing. There is no single way of being deaf, and if the school defines a profile for the Deaf student, we will get involved again in hegemonic discourse and historically approved normal standards. Numerous cultures in the classroom live, interact, and give rise to new cultures.

BIE arises from a social viewpoint in which the function of language is recognized as a means of communication and as a vehicle for intellectual development. It intends to take into account each child's own stories, stories with which the child enters school, as well as experiences, values, and worldviews. The status of languages in deaf education is a political decision that will influence the students.

Defining deaf education is therefore useful in order to design fair and accessible education policies. Understanding deaf education means including Deaf perspectives at school, which indicates the incorporation of other worlds. It also means organizing the school through a regular interchange with a community that has so far been excluded.

What Is the Meaning of Accessibility in Terms of Deaf Education?

Given that schools for the Deaf are part of the mainstream education system, we will try to propose some considerations for their design. An inclusive education system is one that provides members of the educational community access roads to knowledge, the construction of identities, and active participation. Access is defined not only in physical terms but also in its symbolic, cultural, and linguistic aspects. In our country, the most visible progress in terms of accessibility for schools for the Deaf has occurred in the physical designs and, to a lesser extent, in language access. However, school practices are based on symbolic accessibility.

Teachers in schools for the Deaf have understood that visual strategies and the natural language of Deaf people should be part of school. Yet, their practices reveal that the old paradigms still survive: lack of knowledge of the natural language of Deaf people, prejudice on the linguistic legitimacy of sign language, and preconceptions about the intellectual abilities of Deaf people and their ability to be professionally trained and to demonstrate proficiency at school. The results are revealed through the rudimentary educational programs in which the focus is on the teaching of Spanish, the poor sign language skills of teachers, the inclusion of groups of hearing students with language problems in schools for the Deaf, and the fact that certification of primary schooling is only possible if students are integrated into regular schools. Therefore, we consider it indispensable to work in teacher training, empowerment of the Deaf community and awareness of the families. During the visits we have made to schools for the Deaf, we have noticed that physical barriers for Deaf students exist in school mainly due to the ignorance and prejudice of their teachers. But they are also due to the prejudiced notions that Deaf people and their families absorb about themselves.

The organization of accessible educational situations requires ending the images that teachers and principals have of accessibility as referring to the purely physical or architectural. It is imperative to also include the symbolic sphere. We must consider the human and material dimensions: bodies, languages, and cultures.

To make this possible we propose to work on the following issues, which will be briefly described:

1. Teacher education and training
2. Training of professional interpreters
3. Cooperative educational work between hearing and deaf teachers
4. Program design and content of the school curriculum
5. Elaboration of accessible educational materials
6. Family participation

Teacher Education and Training

Teachers have been taught under the banner of rehabilitation, within professional programs that overlap with those related to medicine. In addition, training programs have failed to influence the expected educational changes because of the misconceptions and prejudices that principals and teachers have about Deaf people and deaf education.

The advances that have been made in some teacher training programs respond primarily to politically correct discourses—Deaf rights, language rights, and inclusion of Deaf leaders in schools—instead of revealing a new paradigm of deaf education into the new programs. It is not simply a matter of changing the name of courses or the amount of time designated but changing the way of understanding deaf education.

It is therefore necessary to identify the representations on which teacher practices are based and to inquire about the intention of their actions to recognize the barriers and to be able to act on them. It is not just a mere modification of methods; the passage from the clinical to the teaching perspective implies rather a restructuration of the process of socialization and learning. Awareness is the first step toward change. We propose redirecting the focus of the training programs towards the development of skills and knowledge that derive from learning processes.

Training of Professional Interpreters

Training of LSA interpreters is the first step in the establishment of a "chain of access." It is not just the lack of interpreters but also the lack of qualified training that causes Deaf students in regular schools to obtain only part of the information. Deaf adults find it unfeasible to pursue higher education and Deaf people who attend training courses only receive access to part of the information.

Even today most of the people functioning as interpreters have simply received basic training in LSA. Those are interpreters who perform their tasks in the mass media and in educational, legal, and labor areas. Fortunately, today there are a few professional training programs for interpreters we hope will have a positive impact on the quality of life of the Argentine Deaf community in a few years.

Cooperative Educational Work between Hearing and Deaf Teachers

The joint work between the hearing educational community and the Deaf community is one of the most controversial issues because it entails a definition of the roles and commitment of each of the parties. It is not just about using one language or the other; rather it has to do with a dominant status within the school that has not been questioned so far.

Today, Deaf adults who had been historically excluded from political decisions on education have become essential actors. It must be considered that the same community that had been oppressed in these same schools and by these same teachers is now invited to participate as linguistic and cultural references for Deaf students.

"The Deaf adult" became a recognized figure among Deaf school players. However, this inclusion has been done almost exclusively in physical terms. In order for this proposal to go beyond the mere presence of a Deaf person in school, it would be a good idea to ask ourselves: How is the Deaf community represented in school? How is this new school conceived in terms of the views Deaf people have of education and of the world in general? What kind of training have these adults who are representatives of the Deaf community received in order to work in educational settings with children and to work together with hearing teachers?

Program Design and Content of the School Curriculum

The curriculum is of great significance in the development of the children. It should reflect their values, so that they can go from their personal beliefs to more universal ones. Designing a school for the Deaf not only involves the presence of a linguistic and visual environment that includes the use of both languages but also has to include the teaching strategies used in and outside the classroom, interaction with Deaf adults, and the reformulation of the school curriculum.

In school programs for Deaf students, teachers often implement curricular adaptations. However, these adaptations, which usually end up as content simplifications, have to be carefully reviewed to avoid limiting learning opportunities. A good way to accomplish this aim would be to reformulate the programs so that they contain topics related to the use of technology, the design of fundamentally visual settings, and Deaf history, culture, and languages. School designs also require reconsidering the organization of the school, the criteria for student grouping and the time devoted to the development of the different curriculum areas to favor a significant learning experience for each student. The selection, sequencing, and content organization will contemplate different perceptions of the world where Deaf people are included, involving once again their active participation.

Historically, language teaching has been the main objective in deaf education (Spanish and LSA), a determination that has operated against educational purposes. Even today it is possible to observe the extent to which the development of school disciplines highly depends on the proficiency deaf students have in the Spanish language. Since accreditation requirements include content analysis, reading, and production of disciplinary texts, mastery of written Spanish becomes a concern for teachers thus limiting learning assessment. Spanish is both taken as an object of study and a way to access information. The evaluation tools applied at the end of schooling assess essentially Spanish language skills rather than the acquisition of scientific knowledge included in the curriculum.

This is one of the reasons why the contents are simplified, and this is also why students who finish their primary schooling rarely receive certification for this knowledge. The certificate of completion in schools for the Deaf should be determined by the accreditation of the main fields of knowledge that have been defined in Argentina as Major Learning Cores (Núcleos de Aprendizaje Prioritarios, NAP) or the general education content mandated by the educational system. However, it often happens that, when certifying learning, these are not recognized as valid since it is usually assumed that Deaf students' achievements do not correspond to those required by the regular school, especially in the area of language (Veinberg, 2012).

Elaboration of Accessible Educational Materials

Deaf students attending schools use written material in a second language, Spanish, which becomes a barrier to accessing information and knowledge through books and written materials. For educational resources to be accessible for everyone, it is necessary to rethink the production of materials that are used in schools. Videos in sign language are a valuable resource because their content is transmitted in an accessible language, more so when they are made by Deaf leaders, which guarantees the inclusion of their understanding of the world. In this respect, symbolic accessibility becomes evident; videos made by the Deaf community in their own language help overcome false representations of Deaf people and promote their rights to be recognized as a linguistic and cultural community. The results of this recognition is demonstrated by the fact that schools for the Deaf incorporated Deaf educators within their staff and sign language classes have been included in programs to train teachers of Deaf students. Additionally, physical accessibility makes it possible to transform space and to design accessible technological tools.

Informatics, cybernetics, and information and communications technology (ICT) have opened up endless possibilities previously unavailable to Deaf people. Through these and many other innovations, appropriation of information for Deaf persons has been significantly expanded.

Family Involvement

Families are the most neglected actors in this educational setting. However, fathers, mothers, brothers, sisters, and other relatives who come into contact with the Deaf child from birth are the ones accompanying their development, their decisions, and their way of life. They are strategic allies that are included in this educational process and whose views must be included in every school design.

Best Practices in Deaf Education—Canales

Canales is a civil association founded in 2003 in which deaf and hearing people work toward promoting the rights of Deaf people, especially the rights of Deaf children and adolescents to access quality education. In its first 11 years, they produced 38 sets of accessible educational materials, reached more than 12,000 Deaf children and youth, and trained over 235 Deaf leaders to conduct workshops in schools for the Deaf, coordinate educational projects, and participate in videos on various topics. Over 4,500 people participated in the conferences and training workshops Canales organized throughout the country, including 2,600 teachers and principals of schools for the Deaf and 1,200 children who participated in the workshops. In addition, 970 free materials were delivered to schools, a new document was published to sensitize the medical community, and 450 doctors received advice about the language and culture of the Deaf community.

The working team is made up of teachers of Deaf students, sign language interpreters, project managers, communicators, videographers, designers, storytellers, administrators, illustrators, video editors, web designers, and volunteers.

As discussed in the introduction to this chapter, the lines of action can be summarized as:

1. the design of educational practices to promote Deaf BIE;
2. the production of video materials for access to information and the promotion of reading in LSA; and
3. the training, awareness, and communication related to the education of Deaf people.

The Design of Educational Practices to Promote Deaf BIE

Educational projects developed by Canales are based on the concepts previously described about the meaning of the BIE. The approaches applied in the design, development, and implementation of all our educational projects include certain conditions that are always present in the different stages. All projects include a careful selection of participants, training of Deaf leaders, work with languages, evaluation of the results and the impact, and communication and diffusion of the project for replication. All projects in the process include the involvement of the Deaf community, and collaborative work between Deaf and hearing people and leadership training.

Deaf Community Involvement

In each project and from the starting point, Deaf people are involved in every step of the process, from the design to the evaluation of the final results. In this way, we ensure that training, workshops, educational materials, and reading promotion projects have the imprint of Deaf people who share their experience with everyone on the team, with Deaf children and youth, and with teachers.

Deaf participation not only adds a linguistic richness hardly found in the hearing public whose first language is not sign language but also includes a particular vision in understanding the processes and unique ways of carrying out the activities. Furthermore, the Deaf community is also directly involved in the development and implementation of educational programs and policies.

Collaborative Work between Deaf and Hearing People

Since its early stages, in Canales, the call for participation has been open to both hearing and Deaf people. However, the roles of the team members have transformed over time in different types of projects. The first programs were coordinated by hearing leaders who were actively involved with Deaf people. Today the institution includes Deaf coordinators who have been trained by carrying out these actions. In the same vein, the idea that only Deaf people should be in front of the cameras (as readers or narrators of the videos we at Canales developed) has been challenged. The same Deaf coordinators look favorably at the possibility that both hearing (fluent signers) and Deaf people can participate as narrators in the videos.

However, although this is a proposal we at Canales ought to consider, we understand that at present due to the demanding situation of the Deaf community in Argentina about their rights, it is preferable that they themselves are exposed as referents for students and teachers across the country.

The intensity generated by the exchange between both populations and the creation of joint ideas adds value and expands the meaning of the programs. Sharing experiences each has had on his or her personal story, discussing contents and methodologies, and imagining scenarios and activities to organize before, during, and after each project are some examples of the effects of this cultural encounter.

Leadership Training

Both Deaf and hearing people are trained before each project. In projects that involve the development of educational materials, Deaf people are generally those in front of the cameras. They are trained by experts in each specific topic: sex education, history, rights, ecology, and so on. Some of these projects also include workshops in schools for the Deaf prior to the design of the script for the video filming. The workshops allow us to directly contact the beneficiaries in order to adjust the content of what would later be included in the video in LSA. Participants of each project discuss the content and select relevant topics to include in the final script before the last review by the professional specialists is made.

Direct contact with Deaf children and adolescents offers the possibility of visual strategies to develop naturally during the execution of the activities. This is a great contribution for children who do not find these types of visual behaviors at home with their hearing families, and it serves as a model of interaction for hearing teachers.

Regarding reading books and stories, training of reading "mediators" is very intense. The rupture between Deaf people and written literature has developed over many years. "Deaf people do not read" is a phrase we have run into since we first approached this work with books. Part of the training of reading mediators pointed to distinguish narration from authentic reading. At the beginning, Deaf people working on this process argued that the sign for "telling" a story and "reading" a story was the same because the action carried out with the book was thought to be the same in both cases. Through different workshops, Deaf and hearing readers reflected about the performance of the LSA reading mediators, their training needs, their relationship with books, their relationship with language, their role as reading promoters, and their relationship with children and book selection.

Video Materials for Information Access and Promotion of Reading in LSA

For schools for the Deaf, accessible educational materials are a key resource since most of the time schools do not have Deaf adults on their staff. Nor do they have the necessary tools to assure Deaf children understand the schooling content. As was stated earlier in this chapter, training of teachers in LSA is poor and the material they have is mostly written or acoustic.

Canales has developed a strong line of work for the creation of these materials, since its function goes beyond that of getting information to Deaf students. Accessible materials also provide an opportunity for Deaf children to get in contact with Deaf adults. In many cases, especially in rural areas, this will be the only possibility for them to have contact with a Deaf adult. LSA videos are also a source of inspiration for the development of other school materials used by teachers, interpreters, and students in order to practice and perfect their language. They also serve to introduce topics into the school agendas that otherwise would not be included.

The video productions have experienced progressive modifications, which are based on considerations arising from the joint work between Deaf and hearing people. In the first videos Deaf people refused to incorporate any sound materials. The videos now contain not just voiceover in Spanish but also music, denoting a change in the form of the videos as well as in the meaning they carry. Today, LSA educational videos contain sound effects, voiceovers, and captioning. Videobooks, on the other hand, do not require subtitles because the text is present.

The materials produced by Canales are of various types (Canales, n.d.a):

- bibliographic material for teachers
- medical articles
- written materials with an LSA version
- videos in LSA for access to information
- videos for reading promotion

In the beginning, our activities focused specifically on offering Deaf students materials with which their teachers could work in the classroom. Thus, the first videos are designed based on formal classroom content: Argentine national holidays, civic participation, and sex education. With the same objective, we developed materials for teaching Spanish as a second language that started with a written version and now include accessible versions in LSA.

Other works have been subsequently created as part of a course of action to promote reading that began with the training of Deaf reading mediators. The participation of Deaf people in reading workshops in schools for the Deaf made possible the awareness of their potential as readers, and their relationship with books and literature. It stimulated reflection on the part of teachers on their prejudices regarding the apparent "limitations" of Deaf children's access to books. The cooperation between Deaf and hearing people and interviews with Deaf families to investigate strategies they use to approach books and reading, allowed us to analyze some discussions concerning some of the materials the project has developed.

We at Canales inquired about the ways Deaf children are read to, their experiences with books, their meaning of reading, and their ideas about literature. The joint analysis of common and divergent points between reading in Spanish and reading in LSA, the implications of reading in Spanish as a second language, the complexities of languages, the role of education, literacy, and teacher training motivated the creation of the first books and stories read in LSA (Videobooks) (Zgryzek & Veinberg, 2012) and the book *The Joy of Reading in LSA* (El Placer de leer en LSA) (Zgryzek & Veinberg, 2012). The Canales webpage to date contains a total of 30 books read by Deaf adults (Canales, n.d.c).

In the creation of Videobooks, at Canales, we had in mind that the book is always present and that reading entails direct contact with the written text. Both sign language and reading text and images from the book involve the implementation of visual attention mechanisms. Divided visual attention is one of the particularities of reading in LSA (sign language). The person reading a book in LSA has to coordinate actions such as the movement of the hands while reading in LSA and holding the book and pointing to the pictures. These actions require knowing and properly managing visual strategies so that those who are participating in the reading can follow them. On the other hand, those who are being read to must know where to look at every moment and have to focus their attention on more than one thing simultaneously. They need to know the uses of language to be able to participate, interrupt, anticipate, and follow the thread of the story. The production of accessible versions of the materials used at the school in sign language opens a path to linguistic accessibility and recognizes the need to implement linguistic and visual environments where teachers and students interact through a common language, with teachers fluent in the use of sign language as a tool for communication and learning.

Training, Awareness, and Communication Related to the Education of Deaf People

The first educational projects were designed to respond to the demands of the teachers to support literacy for Deaf students. However, in this process we discovered that the lack of tools for teaching Spanish was a minor detail. There is a critical situation related to teachers of Deaf students due to a lack of pedagogical training as their fields of study have been focused on the field of medicine.

Thus, our work includes the development of workshops with teachers and principals in which they are encouraged to think about their representations concerning deaf education, their career choice, their expectations, and their own experiences as students. It is necessary to develop a suitable training program for a population that needs to view deaf education with new eyes. The Deaf community, teachers, parents, and the "voice" (or hands) of Deaf students have to participate in this educational recreation.

Influencing Public Policies

Educational projects promoted by Canales attempt to transform some of the realities of deaf education in Argentina. The aim is to influence not only in schools for the Deaf across the country but also government agencies and NGOs.

Educational materials in LSA have been included in the netbooks that have been distributed by the national government for all Deaf students. The recommendation by the program of the Ministry of National Education, *Conectar Igualdad,* was made to use the Videobook web site. Additionally, the incorporation of an extension center for teaching Spanish as a second language for Deaf students as part of the basic contents proposed by the Ministry of Education are some of the most concrete evidence of this intervention (Ministry of Education, 2011).

Other activities that have less visible impact are the interventions through workshops with teachers and principals, the influence in the elaboration of curriculum guidelines in many Argentine provinces, and the awareness of people and institutions linked to deaf education, especially regarding inclusive education policies.

Final Words

Through the projects developed by Canales, we intend to generate and display models of intervention and production that agree with what we have described as Deaf BIE. From the beginning we walked numerous routes in search of more inclusive and accessible processes of higher quality that best represent the rights for all. Throughout this path, we faced successful situations and we had to confront our mistakes. Some of our planned actions have not been completed and did not show the results we expected, and some achievements exceeded our expectations.

Our goal is to develop educational practices that can influence policies that promote BIE models for Deaf people. To make that possible, we encourage the inclusion of the language and culture of the Deaf community in school programs, the participation of the Deaf community represented by Deaf leaders in schools, and the active use of the natural language of the students in order for them to generate their own knowledge. Canales' projects always include empowerment mechanisms, leadership training, and inclusion of community members as active participants in the whole process. The joint work with the Deaf community in the development of proposals and educational policies predicts the establishment of a more accessible and equitable school design for Deaf children.

We propose the implementation of strategies for educational intervention that replace socially installed representations of deaf education. This adjustment logically comprises the educational field, the Deaf community, the families, the professionals involved in the area of deafness, and the linguistic policies with the aim of making appropriate decisions. Educational policies have to consider the need for training for the teachers who will be putting these policies into practice. These teachers were previously trained within a context in which Deaf people had no involvement at all and where the focus was solely related to the concepts of impairment and rehabilitation.

Educational institutions have the possibility to design their own school settings and to open them to the Deaf community so that their language is used, their understanding of the world is included, and their identity is strengthened. In addition to being present with its language, the Deaf community ought to actively participate in school decisions, interact with hearing teachers, and become autonomous and committed models for children and young adults.

Canales projects meet the principles we believe should be part of the design of educational policies for Deaf people. We understand that these are the ways that will lead us to an accessible, quality, intercultural, and bilingual school—that is, an inclusive school for Deaf students.

In Argentina we are in the process of building new educational models for Deaf students that are accessible in their symbolic, cultural, physical, and linguistic forms. We come via winding roads from the strong oralist idea historically embraced in our country as a leader of (oral) deaf education in Latin America to the point where we are today. For a real change in education, stereotypical judgments of Deaf people should be changed, and this transformation has to occur in the hearing population and especially in the Deaf population. We will move forward only if we are able to analyze the results of our actions and change the imaginary idea we have built with respect to deaf education during our long history.

References

Canales.(n.d.a). Creciendo enseñas. Retrieved from http://www.canales.org.ar

Canales. (n.d.b). Material propio. Retrieved from http://www.canales.org.ar/materiales_material_propio.php

Canales. (n.d.c). Videolibros en Lengua de Señas Argentina (Videobooks in Argentine Sign Language). Retrieved from http://www.videolibroslsa.org.ar es

Gragnolati, M., Rofman, R. P., Apella, I. R., & Troiano, S. (2015). *As time goes by in Argentina: Economic opportunities and challenges of the demographic transition.* Washington, DC: World Bank. Retrieved from http://wwwds.worldbank.org/external/default/WDSContentServer/WDSP/IB/2015/04/27/090224b082e0f786/1_0/Rendered/PDF/As0time0goes0b0mographic0transition.pdf

Ministry of Education. (2011). *Aportes para la lafabetización en Educación Especial de alumnus ciegos y disminuidos visuals, de sordos e hipoacúsicos* [Contributions for literacy in Special Education of blind, visually impaired, deaf and hard of hearing students]. Buenos Aires, Argentina: Ministerio de Educación de la Nación. Retrieved from http://bit.ly/1IzOwdZ

Veinberg, S. (1996). Argentinien: AnfängeundEntwicklung der ErziehungGehörloser [Argentina: Initiatives and development of deaf education]. *Das Zeichen. Zeitschrift Zum Thema Gebärdenspracheund Kommunikation Gehörlose, 38,* 488–496.

Veinberg, S. (2010a). *Fotografías de la educación de Sordos* [Portraits of education of the Deaf]. IX Congresso Internacional e XV Seminario Nacional. O lugar do conhecimento: identidade, sujeito e subjetividade. Rio de Janeiro, Brazil.

Veinberg, S. (2010b). *Prácticas en educación bilingüe: la promoción de la lectura en LSA* [Bilingual education practices: The promotion of reading in LSA]. IX Congresso Internacional e XV Seminario Nacional. O lugar do conhecimento: identidade, sujeito e subjetividade. Rio de Janeiro, Brasil.

Veinberg, S. (2012). *Orientaciones para la terminalidad de las escuelas rurales primarias para adolescentes y jóvenes CD del NOA y del NEA y de las provincias de La Rioja, San Juan, Córdoba, Santa Fe y Entre Ríos. Particularidades de los alumnos Sordos* [Guidelines for primary school completion in rural schools by teens and youth CD of the NOA and of the NEA and the provinces of La Rioja, San Juan, Cordoba, Santa Fe and Entre Rios. Characteristics of Deaf students]. Informe presentado al PROMER. Ministerio de Educación de la Nación.

Veinberg S., Carracedo, L., & Suchodolski, M. (2015). Educación inclusiva–inclusión educativa: el caso de la educación de los Sordos [Inclusive education–inclusion educational: The case of deaf education]. *Periódico El Cisne Año, 25*(298).

Zgryzek, S., & Veinberg, S. (2012). *El placer de leer en Lengua de Señas Argentina: primeros pasos para el acceso a la lengua escrita de las niñas y los niños sordos* [The pleasure of reading in Argentina Sign Language: First steps for access to written language by deaf children]. Buenos Aires: Bibliografika.

3

Producing and Consuming: Deaf Culture Negotiations in the Contemporary Scene

Lodenir Becker Karnopp, Madalena Klein,
and Márcia Lise Lunardi-Lazzarin

This chapter focuses on the cultural productions of Deaf communities and discusses the power relations involved in the construction of cultural meanings of Deaf identities and differences. It is grounded in the field of cultural studies in education, understanding culture as a battlefield around social meaning, and in the field of Deaf studies, conceiving Deaf culture as a space for dispute and constitution of identities and differences that determine the lives of individuals and populations.

It is worth noting that Deaf people's cultural productions usually involve the use of sign language(s), belonging to a Deaf community, and contact with hearing people—contact that is liable to provide a bilingual and intercultural experience for that community.

Aiming at giving continuity and consolidating research in the area of deaf education, this study has at its core in the analysis of the cultural productions of Brazilian Deaf communities in the different regions of the country, with emphasis on the spaces where an organized Deaf movement is found. Our investigative actions are geared towards analyzing the processes of meaning involved in the production, circulation, and consumption of artifacts of Deaf culture. In so doing, we intend to make the cultural production of Brazilian Deaf communities visible and to contribute to their diffusion. We have prioritized visual recordings available in both printed and digital form—through drawings (illustrations), films/videos, written sign language, translations from Brazilian Sign Language (Libras) to written Portuguese, among other art productions.

This project was supported by a Productivity Grant to Lodenir Karnopp from the Brazilian National Research Council (PQ-CNPq-Process 306626/2012-8).

The chapter will show the analysis carried out in the first stage of the research, with emphasis on the productions of Deaf culture circulating: (i) in formal publishing materials; (ii) on the Internet, especially on YouTube; and (iii) in the course of Letras–Libras. Based on the material produced, this chapter intends to analyze the social processes of meaning involved in the production, circulation, and consumption of Deaf culture artifacts. The analysis of the production of these artifacts has considered the recurrent and singular discourse shown in the material collected. From this collection of discourse, categories of analysis have emerged. They are presented in section two of this chapter.

The Uses of Culture in Contemporary Times

Stuart Hall, a Jamaican scholar living in England, has done interesting analyses about the political and cultural dimensions of globalization and their implications in the constitution of the cultural identities of different social groups. Focusing mainly on aspects of post-colonial diasporas, the author questions the hegemonic forms of understanding culture, stressing, at the same time, its growing importance for the constitution of ways of living and of seeing subjects. From a research field named cultural studies, Hall and other researchers have carried out investigations, which focus on culturally marginalized populations and discuss the power relations involved in the production of meanings and identities. As to that, Silva argues:

> Maybe more importantly, Cultural Studies conceives culture as a field of struggles around social meaning. Culture is a field of meaning production, in which different social groups, occupying different power positions, fight to impose their meanings on society at large. Culture is, in this conception, a disputed field of meaning. What lies centrally at play is the definition of the cultural and social identity of different groups. (1999, pp. 133–134)

In keeping with this epistemological field, researchers involved with deaf education have potentiated discussions that go beyond the disciplinary field of education, rendering cultural themes a privileged locus of analysis and discussion. The emphasis in the centralizing dimension of a universal culture has made it impossible to acknowledge and to give visibility to cultural processes of minority groups, among which are Deaf communities. Thus, since the late 1990s, especially in Brazil, a number of research investigations have constituted other ways of looking at Deaf people and deafness, which has been recognized as the field of Deaf studies.[1]

Analyzing the main narratives of culture, we historically find the opposition nature–culture; culture is what is produced by man, distinct from what is taken as natural and existing in the world. This use of the word *culture* has, according to Canclini (2005, p. 38), "served to distinguish the cultural from the biological or genetic, and to overcome primary forms of ethnocentrism…the political consequence of this definition is cultural relativism." It may be argued that this conception of culture as opposed to nature has led to the way Deaf subjects and groups have been discursively produced throughout history. The emphasis on an alleged fact of nature—the abnormal ear—has denied any possibility of narratives that would inscribe Deaf people as a cultural group capable of producing meanings from their shared experiences.

Considering the close relation that can be established between historical context and Deaf movements, we would like to underline that, on covering some parts of the history of Brazilian Deaf movements, this connection could also be seen. In other words, when Libras was not recognized, or when it was banished from schools and various social spaces, there were also no publishing activities or recognition of Deaf culture. Teaching prioritized the speaking and writing of the Portuguese language. In schools there was neither room for nor acceptance of cultural productions in signs. In spite of that, among Deaf people there circulated signed narratives, jokes, poems, life stories—but in spaces far from the control of those who deprivileged sign language. Specifically in the Brazilian scenario, it is still possible to verify that the reference to a Deaf culture is irrelevant to many people and definitely uncomfortable to some others.

Perhaps it is easy to define and to place, in time and space, a group of people; however, when it comes to reflecting on the fact that in this community specific cultural

---

1. In Brazil the term *Estudos Surdos* (Deaf Studies) was borrowed principally from British groups of investigation (University of Bristol). The field trajectory of investigations and propositions started in the Program of Post-Graduation in Education of the Federal University of Rio Grande do Sul (UFRGS). Inspired by ongoing discussions in the field of Cultural Studies in Education, researchers—deaf and hearing as well—have presented other forms of analyzing the education of deaf people, reversing what was a pathological view to a cultural perspective of difference. The engagement with the deaf social movements is a characteristic of this field, which has brought to the research agenda themes hitherto little explored, such as the power–knowledge relationship, social discourse and representations, and the constitution of the deaf subjects—among others. It is worth noting that Deaf Studies have multiplied in different academic spaces, which explains the heterogeneous production found in the field.

processes arise—or may arise—the rejection of the idea of "Deaf culture" is commonly supported by the conception of a universal culture, a monolithic culture. It does not seem possible to understand or accept the concept of Deaf culture if not through a multicultural perspective, that is, one that looks to each culture in its own logic, in its own historicity, in its own processes and productions. In such a context, Deaf culture is not the veiled image of a hypothetical hearing culture. It is not its reverse. It is not a pathological culture (Skliar, 1998, p. 28). In schools, or in clinical contexts, where sign language and/or Deaf culture are not tolerated, there is, in general, a complete ignorance of the processes and products generated by certain Deaf groups in relation to theater, humor, visual poetry—in short, the cultural production in sign language.

When we state that Deaf Brazilians are members of a Deaf culture, we are not implying that all Deaf people in the world share the same culture simply because they do not hear. Deaf Brazilians are members of Brazilian Deaf culture, as Deaf Americans are members of North American Deaf culture. These groups use different sign languages and have different life experiences; however, notwithstanding the place where they live, one factor that identifies them all is the visual experience. We are not referring, by this, to the compensatory perspectives—usually used to describe Deaf people—which understand that, due to the lack of hearing, they develop the sense of vision. To us the visual experience is related to Deaf culture, represented by the sign language, in a different way of being, expressing, and signifying the world.

Looking, for a Deaf person, is much more than a sense; it is a possibility of *being* something else and of occupying another position in the social network. Looking, understood as a Deaf marker, is what allows one to gaze upon oneself; it is what allows for a reading of the world in different ways, the caring of one for another, the interest in particular things, the interpreting and being in a different manner after a Deaf experience—and finally, looking, as a mark, is what allows for the construction of a Deaf otherness (Lopes & Veiga Neto, 2006).

We do not understand Deaf culture as something situated, closed, or framed. On the contrary, we see it as something hybrid, borderline, in which each group creates "differentiating strategies that organize the historical articulation of features selected from various groups to weave their interactions" (Canclini, 2005, p. 48). We see it in the sense that Heidegger has imparted to cultural places when he considers that "a frontier is not the point where something ends, but, as acknowledged by the Greek, the frontier is the point from which something begins to make itself present" (Bhabha, 2005, p. 19). Deaf culture is present among us, presenting itself, maybe, as a wish for recognition, in search of "another place and of something else," imparting other images and other senses from those so far in existence or from those determined by the hearing culture.

The culture of recognition is of crucial importance to the linguistic minorities that want to affirm their cultural traditions and recover their repressed histories.

However, this fact indicates to us the dangers of fixedness and fetishism of identities within their own calcified culture, in the sense of producing a celebratory view of the past or a homogenized view of the present history. From this perspective, we are not simply opposing Deaf culture to the other cultures but approximating our analysis to the perspective of cultural hybridism, in the sense that "all cultures are involved with one another" and "none of them is unique and pure, they are all hybrid, heterogeneous" (Burke, 2003, p. 53). As an example of cultural hybridism, we can refer the work of two Deaf poets—one of them Brazilian, the other British—analyzed by Quadros and Sutton-Spence. Their poems, in distinct sign languages, identify them as Deaf people and as members of their national communities as well. According to the authors:

> Deaf people's identity and culture are complex, since their members often live in a bilingual and multicultural environment. On the one hand, the deaf people are part of a visual group, of a deaf community that may stretch beyond the national sphere, reaching world level. It is a border-crossing community. On the other, they are part of a national society, with a language of their own and with cultures shared with hearing people of their country. (Quadros & Sutton-Spence, 2006, p. 111)

We have found a vast and diverse cultural production in Deaf associations, schools, and meeting places. Some of these are stories recovered and told by Deaf elders and/or by Deaf storytellers. A small part of this production has more recently been recorded on videotape or DVDs, either in Libras or translated into Portuguese.

Libras is the main identity marker of the Deaf culture. Libras became official in Brazil through Law number 10.436, dated April 24, 2002, regulated by Decree number 5.626, of December 22, 2005, as the result of struggles of the organized Deaf movement in different cities around the country. It has been a struggle for many years, which has mobilized Deaf Brazilians and motivated the exchange/propagation of the language, an indispensable element of the Brazilian Deaf culture. It is a visual–gestural language, the written form of which has just started being employed by users in their everyday life. Sign writing is the form of registering the sign languages, but the work produced under this form is rare (Stumpt, 2008). Additionally, there are few schools that include sign writing in their curricula, so this has not yet become a system widely used by the Deaf community. We believe, however, that, in addition to video (DVD) productions, written sign language is a potential form of recording Deaf culture, since it makes the printing of texts and their circulation in different times and spaces possible.

It is worth stressing that the cultural production of Deaf people involves, in general, the use of a sign language, their belonging to a Deaf community, and contact with hearing people, so that this linguistic and cultural contact is capable of providing a bilingual experience to that community. In this sense, written Portuguese, in addition to sign language writing, is also part of the Deaf world, indispensable to Deaf Brazilians for their schooling, the defense of their rights, and their citizenship. One may think that written records in Portuguese will favor the destruction of the richness of sign language; yet, such a register is not in itself a risk factor, as one can view writing as the search for translation of cultural roots, among other possibilities.

Other forms of documentation, such as filming, are fundamental, in addition to sign writing and its translation into written Portuguese, for the recording of a cultural production that might get lost or suffer changes. In order for a Deaf community to keep an open range of artistic possibilities and options of expression in sign language, visual records are essential, as they allow the creation of visual libraries potentiated by the development of new information technologies.

In referring to Libras we do not mean that this language is used the same way by all Deaf Brazilians. As any other language, it is subject to regional variation, adapting to historical, social, and cultural aspects of the different communities in which it is used. In the same way, artistic and cultural productions are influenced by these aspects. Thus, taking into consideration the non-homogeneity of Libras and of the Brazilian Deaf culture, the lack of records of this variation and of these regional cultural crossings, it becomes more and more urgent to undertake actions that prioritize the collection and analysis of this material in order to constitute a database of reference for studies on Deaf culture and its insertion in the context of regional and national cultures.

Traditionally the expression of Deaf culture requires a close, face-to-face encounter among Deaf people in the same space. This establishes a singular time–space relationship so that the cultural exchanges may circulate through the Deaf communities. Yet, the dissemination of new information technologies has established other possibilities of encounters in which sharing and exchanging meaning have been enhanced. Given these multiple possibilities of production, circulation, and consumption of the Deaf culture, new challenges arise for comparative research in the cultural field.

We can assert that investigations related to Deaf culture have been developing a trajectory in post-graduate programs in education to which Deaf and hearing researchers of varied areas of knowledge converge, thus establishing an interdisciplinary character to research in the field.

Approaches to Deaf Culture Spaces

We describe, next, the methodological procedures followed in the research. Initially, three investigative categories, respecting the actions implicated in the investigational processes, have been defined—namely, "publishing production," which represents cultural products published by established entities and widely distributed; "Internet free-circulating production," which are cultural products available on the Internet; and

"Letras–Libras undergraduate students' production," which are student products such as videos produced in university courses.

These productions have been catalogued in a database in which we, the authors, attempt to describe the details of various productions that fall into the previously mentioned categories. The database recorded several items of analysis, including: title; author; publishing year; publishing house/institution responsible for the production/publication; target public; text typology (informative text, persuasive text, entertainment text); elements in printed material; and elements in multimedia material. In the next sections we present some of the analysis that has been carried out, looking into the effects revealed by the notion of Deaf culture in the analyzed spaces.

Publishing Production

Through the data collected from the material collected from publishing houses or other national institutions, some of the items recorded and analyzed stood out from others. This helped identify differences between different categories of materials. These characteristics will be discussed in this section.

In our first approaches to the research, we considered the publishers' productions, such as books and DVDs, as artifacts to be analyzed. Ninety-seven (97) pieces of work, printed and/or on DVD, were catalogued. There were several publishing houses and institutions responsible for the production and publication of the material, including the National Institute for Deaf Education, Ministry of Education (INES/MEC), the National Federation of Deaf Education and Integration (FENEIS), and other national publishers. The majority of them are located in the region between Rio de Janeiro and São Paulo, which shows a prevailing production in Southeastern Brazil.

The greater number of these productions addresses a target public of children and youth, but teachers have also been targeted. The objectives of these productions for this public usually contain information about deafness. Themes like sign language, the importance of getting to know the Deaf people (and the community), and inclusive processes, among others, are notable in the material collected.

It is worth stressing that, in a number of these materials, a strong medical orientation for dealing with deafness has been detected, which subscribed to a clinical paradigm that attempts to frame Deaf people within a hearing norm. In these materials developed by publishers and other institutions, a large part of the material is created not by Deaf authors but by teachers, speech and language professionals (including audiologists), and other professionals related to both educational and clinical areas. This fact emphasizes that aspects of deficiency and incompleteness as representations of deafness are often present in this category of materials related to Deaf people and deafness.

In this same editorial context, discursive discontinuities are evidenced in which the Deaf movements, through their leaders, struggle over issues related to the political and identity recognition of Deaf people. In the catalogued work, aside from the clinical representations, there are pieces of work that show the presence of Deaf characters, sign language interpreters, and elements of Deaf culture. The predominance of visual aspects helps guarantee the creation of other ways of looking at deafness.

We have verified that the greatest rate of production occurred between 1999 and 2010, a time when Deaf movements fought for the recognition of being Deaf as a cultural difference. At the same time, educational policies fomented the discussions and debates around the inclusion of Deaf children in the regular schooling system, rather than educating them in schools for the Deaf. The evidence related to the kinds of materials described in the previous paragraph can possibly create different meanings in this battlefield. Sign language, visual approaches, and sign language (Libras) interpreters, for instance, can be considered as parts of Deaf culture and resistance markers. But they also can represent pedagogical "aids" that make the insertion and integration of Deaf students in general school spaces together with hearing students possible.

The issues so far raised provoke the continuity of the analyses and allow significant intersections with the other categories previously mentioned. In order to do this, we will show some specific traits in the sequence of this chapter, at the same time pointing out possibilities of articulation in the analysis of the other artifacts either found in free circulation on the Internet or produced by Letras–Libras students in universities.

Internet Free-circulating Production

The material analyzed from videos collected from YouTube marks the free Internet circulation of Deaf cultural productions. By means of the visual recordings in artistic categories, such as performances, advertisements, jokes, and other displays of Deaf people, we can infer that these productions serve as guidelines for the constitution of Deaf identities.

In the set of material collected up to the present, we are able to visualize a diversity of content. The videos produced by Deaf associations, for example, rely on the diffusion of events for the Deaf community and other interested people. The videos produced by Deaf leaders from different regions of the country have the diffusion of sign language as a central theme, be it through jokes or stories. In other videos analyzed, the content is more on an informative level. For example, it is more concerned with public service announcements about, for instance, tax reduction for car purchases or stickers for the identification of Deaf drivers. There is also a good number of videos that publicize bilingual software—in which elements of Deaf culture, like the flashing light doorbells, stand out—or that present theater pieces in sign language.

The categorization of the data collected showed the recurrence of a few elements. In approximately 34% of the videos analyzed, we noted the participation of hearing people in the video production, as well as the subtitles, background sound, and narration. However, the involvement of Deaf people can be observed in all the productions collected, as well as the fact that the materials' target is people fluent in Libras.

This use of Libras in these productions shows that deafness has been narrated based on a discourse of linguistic cultural difference. In this sense, Deaf people represent their identity as legitimate within Deaf culture. It is up to them to develop "the place…to build their subjectivity so as to ensure their survival and to have their status quo, in face of the multiple cultures, multiple identities" (Perlin, 2004, p. 78).

This place is discursively invented; that is to say, Deaf subjects produce themselves, but they are also produced by a vast discursive network, which positions them in certain places. In this perspective, another look at these data is worthwhile. We understand that the degree of participation by hearing people in the making of the videos points to a broader dimension of the target public, with the issues of deafness being also addressed to hearing Internet users.

Based on this, it is possible to state that the discourses, which circulate in the analyzed videos, are producing certain forms of understanding of Deaf culture. This means that this notion is no longer taken as a fixed and stable reference—for example, the idea that Deaf culture would be limited to the use of sign language. It can be observed that Deaf people themselves have been producing and enlarging the meanings of what is considered Deaf culture by means of cultural hybridism.

Another prominent aspect of this analytic view is the authorship of the videos. There is a great incidence of participation of Deaf associations, schools for the Deaf, Deaf theater groups, and independent Deaf actors, with a large number of published productions. By that we want to stress that what is consumed as Deaf culture still needs to be legitimated by Deaf representation. This becomes more evident when we realize that representation can only be understood in a game of power relations in which meanings are produced by certain discursive practices. In other words, the right of representing, constituting, and presenting the Deaf cultural image is intimately related to the place these subjects occupy in the cultural scene.

This configuration allows us to say that the different forms of production of Deaf culture analyzed in the research are not only interfering in the way the notion of Deaf culture is signified in the present time and space. These displacements in the way of understanding Deaf culture have also been producing Deaf subjectivities that are convenient for contemporaneity. It is possible to perceive that the use of this culture can be articulated with the convenience of the forms of being Deaf, because "the convenience of the culture supports performativity as the fundamental logics of today's social life" (Yúdice, 2004, p. 50). We are referring here to the ways of acting, negotiating, and resisting socially that are adopted by Deaf subjects in order to remain culturally different.

The Production of Letras–Libras Undergraduate Students

As part of this project, we catalogued narratives and poems from Letras–Libras undergraduates in a distance learning course in 2008, disseminated through the Federal University of Santa Maria. Students from different regions of Brazil and 15 different universities produced final papers for a Deaf Literature course. The work was developed in different centers used by the course and was done either individually or in groups of four students, resulting in 183 productions. The aim of the Letras–Libras training is the development of both teachers and sign language interpreters. Facilitators for the distance education course included course teachers, tutors, and monitors who interacted with different regions in the country in the distance education modality. Teaching is bilingual in the Virtual Learning Environment (AVEA) and the material available for the students is in Libras and Portuguese. The centers in the different regions provided the final student productions on DVD and included: the Federal University of Rio Grande do Sul (UFRGS), the Federal University of Espírito Santo (UFES), the State University of Pará (UEPA), Goiás Federal Institute of Education and Technology (IFETGO), the University of Brasília (UnB), the Federal University of Paraná (UFPR), the State University of Campinas (Unicamp), the Federal University of Santa Catarina (UFSC), the Federal University of Rio Grande do Norte (UFRN), and the Federal University of Grande Dourados (UFGD).

The empirical data analyzed consisted of the literary production (narratives and poems) in Libras by students in the Deaf Literature course, which integrates the curriculum of the Letras–Libras course. We do not see these narratives only as "a passive field for the mere recording or expression of existing meanings" (Hall, 1997, p. 47). The meanings are historically built, and what is narrated by Deaf people is inscribed in the discursive terrain that is possible in our time. The catalogued material showed us the productivity to be found in the creation and strengthening of certain features in the literary productions in Libras. The students' productions were marked by the experiences of Deaf people relating to the use of sign language and its insertion into family and school environments, settings where stories are exchanged mainly in the Portuguese language. The majority of the students chose to translate fables and popular stories into Libras, such as "The Frog and the Ox," "The Rat and the Elephant," and "Hansel and Gretel," among others. The productions could be characterized as cultural translations of narratives or poems by Aesop, La Fontaine, Hans Christian Andersen, as well as Brazilian children's author Monteiro Lobato, Brazilian poet Vinícius de Moraes, and biblical texts. Other students, however, created more detailed narratives; some of them related to their life experiences, including social and school experiences.

As to the textual typology, all of the 183 pieces produced have an entertaining quality consisting fundamentally of folkloric texts (fables), humorous texts (anecdotes, jokes), narratives (tales, fairy tales), and poems. This tendency is due to the type of work designated by the discipline of Deaf Literature, which asked for literary production in Libras or the translation of a literary piece into Libras. The lengths of productions by the students were from 1 to 15 minutes.

In general, the students demonstrated a preference for narratives and poems translated into sign language. Among the productions, the ones with Deaf culture markers stand out. These included those containing lessons for life, those that stimulate imagination and playfulness, and those that prioritized performances in sign language. The majority of the videos show the signer in the foreground providing a clear view of the signing in Libras. Some of the works also used were illustrations, performances, and subtitles for the story narration. We want to highlight the aesthetic use of signs with emphasis on classifiers and on linguistic expressiveness in the production of stories and poems.

Fables were the favorite narrative form. We presumed that time was the factor in the selection of fables. However, it is possible that there was a preference for texts displaying life lessons or containing a concluding "message." The texts teach, touch, provoke, encourage success in life, and demonstrate equality for all. They are also examples of goodness, humility, and affection and show what is right in life, with a moral.

The narratives and poems presented by Deaf people can be seen as tools of resistance and as cultural markers, as the Deaf subjects affirm their legacies through their productions. In this way, the possibility is open for knowing or recognizing other ways of living and of narrating what has been lived, conferring visibility to many invisible protagonists, based on the stories that are translated, adapted, and invented.

Negotiations of Deaf Culture—A Final Note

The visual recordings identified by this study offer the possibilities of opening opportunities for sharing and exchanging meanings among Deaf communities, both in face-to-face and virtual spaces. In the context of the research we have considered published production of books and DVDs as one category of the artifacts to be analyzed. Ninety-seven have been catalogued, either in print or on DVD. The collection has been achieved through book donations and through surveys of the websites of publishers where we primarily accessed catalogues or e-books. In Brazil, the majority of these products have been distributed to educational institutions by the Ministry of Education. The productions were focused on entertainment or informational material and primarily targeted children. Some of the material on DVDs or CDs included sign language, and some used subtitles in Portuguese.

The investigation has also used the virtual environment of YouTube where videos are posted and freely accessed by Internet users for data collection. Regarding the categories of the analyzed videos, there were works of art, performances, advertisements, jokes, and other displays by Deaf people, which supported the construction of Deaf identities and difference. In this space, as well, productions with either an entertaining or informative character were found. Participation of the hearing public could be identified in the production of subtitles, background sound, and narration. This fact supports the idea that discourses about Deaf culture are articulated within a power and knowledge network in which cultural meanings are constantly negotiated in order to mark out spaces that may legitimize what should be considered Deaf culture.

The other materials analyzed were the productions of narratives and poems in Libras, developed by Deaf and hearing students in the distance learning Letras–Libras course. One hundred and eighty-three products were catalogued involving over 300 students at 10 course centers, in Belém, Brasília, Campinas, Curitiba, Dourados, Florianópolis, Goiânia, Natal, Porto Alegre, and Vitória. The material produced by the students is quite diverse and targets sign language users of different age groups. These productions demonstrated that aesthetic effects were given priority in telling a story or producing a poem in sign language. The poems presented in Libras accentuated facial and body expression, with rhythm and rhymes unique to sign language, giving emphasis to an aesthetic use of hands, location, and movement. Additionally, the students showed preference for narrative texts in countrywide circulation, particularly fables and stories, in which they inserted elements of Deaf culture. These narratives predominantly related to "lessons for life."

In analyzing the material, we have observed that the discourses around Deaf culture serve as a base or as support for claims of Deaf identity and difference in public spaces. Since culture allows creating spaces where people feel "safe" and "at home," Deaf culture is more than simply a gathering of ideas, narratives, and materials. It is founded upon difference, which works as a resource. As Yúdice (2004, p. 43) states, "the content of culture shrinks in importance whereas the utility of the claims for difference as a warrant gains legitimacy. The result is that politics win over the content of culture."

References

Bhabha, H. (2005). *O local da Cultura* [The location of culture]. Belo Horizonte, Brazil: Editora UFMG.

Burke, P. (2003). *Hibridismo Cultural* [Cultural hybridity]. São Leopoldo, Brazil: Editora UNISINOS.

Canclini, N. G. (2005). *Diferentes, desiguais e desconectados* [Different, uneven and disconnected]. Rio de Janeiro, Brazil: Editora UFRJ.

Hall, S. (1997). A centralidade da cultura: Notas sobre as revoluções culturais do nosso tempo [The centrality of culture: Notes about the cultural revolution of our time]. *Educação e Realidade, 22*(2), 15–46.

Lopes, M. C., & Veiga Neto, A. (2006). Marcadores culturais surdos quando eles se constituem no espaço escolar [Deaf cultural markers when it is part of school space]. *Revista Perspectiva, 24* (especial), 81–100.

Perlin, G. (2004). O lugar da cultura surda. In A. Thoma & M. Lopes (Org.), *A invenção da surdez: cultura, alteridade, identidade e diferença no campo da educação.* Santa Cruz do Sul: EDUNISC, 73–82.

Quadros, R. M., & Sutton-Spence, R. (2006). Poesia em língua de sinais: Traços da identidade surda [Poetry in sign language: Features of deaf identity]. In R. M. Quadros (Ed.), *Estudos Surdos I* (pp. 110–165). Petrópolis, Brazil: Arara Azul. Retrieved from www.editora-arara-azul.com.brParteA.pdf

Silva, T. T. (1999). *Documentos de Identidade: Uma introdução às teorias do currículo* [Identity documents: An introduction to curriculum theories]. Belo Horizonte, Brazil: Autêntica.

Skliar, C. (1998). *Surdez: Um olhar sobre as diferenças* [Deafness: A look at the differences]. Porto Alegre, Brazil: Mediação.

Stumpf, M. R. (2008). *Escrita de Sinais III* [Sign Writing III]. Florianópolis, Universidade Federal de Santa Catarina. Retrieved from http://www.signwriting.org/archive/docs6/sw0569-BR-2008-StumpfELSIII.pdf

Yúdice, G. (2004). *A conveniência da cultura: Usos da cultura na era global* [The expedience of culture: Uses of culture in the global era]. Belo Horizonte, Brazil: Editora UFMG.

4

Bilingual Inclusive Deaf Education: Research in the Public Education System

Cristina B. F. Lacerda

Brazil's current National Education Policy is defined based on a number of national and international documents (Brazil, 1988, 1990, 1994, 1996, 2001a, 2001b, 2001c; UNESCO, 1998; United Nations, 2006) and determines that inclusive education is the most suitable form of teaching special education students, consistent with various international debates. This policy describes inclusive educational processes as "a political, cultural, social, and pedagogical action undertaken in defense of the right of all students to be together with others, learning and participating without any kind of discrimination" (Brazil, 2008, p. 1). Rooted in human rights, the policy aims to pair equality and difference as inseparable values that constitute our society and, therefore, considers that educational actions to be established and implemented must overcome exclusion inside and out of school (Brazil, 2008). To that end, the inclusion of all students, including those considered disabled, into the regular education system is defended, and schools are to organize themselves accordingly, ensuring the necessary conditions to provide quality education for all (Brazil, 2001a).With regard to Deaf students, the inclusive education policy also needs to consider two other official documents that guarantee the recognition of Brazilian Sign Language (Libras) as a legally recognized means of expression and communication and the right of Deaf people (Brazil, 2002). Therefore, according to the policy, education practices are to be developed in school environments in order to ensure that bilingual deaf education is provided (Brazil, 2005). In general, bilingual deaf education believes that Deaf students should learn sign language as the first language (L1) from Deaf adults who are users of the language and active participants in the educational process. When Deaf

The research in this article was financially supported by Fundação de Amparo à Pesquisa do Estado de São Paulo (FAPESP) proc. 2012/17730-9. I would like to thank, particularly, bilingual teachers Julia Caroline de Araújo Almeida and Elaine Aparecida Machado de Agostino for their help in producing this article.

50

professionals are not available, the legislation provides for the participation of bilingual (Libras–Portuguese) hearing adults with a documented fluency in Libras.

Reconciling, the National Education Policy, which calls for inclusion and existing laws regarding linguistic, social, and educational rights of Deaf people, with the various interpretations of these laws and national policy, is challenging. There are different views regarding the needs of Deaf students and how to provide these students access. In Brazil, basic education is organized as follows: Early Childhood Education for children from 0 to 5 years old; Primary Education I for children from 6 to 10 years old; Primary Education II includes students from 11 to 14 years old; Secondary Education includes youths from 15 to 17 years old. The next education level is Higher Education, which is offered by universities, university centers, and faculties.

As a result, different inclusive education projects have been created. They do not always ensure that Deaf students' linguistic needs are taken into account, a critical consideration to make teaching and learning effective. There are also economic factors related to the training of professionals, hiring of specialists, and the organization of the school, when implementing an "egalitarian" education for all. Moreover, the law does not provide any sanctions for those who do not follow it, resulting in ineffective school experiences. Consequently, educational inclusion, although established by law, is implemented according to the feasibility determined by the administration of each site, who determine how "inclusion" is understood, and with no guarantee of meeting minimum requirements.

Conducting a bilingual inclusive program for Deaf students requires that certain principles be respected and put in place. Otherwise, Deaf students' language development, key for any learning to take place, is jeopardized. For educative practices to be considered inclusive and bilingual, they must consider language development the foundation for higher psychological processes. Additionally, interaction with Deaf adults who support the full development of Deaf children's language by immersing them in sign language and Deaf culture is critical. These Deaf adults must be fluent users of Libras and active in the Deaf community. It is essential that Deaf students in regular classrooms have Deaf peers in the same class to avoid linguistic isolation and a lack of interaction with peers that can marginalize Deaf students from socializing and learning processes (Góes & Tartucci, 2002).

The relationship between language development and learning written Portuguese as a second language is central in inclusive, bilingual proposals for Deaf students. Bilingual interlocutors must lead the process of learning Portuguese and provide the opportunity to learn the various uses of written language in the context of how meaning is constructed in Libras. These interlocutors must take into account that language development and learning processes actually begin with various reading practices, through activities that emphasize visual learning, including those that activate symbolic domains to build new knowledge (Lodi, 2010a, 2010b); in addition, curriculums should be implemented encompassing the socio-cultural diversity existing in the school. Therefore, the curriculum must guarantee the inclusion of Deaf ways of signifying the world, as well as courses in Libras for all.

In order for these processes to occur as expected, bilingual education has to be implemented from early childhood education. At this educational level the child experiences the period of development that is the foundation for their development, which is built through the relationships established with others (peers and adults) and by experiences via language in the school environment and outside of school. However, despite the critical importance of early education and Brazilian laws, which designate education should begin at this age, there are few early childhood educational opportunities for Deaf students. As a result, Deaf students start school with little language development and, therefore, with limited possibilities to acquire the knowledge circulating in the school.

Guidelines for ensuring Deaf people the right to education in Brazil can also be found in Decree 5626/05 (Brazil, 2005). As determined in Article 22 and Article 23 Paragraph 2 of the Decree, the inclusion of Deaf students in both public and private education systems are to be ensured through the organization of:

> I-bilingual education schools and classes open to both Deaf and hearing students, with bilingual teachers, in early childhood education and the early years of primary education;
>
>   II-bilingual or ordinary schools in the regular education system, open to both Deaf and hearing students for the later years of primary education, secondary education, or vocational education, with teachers of the various subjects aware of Deaf students' linguistic uniqueness, in conjunction with Libras-Portuguese interpreters and translators. (Brasil, 2005)

It is worth highlighting that, for the early years (i.e., early childhood education and early primary school), children should be allowed access to curriculums in their primary language, Libras, with the presence of a bilingual teacher. During the later years of primary and secondary school, each classroom with a signing Deaf student enrolled has Libras interpreters. Teachers of the various subjects are to be aware of Deaf students' linguistic uniqueness and keep in mind that classes will have an additional adult in the classroom (i.e., a Libras interpreter, whose role and styles of work may be unfamiliar). Additionally, teachers must recognize that Deaf students have a very different relationship with Portuguese than do hearing students.

Moreover, this Decree is relatively recent, and there are few courses on a higher education level to train Libras interpreters for various educational levels. The presence of these professionals in classroom are not free of conflicts arising from the relations between teachers and Libras interpreters, teachers and Deaf students, and Deaf students and Libras interpreters. Also, as Libras interpreters have only recently been professionally recognized, a mistaken view persists that simply knowing Libras is enough to work as an interpreter (Almeida, 2010).

Working as an interpreter requires a differentiated knowledge both of Libras and Portuguese and of the articulation processes specific to each of them. It also requires learning to experience another culture as an outsider in order to be able to put it into dialogue with their own culture (Lodi & Almeida, 2010). This process implies a relationship between languages and cultures (Sobral, 2008). In the school environment, the interpreting professional should also master the different terminology that constitutes each subject area, language that may be unfamiliar to them and unknown to the students. Therefore, it is not only teachers who require guidance about Deaf students' linguistic needs but also the Libras interpreters, who also require appropriate training for educational positions.

Deaf adults cannot be overlooked in these formative processes and should be present on each educational level in classrooms where Libras is the language of instruction (i.e., early childhood education and early years of primary education) and in the classrooms with Libras interpreters (later years of primary and secondary education). This professional should be the ideal interlocutor who can not only help Deaf students in language development and sign language acquisition but also serve as an adult role model, representing equality and capacity, and whose views could be decisive in the construction of a positive self-concept in students.

The training of this professional is also provided for in Decree 5626/05, which defines that the professional who teaches Libras should preferably be a Deaf person and should hold a degree in Pedagogy or higher education training in primary school teaching[1] although a secondary education diploma in teaching suffices for primary teaching. For later years of primary and secondary school, a higher education degree is required.

However, if we examine the historical processes of education for Deaf students, we will find that Deaf professionals with such qualifications are still a minority in the country. Most of them are concentrated in state capitals where more educational offerings has always existed (without necessarily implying better quality education), while a minority lives in smaller cities in the interior of the country. Therefore, in order to make the participation of Deaf professionals viable in Deaf children's education, the hiring process cannot take for granted, even today, training for these professionals

---

1. In Brazil, the latter is a degree obtained from a post-secondary program, called *curso normal superior*. These programs are at the secondary, pre-university level. They are similar to the normal schools in the nineteenth-century United States for training primary teachers (Ravitch, 2003).

included in the Decree. Fortunately, this reality is beginning to change as Deaf people increasingly demand higher education, and hopefully, in the coming years, we will have professionals suitably trained for this role. However, regardless of the availability of training, Deaf adults have experienced inadequate education during their lives, and because the higher education still privileges hearing students, many Deaf professionals function in environments that fail to engage in a continual reflection about their roles.

Santos and Gurgel's (2009) point out that this difficulty stems from the very conception of the role of this professional. Even today, it is not rare to see the teaching of Libras begin with lists of words, the naming and repetition of signs, and an inflexible educator who fails to consider students' knowledge and their development and learning processes. Therefore, in hiring Deaf professionals to work in schools, thorough and on-going on-the-job training should be provided "so the professional can build a respected profile as a language teacher and an educator concerned with the uniqueness of each group he/she will oversee" (Santos & Gurgel, 2009, p. 55).

In view of these circumstances, thinking about inclusive processes for Deaf children requires the following actions: the continuous training of teachers and other professionals who work in the school so they can understand Deaf students' linguistic and socio-cultural needs, and the hiring and on-the-job training of Deaf educators and professional Libras interpreters. Additionally, Libras must assume the status of a first language in learning processes of Deaf students, along with the necessary curriculum and methodology adaptations, and contact with other Deaf students must occur so that both the academic and social development of the included (integrated) Deaf children can be achieved.

Therefore, when we talk about inclusive schools for Deaf students and providing for their bilingual characteristics in the school environment, it is necessary to reflect on how public schools must thoroughly change the way they work with Deaf individuals. From this perspective, we developed a bilingual inclusive education program, with the participation of both the municipal government and the Universidade Federal de São Carlos, which has been operating since 2011 in the city of São Carlos, São Paulo (SP). São Carlos, in the state of São Paulo, has a population of over 238,000, and is an academic, technological, and industrial center that contributes to scientific research and professional training in various fields of study. The program is also supported by research agencies concerned with the need to train professionals and meeting Deaf students' educational needs.

Intervention and Research Context

In order to implement our project on Deaf students' inclusion, the Department of Education of the city of São Carlos established a condition that the project be done in the city's public schools. There were few bilingual professionals available in the city, so we had to work with professionals from the municipal school system, even though not all of them had the knowledge required for the actions that would be developed, using as much as possible the municipal system's available resources.

Officials from the city of São Carlos, SP, and researchers at the Universidade Federal de São Carlos formed a partnership to implement a Bilingual Inclusive Education Policy for Deaf children in the city. To that end, a plan of intervention and research was proposed to achieve the following goals:

1. Creating school-centers in the city prepared to work with Deaf students in early childhood education, primary education, and youth and adult education, using a bilingual inclusive program for Deaf individuals in accordance with Federal Decree 5626/05.
2. Seeking satisfactory education results for Deaf students by incorporating Libras into the school environment, rethinking methodologies, and developing pedagogies appropriate for these students at two municipal schools: an early childhood education unit, and a primary and youth/adult education unit (Educaçao de Jovenes e Adultos [Youth and Adult Education; EJA]).
3. Offering training to the whole team working at the schools concerning specific aspects of Deaf persons' language development, Deaf students' learning processes, the particularities of Libras enunciative–discoursive processes, and interaction processes of Deaf students included into the various social practices occurring in the schools.

In 2015, there were two students enrolled in early childhood education (two to five years old), ten students in the first stage of primary education (six to ten years old), eight on the second stage of primary education (11 to 14 years old), and two adults in EJA.

Organization of the Educational Program

At the end of 2011, we began our work in partnership with the Municipal Education Department, which found schools in their system that were interested in having the bilingual inclusive education program and had enough personnel, physical space, and school hours available. The Secretary of Education sent out an internal memo to teachers who were proficient in Libras and interested in working as bilingual teachers, to join the program. Thus, we proceeded to implement the educational model of classrooms with Libras as the language of instruction for Deaf children enrolled in early childhood education and the early years of primary education.

In this process, the classroom teacher, who must be bilingual, in partnership with the school administration, discussed the appropriate pedagogical strategies for Deaf students that would develop the same content taught to hearing students in classrooms where Portuguese was the language of instruction. Equivalent content allows the organization of parallel school activities (i.e., for Deaf and hearing students), giving Deaf children the same educational opportunities and, therefore, ensuring school and social inclusion and coexistence in diversity.

With the purpose of making the schools bilingual, with both Portuguese and Libras circulating in the school environment, Libras classes were offered to teachers and Libras classes for hearing children were taught by the bilingual professionals.

Although the presence of a Deaf adult was necessary in school activities, particularly with young children acquiring Libras, there was no Deaf adult available for that position in the city. In order to solve this problem, Deaf adults were often invited to visit the schools and speak to the Deaf students and their families as a way of minimizing the absence of these professionals. It was not until 2015 that a Deaf bilingual teacher (who had just graduated in Education) joined the school's team and began to collaborate in the teaching activities.

The second part of the project related to students enrolled in the later years of primary education and youths and adults enrolled in EJA. It called for inclusion mediated by Libras interpreters to provide access to the ideas and content developed by the teachers according to the curriculum guidelines for each year.

Considering also Deaf students' characteristics regarding the learning of Portuguese in primary, secondary, and adult education, these students participated in Portugueseas-a-second-language classes at specific times. These educational spaces included a bilingual teacher, who specialized in deaf education, and a professional Libras interpreter who worked together in planning and conducting the classes in order to provide more individualized attention to students.

In addition to these activities designed and developed for Deaf students, Libras classes taught by bilingual teachers were offered to their families, thus allowing families to understand the characteristics of this language and relate in the best possible way to their children by using sign language in out-of-school environments.

A third aspect focused on all professionals involved, regardless of the educational level in which they worked. Biweekly meetings were held with the program team, the Libras interpreters, and the teachers who had Deaf students in their classes in order to discuss the learning process of those students, help with the planning of suitable activities, and achieve a greater understanding of each student's educational process.

In view of the broadness of this research, which has been conducted since 2011, we have determined the following methods for data collection: (1) filming the activities in the classroom, in the Libras classes for the families, and in the classes of Portuguese as a second language, (2) field note diaries kept by the researchers about their activities, and (3) interviews with program participants. Written records of training meetings were also kept, which allowed reflecting on the effects of the training provided to all professionals involved and the suitability of the classroom practices. The records also allowed examination of Deaf students' academic, socio-affective, and language development, as well as their interactions with both Deaf peers and hearing students in the school environment. This reflection on how the bilingual inclusive program for Deaf students has developed over the last four years also enabled a critical look at the practices involved. It has provided understanding of how the proposed model has or has not met Deaf students' needs, and whether it has achieved the goals proposed in the national policy for educational inclusion.

Reporting Experiences to Contextualize Actions

Researchers closely monitor bilingual teachers involved in the education of the Deaf students and hold training meetings on an ongoing basis. These meetings are a space for reflecting on pedagogical practice. The bilingual teachers who work in the first stage of primary education (students aged six to ten) are supported by the research-funding agency and receive a grant to support deeper reflections on their classroom practices. Currently in our intervention, teacher reports focus on the teaching of Portuguese as a second language, and indicate the importance of working with various text genres in teaching literacy to Deaf students. For the purposes of this article, we will describe a few classroom activities and practices in Primary Education I that we consider exemplars of the activities that have been conducted.

Focusing on the Classroom

Due to the small number of Deaf students enrolled in São Carlos' municipal school system, all Deaf students old enough to attend the first stage of primary education were placed in the same school (Escola Polo). Because it was not viable to set up several classrooms with only a few students in each, they were placed in a single classroom with two bilingual teachers. Each teacher is responsible for a cycle: Cycle I—first to third grade (six to eight years old), or Cycle II—fourth and fifth grades (nine and ten years old), but both were equally responsible for the whole group. Currently, five students are enrolled in Cycle I and five in Cycle II. In a multi-graded context, while each teacher has the opportunity to follow students more individually and plan according to each student's need, the teacher cannot forget the entire range of topics and content to be addressed and should promote occasions in which older and younger students can exchange experiences, learn from each other's difference, and grow through these relations.

Many students start school without fluency in sign language, while others have learned it by interacting with Deaf peers in contexts outside of school (e.g., religious groups, community associations, family). However, the majority starts school using only home signs and a few Libras signs. In this context, conversational exchange between peers becomes even more necessary to support the acquisition and development of sign language. It is also worth noting that Deaf students who started primary education having participated in the early education part of the bilingual program enter first grade with a fluency in Libras that makes them stand out, indicating that such bilingual practices we have offered have advanced the acquisition and development of Libras.

Regarding the multi-grade issue, we should consider the teachers' difficulty in planning activities that consider the heterogeneity of learning needs, sign language mastery, and ages. Another challenge is the harmonious relationships that teachers must establish among themselves to accomplish multiple tasks including: the joint planning of classes, making needed changes to the plan, task division, maintaining constant communication for the sake of making decisions, and adopting practices and positions of mutual support in front of students and parents by not discrediting colleagues and by establishing an ethical and professional relationship.

ORGANIZING THE ACTIVITIES

In the beginning of each school year, bimonthly plans are designed based on a Yearly Teaching Plan. Over the year, weekly plans are designed based on the bimonthly plans. The weekly plan encompasses activities common to both Cycles I and II as well as specific plans for each cycle. The specific activities are designed and developed by each teacher for the students from the cycle he/she is working with.

In preparing classes based on the proposed goals, the teacher should decide on the following: the best way to present the content in sign language, and whether there are specific signs the teacher must learn to teach the content. Additional considerations include determining the most appropriate visual aids to support students' understanding of content, the need for printed material and content of that material, methods for recording the new content, and how many classes will be required to cover the content. Also assessment must be planned to assess learning as well as the suitability of the methods adopted. These choices should be made during the planning in order to achieve the goals.

The activities done in common by both Cycles are planned by the two bilingual teachers, according to a division of tasks. It is important to design activities that are appropriate for both older and younger students, as well as adapting both the vocabulary to be employed and the methods and materials to be used.

Last school year, the work was organized as follows: daily activities began with all students together and a new topic was presented each day under guidance of one of the teachers. Then the activities related to the topic were done in separate groups (Cycles I and II) under the guidance of the respective teachers. Each teacher focused her work with the group based on the plan for that particular class. Thus, the teacher was able to present a new content, carry out activities with the students, clarify misunderstandings, and conduct assessments.

As an example of an activity, we will look at activities related to fairy tales, a central topic during the bimester (a two-month period). The contents were organized to explain the different genres of texts. We chose fairy tales because they are interesting to students, in addition to being in the yearly curriculum plan for Cycle I Primary Education. Additionally, this genre had not yet been part of the curriculum and teaching activities for this class.

We chose to work with *Snow White and the Seven Dwarfs*. Various narrations of the story were presented in sign language. The idea was to show students videos with different narrators, thus giving greater visibility to the various ways of narrating a story in Libras. Exposure to diverse narratives can help widen students' ways of expressing things in Libras. In addition, watching a video with a sign language narrative fosters Deaf students' reading habits. They experience different narrations, different ways of saying things in their language, and due to the nature of video, they can repeatedly view the text providing possibilities to reflect about their language.

The students were enthusiastically engaged, which allowed the conducting of several activities related to the fairy tale. The following points were explored in these activities: the concept of a character's personality and physical traits, urban and rural landscapes, the notion of time and space (the tale's sequence and settings), and grammatical features of sign language, such as facial/body expression and the use of classifiers, among others.

After the experience of watching different versions of the tale in Libras, the students were invited to illustrate the passage they had liked most. The act of drawing involves the important domain of symbolic adoption that can enhance students' comprehension of aspects of the text that are being presented to them. Drawings by two students are shown below:

Drawing was explored throughout our work with the fairy tale, and students showed more details and elaborate aspects of the characters through dramatizations and by

FIGURE 1 Left, drawing by M., a male student, Cycle I. Right, drawing by G., a female student, Cycle II

recounting the story themselves, indicating their potential for deepening those aspects related to Libras and the narrative. In order to explore the traits of each character and establish a relation with aspects of ethnic, racial, and identity diversity—subjects also proposed for this education level—the teachers focused on the physical and psychological features of the characters and the implications of these characteristics for social relations. Both drawings and descriptions in Libras were explored so as to highlight the physical characteristics, facial and body expressions, and clothes seen by the students as they watched the videos about the tale. Drawing was used to prompt students to identify the characteristic features of the various characters, and based on the drawings, the teachers were able to better understand students' perceptions, thus helping them deepen their perceptions and understanding of the characteristics and how to express them.

For example, they were invited to draw and/or express in Libras the Snow White characters Sleepy, Bashful, and Grumpy, three of the seven dwarves. This activity revealed several students didn't understand how to observe and note the details of a particular character, and even after they understood the characteristics of each one, they were not able to explain them in Libras. Some students did not show a range of elements in their facial expressions, and that became an activity for the whole class.

Out of this activity came another; the students themselves proposed staging Snow White and the Seven Dwarfs. The students then set about developing the script, choosing the characters they wanted to play, making the scenery and costumes, which was a collective project undertaken by both cycles. The teachers used this activity to further explore body and facial expression, as well as different ways of delivery in Libras.

Figure 2 The Evil Queen learns from her Magic Mirror that she is the most beautiful.

FIGURE 3 The Hunter threatens to kill Snow White; she begs him not to do it. (An expression of fear and supplication.)

FIGURE 4 Theater performance for the school community and families.

The students' interest in the fairy tale and rehearsals spread to the parents attending the Libras study group at the school. The parents then decided they too would stage a version of the tale in Libras for the children, which promoted intensive work with sign language and effective discussions among hearing parents and Deaf children about the themes in the fairy tale. Both the children's and the parents' performances for the school community were scheduled for the same date so everyone could attend and interact with one another.

Portuguese-as-a-Second-Language Activities

During the work with the fairy tale, various activities involving reading and writing in Portuguese were proposed. The teachers started by showing the students a narrative text of the tale in Portuguese and asking them to indicate the words they knew.

After that, the students were prompted to read the text individually. As a new topic or content is approached, the starting point is always sign language, because:

> knowing a certain discursive genre in Portuguese means having contact with it in a significant way, primarily in Libras and later in Portuguese, and this relation of Libras to the second language should primarily occur through reading. (Lodi, 2012a, pp. 171–172)

The text was used as a basis for the work with Portuguese vocabulary and grammar, while understanding the importance of reading activities, since "literacy practices are closely linked to READING contexts. Without reading, there is no significant writing and, therefore, no literacy can take place" (Fernandes, 2006, p. 9). The students were also given different versions of the Snow White story in a "reading box" so they could freely refer to them at breaks between class activities. The main purpose was to allow free reading time according to the interest of each student. Gradually, they formed pairs and even groups to share their reading of the texts in Portuguese. They asked classmates with greater language mastery and teachers the meaning of unfamiliar words; first, they tried to read word by word, and the work was progressively directed to the importance of seeking meaning in the text, even though they might not know every word. Here, the work was focused on aspects of the multiple meanings of words, as well as the different ways of saying things in Portuguese and Libras (contrasting aspects between both languages). Lodi affirms that:

> importance should not be placed on the word itself, but rather on the meaning it carries, the different contexts in which the word is used, thus implying various ways of enunciating in Libras. (Lodi, 2012a, p. 173)

Free reading time fostered much learning. The students established relations with content dealt even in other subjects and deepened their knowledge of Portuguese grammar and spelling. Writing activities were proposed to complement the reading activities, beginning with collectively written pieces in order to produce greater student confidence, and later, individual writing. The knowledge created about the tale narrated and discussed in Libras gave students more confidence to write. They knew what they wanted to write and were taking the risk.

Prior to rewriting the tale individually, the teacher proposed as one of the activities that students draw a sequence of the facts they intended to narrate in the form of comics. The goal was to have students express themselves initially through drawing, which for many was the easiest form of expression, since "in this perspective, drawing is understood as the way children reflect their knowledge, thus giving sense to their ideas, the products of their thoughts" (Lodi, 2012b, p. 187).

By making the drawings, the students felt confident to produce their own texts, and some students wrote texts several pages long. The texts reveal the students' interest in writing and a quite comfortable relationship with writing in Portuguese. The students' writings also showed elements of correct usage of Portuguese, as well as very clear, consistent, and cohesive sentences and sequences of ideas. However, there were still passages in ungrammatical Portuguese and mistakes in standard language use. But what was important was that students were actually writing—putting themselves in the position of writers of Portuguese—which allowed teachers to intervene, make suggestions, and foster the expansion of their knowledge.

At the end of the bimester, formal examinations were conducted covering the period. Our position in this project has been one of continuous assessment, taking into account students' various products during all school activities. While conducting formal examinations ("test day") meets a bureaucratic demand of the municipal education system, it is also a systematized assessment event that provides the teacher with information about other aspects of his or her students' learning. These formal assessments seek to replicate content already covered in the classroom so they are familiar

FIGURE 5 Tale illustrated by Ma, a female student.

to students. The main focus of the assessment activity was reading and understanding Portuguese. The students took the test with no outside help. It was the first experience in which they were to read the entire assessment by themselves, including the exercise instructions, and answered the questions corresponding to their comprehension.

We observed that several students were capable of reading the texts and instructions, generally answering in a coherent manner and demonstrating good performance on questions related to reading, comprehension, and grammar. Even though their texts required corrections and changes in the written Portuguese and did not always adhere to the topic suggested, they exhibited good performance considering their history of producing individual written texts.

At our meetings, we reflected on the practices effected by teachers and researchers and developed a list of both gains and aspects to be improved. In considering the positive aspects of the process, we noted that the topic "Snow White and the Seven Dwarfs" allowed students to work with a number of types of texts: lists, invitations, recipes, drama, scripts, among others. Teachers were able to explore structural characteristics of texts and genres and social roles of genres with the students. However, we determined that the fairy tale genre was not sufficiently explored, because only one fairy tale was explored, which did not permit a more refined analysis of the genre.

Additionally, in order to work with the fairy tale genre, it was necessary to consider how to approach the content in sign language. When we consider Deaf children's learning process, particularly regarding literacy, there is an enormous methodological distance from approaches to teaching Portuguese to hearing children. Therefore, it is necessary to study and reflect on the characteristics of fairy tales related in sign language, which are quite different from Portuguese. How this content is approached and presented greatly impacts its comprehension by students and merits further study.

Understanding that the languages involved in the bilingual learning process are different and that discourse genres for each language are also differently marked indicates that simply making adaptations and transferring content from one language to another is not enough. The student can only understand a text when he or she can actually understand the genre, its features, and its social role. Lodi warns us that:

> it is no enough to master the language if we are to move around/master a genre.
> Ignoring the genre and the sphere where it circulates can often become a barrier
> to understanding a text. (Lodi, 2006, p. 191)

Bilingual teachers need to engage in continuous study so that their classes are well planned. Rethinking practice on a daily basis is essential to be effective in planning teaching and learning. There is always something that can be utilized, something to be discarded, and something to be improved. The meetings between teachers and researchers have often allowed for reflection to change the practice in the classroom when necessary.

Currently, classroom activities have been directed towards exploring a single theme intersecting across disciplines in order to increase students' confidence in their mastery of the theme and help improve their learning performance. Project learning has been adopted to eliminate boundaries between subjects and foster contextualized, significant learning and has emerged as a promising path. It is a new challenge to be faced, a new way of understanding the learning process and revising assessment methods to assure meeting the goal of effective literacy for the Deaf child. As reflected in Fernandes' words, we intend to continue this work to improve the literacy of Deaf children, challenging ourselves in a new, more contextualized methodologies, and always reflecting on the steps taken.

> Reading does not happen by simply recognizing and understanding isolated words. The activity occurs in broader linguistic contexts in which the words combine to form assertions. Simply recognizing and memorizing the external form of the word does not guarantee it is understood, as the context is what will define its meaning. (Fernandes, 2006, p. 10)

A Few Considerations

The Inclusive Bilingual Project presented here continues its activities. Because it was created in a medium-size city in the state of São Paulo, professionals with the required qualifications have not always been available for this work. Training activities are provided on an ongoing basis for bilingual teachers, Deaf instructors, and sign language interpreters, in addition to the more general training provided for the professionals working in the schools.

Over the course of this research project, we have gathered a large set of data that have been systematically treated. Themes of interest to us are: the development of language by Deaf students, teaching methodologies used by teachers to teach different subjects and content with emphasis on the role of Libras, and adapting assessment to better manage the development of Deaf students. Developing new research studies is key to the advance practices most appropriate for Deaf students. Finally, this project has also served as a reference point for other education systems that seek to implement bilingual inclusion programs for Deaf students.

References

Almeida, E. B. de. (2010). *O papel de professores surdos e ouvintes na formação do tradutor e intérprete de Língua Brasileira de Sinais* [The role of deaf and hearing teachers in the training of the translator and interpreter of Brazilian Sign Language]. (Master's thesis). Universidade Metodista de Piracicaba, Brazil.

Brazil. (1988). *Constituição da República Federativa do Brasil* [Constitution of the Federal Republic of Brazil]. Brasília, Brazil: Senado Federal.

Brazil. (1990, July). Lei nº 8.069: Dispõe sobre o estatuto da criança e do adolescente e dá outras providências [Law No. 8.069: Dispositions on the state of children and adolescentes and other measures]. *Diário Oficial da União*. Brasília, Brazil.

Brazil. (1994). *Declaração de Salamanca e linhas de ação sobre necessidades educativas Especiais* [Salamanca declaration and lines of action on special educational needs]. Brasília, Brazil: CORDE.

Brazil. (1996). Lei nº 9.394: Estabelece as diretrizes e bases da educação Nacional [Law No. 9.394: Establishing the guidelines and bases of education]. *Diário Oficial da União*. Brasília, Brazil.

Brazil. (2001a). *Diretrizes nacionais para educação especial na educação básica* [National guidelines for special education in elementary school]. Brasília, Brazil: MEC/SEESP.

Brazil. (2001b). Lei nº 10.172: Aprova o plano nacional de educação e dá outras providências [Law No. 10.172: Approval of the national plan for education and other measures]. *Diário Oficial da União*. Brasília, Brazil.

Brazil. (2001c). *Decreto nº 3.956*. Promulga a Convenção Interamericana para a Eliminação de Todas as Formas de Discriminação contra as Pessoas Portadoras de Deficiência [Promulgation of the InterAmerican Convention for the Elimination of All Forms of Discrimination against People with Disabilities. Guatemala].

Brazil. (2002l). *Lei nº 10.436*. Dispõe sobre a Língua Brasileira de Sinais e dá outras providências [Provisions for Brazilian Sign Language and other measures]. *Diário Oficial da União*, Brasília, Brazil.

Brazil. (2005). *Decreto nº 5.626*. Regulamenta a Lei nº 10.436, de 24 de abril de 2002, que dispõe sobre a Língua Brasileira de Sinais—Libras, e o art. 18 da Lei nº 10.098 [Regulation Law No. 10.436, of April 24, 2002, which provides for the Brazilian Sign Language—Libras, and Art. 18 of Law No. 10,098]. *Diário Oficial da União*, Brasília.

Brazil. (2008). *Política nacional de educação especial na perspectiva da educação inclusiva* [National policy on special education in an inclusive educational perspective]. Brasilia, Brazil: MEC/SEESP.

Fernandes, S. (2006). *Práticas de letramento na educação bilíngüe para surdos* [Literacy practices in bilingual education for the deaf]. Curitiba, Brazil: SEED.

Góes, M. C. R. de, & Tartuci, D. (2002). Alunos surdos na escola regular: as experiências de letramento e os rituais da sala de aula [Deaf students in regular schools: Literacy experiences and room rituals in the classroom]. In A. C. B. Lodi, et al. (Eds.), *Letramento e Minorias* (pp. 110–119). Porto Alegre, Brazil: Mediação.

Lodi, A. C. B. (2006). A leitura em segunda língua: práticas de linguagem constitutivas da(s) subjetividade(s) de um grupo de surdos adultos. [Reading in a second language: Language practices of forming of subjectivity of a group of deaf adults]. *Caderno Cedes* [Cedes Notebook], *26*(69), 185–204.

Lodi, A. C. B. (2010a, May). *Princípios para a educação de alunos surdos* [Principles for the education of deaf students]. Presentation at the Fórum Permanente de Educação, Linguagem e Surdez. Rio de Janeiro, Brazil.

Lodi, A. C. B. (2010b, December). *O processo de escolarização das pessoas surdas: Princípios* [The process of schooling deaf people: Principles]. Presentation at IV Seminário Nacional de Educação Especial e III Encontro Nacional de Pesquisadores em Educação Especial e Inclusão Escolar. Uberlândia, Brazil.

Lodi, A. C. B. (2012a). Ensino da Língua Portuguesa como segunda língua no AEE [Teaching of Portuguese as a second language in the AEE]. In L. C. Da Silva & M. P. Mourão (Eds.), *Atendimento educacional especializado para alunos surdos* (pp. 161–176). Uberlândia, Brazil: EDUFU.

Lodi, A. C. B. (2012b). Ensino da Língua Portuguesa como segunda língua no AEE: dialogando com atividades [Teaching of Portuguese as a second language in the AEE: Dialogue with activities]. In L. C. Da Silva & M. P. Mourão (Eds.), *Atendimento educacional especializado para alunos surdos* [Specialized educational services for deaf students] (pp. 177–191). Uberlândia, Brazil: EDUFU.

Lodi, A. C. B., & Almeida, E. B. de. (2010). Gêneros discursivos na esfera acadêmica e prática de tradução-interpretação em Libras-Português [Genres in the academic sphere and practice of translation-interpretation in Libras-Portuguese]. *Tradução & Comunicação, 20*, 89–103.

Lodi, A. C. B., Souza, J. R. de, & Padilha, A. M. L. (n.d.). *Educação Inclusiva: o que pensam professores de educação infantil sobre a presença de alunos surdos* [Inclusive education: What preschool teachers they think about the presence of deaf students]. Unpublished paper.

Ravitch, D. (2003). *A brief history of teacher professionalism*. White House Conference on Preparing Tomorrow's Teachers. Retrieved from http://www2.ed.gov/admins/tchrqual/learn/preparingteachersconference/ravitch.html

Santos, L. F. dos, & Gurgel, T. M. do A. (2009). O instrutor surdo em uma escola inclusiva Bilíngüe [The deaf teacher in a bilingual inclusive school]. In A. C. B. Lodi & C. B. F. de Lacerda (Orgs.), *Uma escola duas línguas: Letramento em língua portuguesa e língua de sinais nas etapas iniciais de escolarização* [A two-language school: Literacy in Portuguese and sign language in the early stages of schooling] (pp. 51–64). Porto Alegre, Brazil: Mediação.

Sobral, A. (2008). *Dizer o 'mesmo' a outros: ensaios sobre tradução.* [To say the "same" to others: Essays on translation]. São Paulo, Brazil: Special Book Services Livraria.

UNESCO. (1998). *Declaração Mundial sobre Educação para Todos: Plano de ação para satisfazer as necessidades básicas de aprendizagem* [World Declaration on Education for All: Action plan to meet the basic needs of learning]. Retrieved from http://unesdoc.unesco.org/images/0008/000862/086291por.pdf

United Nations. (2006). Convention on the Rights of Persons with Disabilities. Retrieved from: http://www.un.org/disabilities/convention/conventionfull.shtml

5

Deaf Educators: Linguistic Models in an Intercultural–Bilingual Educational Context

Verónica de la Paz Calderón, Maribel González Moraga, and Fabiola Otárola Cornejo

The main difference between these pedagogical approaches and yours is cultural, Deaf people look at Deaf children as future leaders of their communities. The better they are educated, morally, spiritually as well as emotionally, the better members of the community will be; better ambassadors able to break barriers that separate the Deaf and the Hearing worlds. (Ladd, 2005, p. 14)

It is difficult to accurately assess the current Deaf population nationwide due to the lack of specific data. According to the First National Study of Disability in Chile (Fondo Nacional de la Discapacidad, 2004), there were 292,720 Deaf people. Of these, 10,000 were school age. Furthermore, the study reported 7,489 Deaf boys and girls between the ages of six and 14. However the study does not indicate the schooling situation for 5,079 of these Deaf children. According to the 2012 census, the Deaf and hard of hearing population had grown to 488,511 (Instituto Nacional de Estadísticas, 2012). The 2012 census findings were later rejected because of a series of problems in securing and treatment of data.

In Chile, school age Deaf children are provided two educational settings: special education or inclusive education. The first option offers early childhood programs and elementary schools for children who are Deaf. The second consists of a School Integration Program (PIE, its Spanish acronym), which provides specific support and curricular adaptations within regular schools based upon the characteristics of the integrated students.

This project received funding from the CONICYT PAI/INDUSTRIA 79090016.

The INDESOR (Institute of the Deaf) registry indicates that in July 2015, there were 677 school programs offering PIE in Chile, which reported an enrollment of 1,305 Deaf students (A. Pérez, personal communication, July 10, 2015). Additionally, there were 20 special schools with 626 students with hearing loss in eight (of the 12) regions of the country (MINEDUC, 2015). Twenty of the schools with PIE have a Deaf adult on the staff and six of the special schools for the Deaf have a Deaf person in theirs (MINEDUC, 2013).

A Short Historical Account

Deaf education in Chile began approximately 150 years ago and has been strongly influenced by educational canons originating at the Milan Congress in 1880. Its main goal for decades, therefore, has been oral skills development. In its early years, medical staff was primarily in charge of the schools due to a lack of qualified teachers. These doctors filled the void and considered Deaf pupils from a medical perspective.

Early efforts to offer elementary deaf education goes back to 1852 (Caicedo, 1988) when the first school for "deaf mutes" in South America was established in Chile. Its school program was very similar to that of a regular elementary school. This school remains active today under the name of the Anne Sullivan School and currently offers a traditional oral development model. In the past, due to a lack of local specialized teachers of Deaf students, Chilean teachers traveled to Argentina and Mexico as early as 1962 for training in the Oral Model. Upon their return they implemented this approach entrenching the oral method. (Carmona, Sauvalle, Ulloa, & Venegas, 2003).

In the early 1960s, schools for the Deaf were established throughout the country. These schools concentrated on oral language development, and it was not until the 1980s that a regular educational program was systematically incorporated. In 1990, new programs of study were created for students with a hearing loss that maintained a deficit focus and a non-contextualized curriculum (Herrera, Alvarado, & Puente, 2010). These programs remain in use today in the majority of schools for the Deaf in the country.

In 1996, Chile revamped its curricular framework by Supreme Decree of Education Number 40 (Decreto Supremo de Educación en Chile, 1990). This decree brought new curricular frameworks for early education, elementary, and secondary schools but not to special education, which continued to focus on a rehabilitation approach. Between 1998 and 2003, schools faced new policies on school integration disseminated via teacher training and increased financial support for school integration projects.

Special schools do not offer a full curriculum for those capable of completing a high school program and schools with PIE, the majority of these educational centers, do not provide an adequate environment that is responsive to the cultural and linguistic characteristics of the Deaf student. In 2006, Chilean Sign Language interpreters were incorporated in the PIE schools. Although most of the interpreters have average competence in LSCh, they lack formal training as school interpreters. In 2010, Article 26 of Law 20422 (Biblioteca del Congreso Nacional de Chile, 2010) recognized LSCh as a means of Deaf communication. Additionally, in 2013, a Chilean university granted the first graduate degree for interpreters of LSCh, creating the first professionals in the field.

There has been an effort toward a bilingual–bicultural education in schools for the Deaf since the beginning of this millennium. However, its focus was more on bilingualism than the bicultural aspects. Bilingual–bicultural education efforts have not wholly considered the cultural elements of the Deaf community and the important role that Deaf adults play in these school environments.

In spite of the progress achieved in the past decade, Deaf students continue to face social integration rather than full academic integration in secondary school. Deaf students have not had full access to curriculum and have experienced limited participation in the teaching–learning process. Inclusion of students with special educational needs in the system of public education has gained momentum, and due to the increasing number of cochlear implants, a growing number of children and young adults are attending general education schools under PIE. Most of these students have curricular modifications dealing primarily with the hearing loss rather than the characteristics and needs of Deaf students.

This is an overview of what Chile currently offers its Deaf students. We believe that these options fall short because current curriculum does not reflect respect for, the importance of, nor acceptance of the Deaf community with its own values and traditions. In 2006, this context and reality led to a new academic project at the Dr. Jorge Otte Gabler Instituto de la Sordera (Institute of Deafness) in Santiago.

The Educational Project at Dr. Jorge Otte Gabler School for the Deaf

The Instituto de la Sordera is a private, nonprofit corporation created in 1957 primarily to train young Deaf people who had no prior formal schooling for employment. Volunteer staff, trained by the doctors who established the institute, ran the program. In 1998, this institution became partners with the Research Center of the Metropolitan University for Educational Science. The primary goal was to offer comprehensive services and orientation to Deaf people, including education, research, and hearing diagnosis embedded in a diverse society and compatible with the characteristics of the

Deaf community. This goal is achieved through three main components, which are part of the Instituto de la Sordera (de la Paz & Salamanca, 2014, p. 15):

- Dr. Jorge Otte Gabler School for the Deaf
- Hearing Diagnostic Center
- The Deaf World Resource and Research Center

Deaf children and young adults from the Metropolitan Region, primarily from low-income families, attend this school, which offers a wide range of academic programs from early infancy to high school. It has four levels:

1. Early Education: serves children ages zero to seven. It includes an early intervention (early attention) program, preschool program for children with multiple disabilities and five levels, which include one through four plus preparatory.
2. Elementary Education: serves students between ages six to 15 or grades one to eight. Additionally, there is programming for students with multiple disabilities.
3. Secondary Education: serves young adults 15 to 19 years of age. This program offers levels one to four, but at this time is in the process of being approved by the Department of Education (MINEDUC, 2013).
4. Vocational or Transition to Adulthood: serves young adults 16 to 24 years of age with multiple disabilities (INDESOR, 2014).

This school has taken the lead in deaf education nationwide by implementing an intercultural–bilingual model that provides an excellent opportunity for training future professionals in the area of deafness.

The school's mission is to enable Deaf students to integrate into the society to which they belong by offering them an open and pluralistic education firmly grounded in bilingual–bicultural education principles that focus on promotion of intercultural relations between hearing and Deaf people. These interactions promote and value Deaf culture and its language. Furthermore, the school has made a firm commitment to make this approach to teaching and learning an option for all Deaf children, Deaf adults, and their families in order to enable them to find their rightful place in an ever-changing Chilean social and cultural life as well as to contribute to a society based upon respect for diversity. The school has its own curricular plans and programs that have been approved by the Ministry of Education (MINEDUC). Dr. Jorge Otte Gabler School faculty developed the curriculum and all of the program plans following the Curricular Foundations of Education Guidelines of the Supreme Decree of Education Number 40 (Decretos Supremo de Educación en Chile, 1996) and adhering to the concepts of interculturalism and bilingualism.

Grosjean (1982) defines bilingualism as the regular use of two or more languages. These languages in terms of Deaf people refer to the language of signs and the language used in their country of residence, be it spoken or written. This implies that sign language has been recognized as the primary language of Deaf people; in turn, the learning of the language used by hearing people is their second language and acquired primarily through reading and writing (Johnson, Liddell, & Erting, 1989; Svartholm, 2010).

Interculturalism refers to the interactions of diverse communities and assumes a positive view of the uniqueness of each person (Zuñiga & Ansion, 1977).[1] This concept creates an important challenge for a modern educational project in a world in which cultural diversity is becoming more common and intense. Interculturalism includes promoting horizontal and reciprocal relations as a way to encourage continuous and mutual learning.

Intercultural education respects, celebrates, and recognizes diversity as a norm. Students acknowledge diversity in lifestyles, traditions, and worldviews as facts that enrich us all. Consequently, living together enhances our own culture through interaction with other cultures (Saéz, 2008). Intercultural pedagogy provides the tools for teachers and students to communicate intellectually and affectively, reflecting on personal interests and participating actively in the construction of their own life projects.

Intercultural pedagogy offers a pathway for students to preserve, develop, and express their own culture and at the same time develop cognitive and social skills and age-appropriate competencies as defined by the school curriculum. These competencies in turn will enable students to participate on an equal footing in a global society. Consequently, in an intercultural approach, academic content must include both themes emanated from the culture of the majority as well as themes from the minority or that of the student population. This never means that Deaf students would have to learn the language and the culture of the majority at the expense of their own.

Most Deaf children and adults have parents who are hearing (Marschark, Tang, & Knoors, 2014). Therefore, it is important that these children experience meaningful and contextual scenarios where Deaf adults are present. Deaf adults act as linguistic models providing authentic communicative and linguistic competencies via sign language. It is in school and not at home where Deaf students of hearing parents are exposed from early age to their culture and to its core, sign language. It is at school through interaction with peers and with Deaf adults that children discover and forge their identity (de la Paz, 2012). Combining Deaf educators' knowledge of the dynamics of the Deaf community and the experience of students as they grow provides the necessary support that enables Deaf students to have positive experiences in school, which increase academic progress.

---

1. *Interculturalism* is a phrase used more commonly in Latin America than multiculturalism. The two concepts are related and overlap, but there are some differences (see Zúñiga & Ansión, 1977).

The Role of Deaf Educators

Historically, hearing people have defined what and how to teach Deaf people. Naturally, the concept hearing people have about deafness has influenced content selection, methods of teaching, and philosophical orientation of all schools for the deaf worldwide (Ladd & Gonçalves, 2012). There is little research on the role of Deaf educators (regardless of their position) in schools for the deaf. Most studies have been done in Western Europe, the United States, and more recently in Brazil. Based on this research, it appears that "the specific roles played by Deaf adults, vary and have different significance based upon the educational context such as (regular school or schools for the Deaf), the educational approaches of the schools and the position of the Deaf adult (teacher aide or teacher)" (González, 2014, p. 7).

Commonly, Deaf educators function as assistants (co-educators) to hearing teachers. They are responsible for teaching sign language to Deaf students, promoting a cultural identity, aiding in the development of self-awareness in students, and assisting students with academic matters. In addition, they teach sign language and Deaf culture to hearing parents and members of the school community (McKee, 2003; Santini, 2001).

Deaf educators who work in bilingual schools for the deaf find, even though they support the bilingual model, these institutions lack sufficient pedagogical guidance and support to aid them in their work with hearing teachers toward this common cause (Santini, 2001). This observation goes hand in hand with the perception regarding the status of sign language versus the oral–written language, which affects the status of Deaf educators versus hearing teachers. Consequently, the result is that hearing teachers hold a more active and powerful position where they lead and make decisions regarding the education of Deaf students (Santini, 2001; Young, Ackerman, & Kyle, 1998).

Deaf Adults as Educators in Special Schools for the Deaf in Chile

The bilingual–bicultural model of deaf education, which was introduced in schools for the deaf in Chile nearly two decades ago, opened the doors to Deaf adults to become active participants in deaf education. Initially, their main task was to provide support to hearing teachers within the classroom.

As Mahshie (1995) points out, professionalization of Deaf communities is directly related to the quality of education they received and their access to universities to gain academic knowledge needed for a career as teachers. In Chile, in general, Deaf educators currently working in schools do not possess a professional degree. Some of them hold a technical degree (similar to an associate degree) in special education and some are enrolled in such programs (Sierralta, 2010). Deaf adults who possess university (professional) degrees have been recently incorporated into the educational system as teachers, creating new positions for Deaf adults in schools.

Deaf Educators in an Intercultural–Bilingual Context at Dr. Jorge Otte Gabler School

The first Deaf adults who were brought into the school community in 1998 were people who had barely completed high school. However, they were community leaders with strong Deaf identities and fluency in LSCh. Most of them were products of an oral tradition and grew up in an era when sign language was not recognized as the natural language of the Deaf community in Chile.

As time progressed, the role and duties of Deaf educators have changed in response to transformations that have taken place in the school. Construction of the role has been a process in which there has been constant negotiation, dialogue, and exchange to adjust needs, competencies, and expectations of Deaf adults and the requirements and needs of the school (González, 2015).

While working at the school, Deaf teacher assistants have completed secondary school and some have gone on to higher education and/or taken specialized coursework in specific areas. The school has also become a training ground for "growing" its own teachers as areas of need such as managing specific content areas and as new teaching strategies have developed (González, 2015).

Duties of Deaf Educators

Deaf educators have identified two main responsibility areas among the multiple tasks they perform (Ortuzar, 2015): activities related to sign language acquisition and learning, and social and community work. The first area focuses on teaching and promoting the use of LSCh among students and their parents in academic and nonacademic activities. The second area refers to the comprehensive participation of Deaf adults as social and linguistic models. In other words, the aim is to pass on the cultural heritage, foster meaningful interactions and cooperation among families and the Deaf community, provide orientation to parents, and keep abreast of activities that pertain to the Deaf community at the national and international level (Ortúzar, 2015).

Deaf educators employed in schools today act as either teachers or teacher assistants. Out of nine Deaf educators at Dr. Jorge Otte Gabler School, seven are teacher assistants and two are regular teachers. Although Deaf teacher assistants do not possess a professional degree, they support the work of the regular teacher, a hearing person, within the classroom or work with groups of students on specific topics. Some have degrees from a technical college or have taken specialized training. Although they lack degrees in education, these assistants have years of experience position in a school environment and have taken advantage of on-the-job training (González, 2014). These teacher assistants work at the early intervention, preschool, and elementary levels.

In early intervention, Deaf assistant teachers focus on supporting Deaf children's LSCh acquisition by interacting directly with the babies and toddlers (aged three and younger) and serve as role models for communication and interaction. Parents and members of the children's extended families also participate in the activities, which enable them to learn from the Deaf adults. In preschool, the Deaf teacher assistants lead routine activities, educational games, and storytelling, which favor an early acquisition of LSCh in a natural context.

At the primary level (up to eighth grade), hearing teachers and Deaf teacher assistants work as a team and both are responsible for modeling the two languages as used in the classroom. Deaf assistant teachers also organize sports, art activities, and acting workshops as elective subjects for elementary and secondary students and provide LSCh courses for school personnel and students' parents and guardians.

Deaf educators, who hold a professional degree in education, work as teachers with their own classrooms. They are responsible for teaching content areas and LSCh at the elementary and secondary school levels. In addition, they partake in the design and creation of the LSCh curriculum as the first language (L1) for all school levels.

Profile of Deaf Educators

In order to create an effective intercultural–bilingual deaf education program, there are essential characteristics that a Deaf teacher should demonstrate (Ortúzar, 2015).

a. Pride in being Deaf
b. Fluency in sign language
c. Active in the Deaf community
d. Ability to write clearly and correctly
e. Interest in teaching
f. Willingness to learn, integrate, and apply diverse methodologies
g. Willingness to live in an intercultural environment (p. 8)

This is an ideal description of the Deaf educator. There are many other desirable characteristics, which depend on motivation, competencies, attitudes, and experience of the current group of Deaf educators.

Pedagogies developed by Deaf educators have much in common in terms of values, beliefs, and attitudes toward education of Deaf children (Gonçalves, 2009; Ladd & Gonçalves 2012; Sutton-Spence & Ramsey, 2010). Deaf educators appear to develop pedagogical approaches from their cultural intuition, although they may not be conscious of this and not recognize the source of these strategies (Ladd, 2013).

Intercultural Educational Practices

It is a challenge to develop an intercultural environment, and doing so entails a great deal of energy and effort. It requires that a person move from a bicultural framework with an established set of roles, one role being that of colonizer and the other being the colonized, to an intercultural environment where all the participants have the same value as human beings with rights and responsibilities. When the Dr. Jorge Otte Gabler School began its bilingual–bicultural project in 1998, the importance of incorporating Deaf adults who would transmit their culture to students on a daily basis was understood. Deaf adults would support students' successful adaptation to both hearing and Deaf cultures. Over time, the school community realized that while there was a heavy emphasis on bilingualism, Deaf culture was absent from the school curriculum. The idea of an "intercultural" school emerged from this realization, and the school adapted a curriculum in which Deaf culture is present throughout the school and everyone respects the characteristics and needs of others.

The curriculum was modified to include aspects of Deaf culture, including history, traditions, stories, biographies of Deaf leaders and heroes, identity development, and more. In addition, a comprehensive LSCh class was set up at the national level; Deaf educators were welcomed to join faculty meetings; new ties with the Deaf community were developed; and the Deaf World Resource and Research Center was created at the Instituto de la Sordera in order to disseminate accurate information at the national level.

Challenges related to the encounter of these two cultures still exist today. Effective communication continues to be a real challenge. However, over time, it has become exceedingly clear that Deaf adults are central and indispensable in schooling that provides Deaf students with the best educational opportunities.

Deaf Educators as Linguistic Role Models in an Intercultural–Bilingual Context

We have emphasized that the success of a school with an intercultural–bilingual component requires, at its core, a team of Deaf adults. Having educators from both communities ensures that students develop a range of cultural values and necessary linguistic resources, are taught academics in an accessible language, and acquire competencies in the oral language that may enable an easier integration in Chilean society.

Deaf educators within an intercultural–bilingual school act as linguistic role models not only because they are fluent in sign language but primarily because they possess a particular life experience and perspective that is different than those of hearing teachers. Central to this is the fact that Deaf individuals construct their reality and learning in a visual–spatial modality, which is reflected in their interactions within the Deaf community and particularly in their language.

Sign language is typically constructed and expanded by exchanges within the Deaf community. These exchanges convey a wealth of linguistic resources based on visual experiences. These are valuable tools in the communication, curricular, and cultural processes in an intercultural–bilingual school. Eye gaze, hand and body movements, gestures, and signs are all part of an educational space (Skliar & Quadros, 2005).

The following section deals with concrete pedagogical actions closely related to LSCh development that Deaf educators use at Dr. Jorge Otte Gabler School.

Deaf Educators' Role at Different Educational Levels

Deaf educators, as linguistic models, perform in a diverse fashion at each educational level in the school. Thus, their main function, to facilitate acquisition of LSCh as the first language, is achieved by conducting age-appropriate activities in concordance with the desired goals for each level.

The following are some of the objectives and strategies that Deaf educators develop in each school level. These curricular and didactic elements are actually included in the school's plans and programs. It is possible to observe the variety of linguistic actions Deaf teachers and teacher assistants apply based on the student's characteristics and that of his or her family.

Early Intervention Level (Atención Temprana)

At the early intervention level, the purpose of play activities is to develop hand–eye coordination skills that are important for the acquisition of more complex linguistic behaviors. As children's competency increases, they become eager to start and maintain a conversation in a visual–gestural modality.

By making a connection between linguistic theory and educational practice, Ladd and Gonçalves (2012) describe six steps in which Deaf educators guide children toward bilingualism: (1) starting the cognitive engine, (2) utilizing visuo-gestural-tactile modalities, (3) creating a safe Deaf space, (4) the language development stage, (5) Deaf children's place in the world, and (6) moral and intellectual guidance on how to live in the world (pp. 16–18). These stages can be easily observed in Deaf educators' pedagogical practices at school. Although it is relevant to mention that this is a hypothetical model based on "typical" Deaf children, and it does not consider the case of Deaf children with multiple disabilities. These steps can be readily observed in the educational process at the Dr. Jorge Otte Gabler School.

At the early intervention level, Deaf educators provide guidance and support to stimulate Deaf students' cognitive abilities. They do this, first, by recognizing and naming items in the surrounding physical and social environment, and most importantly by teaching the children to notice the world around them.

TABLE 1: Early Intervention

Age: 3 months to 2 years	
General Linguistic Objective	• Encourage acquisition of LSCh through natural and direct interaction.
Specific Linguistic Objectives	• Develop attention span, guided mainly to the use of signing space and gazing. • Provide support and orientation to families with children who have recently been diagnosed deaf. • Model for parents different interactive techniques and games they can do at home. • Facilitate an adequate process to develop ties between caretaker and the Deaf child.
Teaching-Learning Activities and/or Strategies	• Lead play activities that attract the Deaf child's attention toward the adult's face. Employ facial expressions, mouth and lip movements, etc. • Guide gaze and attention to physical space in which interaction takes place; gradually focus on sign space. Lead games (facing the child) that require hand-eye coordination in six different orientations. • Pay attention to movement of hands and body. Use slow, long, and repetitive motions so the child can imitate them. • Introduce attention getting techniques: touch the child's shoulder or leg or wave your hand in front of the child to get his/her attention. • Introduce basic LSCh; focus on semantic fields that are more frequent and functional: family, food, toys, animals, house items, etc. • Introduce appropriate, spontaneous conversation of other Deaf adults in LSCh.

Preschool Education (Educación Pre-Escolar)

The focus of activities at this level is communicative interaction geared to the development of visual ability and intended to introduce basic elements for sign language development, including gestures, eye gaze, and first signs. The program aims to establish a natural environment where all communication is in sign language. Children who achieve linguistic competencies at this level are promoted to Educación Básica (Basic Education), which is the elementary education program.

TABLE 2: Preschool

	Age: 3 to 5 years, 9 months
General Linguistic Objective	• Develop communication competency, enhancing expression of feelings, emotions, needs, events, and ideas, through progressive and adequate use of LSCh.
Specific Linguistic Objectives	1. Strengthen use of LSCh through increased vocabulary and use of appropriate linguistic expressions. 2. Model interactive communication in playtime and daily activities. 3. Expand conversation topics and communicative interaction in a variety of spaces. 4. Reinforce the correct use of sign-space, appropriate facial expression, and body movement as key elements of communicative competencies. 5. Encourage respect and appreciation for cultural differences and different means of communication, be it with hearing or Deaf families. 6. Instill a positive attitude toward both hearing and Deaf cultures.
Teaching/Learning Activities and/or Strategies	• Conduct games and play activities that require children to communicate through mime, gestures, body movements, eye-face expressions, etc. Activities such as: work stations, greetings, storytelling, and snack time. • Tell stories and narrate personal anecdotes in order to model discursive style. Gradually demonstrate the wealth of linguistic resources that LSCh offers. • Model and incorporate into daily routines etiquette, social manners in terms of greetings, expressing appreciation, turn taking, asking for permission, etc. • Create activities that allow application of LSCh with their peers and Deaf adults. • Foster learning activities where children can learn new concepts not only from adults but also from their peers. • Boost curiosity for exploration of their natural and cultural environment creating a safe surrounding where children can develop a healthy persona.

According to Ladd and Gonçalves (2012), during the first two years of preschool, Deaf educators work on visual, gestural, and tactile development, which is fundamental in sign language. They guide children in every step of the process in the acquisition of sign language and promote communication through body language and eye contact.

During the third school year, Deaf educators increase safe spaces for children to feel free, comfortable, and able to express themselves (González, 2014). This is also the time when they begin to help the children develop strategies to address negative attitudes of hearing society that could affect their participation in the hearing world.

Elementary Education

Elementary or primary school is the longest period of schooling, covering from first to eighth grade. There are two cycles, each consisting of four years or grades (Just Landed, 2015). During these years, students go through many linguistic changes, which require the attention of Deaf teacher assistants and Deaf teachers in LSCh classes (L1). Optional workshops and formal and informal activities are offered for the development of Deaf culture and LSCh. Students acquiring the needed linguistic competency are able to move up to Educación Media (Secondary Education).

Teachers and teacher assistants at the elementary level at Dr. Jorge Otte Gabler School focus on stages four and five, which deal with students' acceleration in language learning and learning their individual place in the world (Ladd & Gonçalves, 2012). In the first cycle of Elementary Education children are between six and nine years of age and Deaf educators put extra energy into supporting children's expansion of LSCh skills. While these young signers may lack agility, their emotional development and level of interest prompt the Deaf educators to expand conversational topics and the children's range of expression in LSCh.

In the second cycle of elementary education, the boys and girls are between 10 and 14 years of age. Self-identity becomes highly important for students. Deaf teachers and teacher assistants provide support in the construction of a Deaf identity and find a definition of the role they play in society. Deaf educators offer strategies to cast a positive light on the differences between the Deaf and hearing worlds (Ladd & Gonçalves, 2012).

Middle/High School (Educación Media)

Secondary school in Chile is compulsory, prepares students for either university or technical school, lasts four years, and is organized into two two-year cycles (Just Landed, 2015). In secondary school, Deaf teachers provide students with firsthand experience and advice that contributes to the formation of the next generation of Deaf adults in Chilean society.

TABLE 3: Elementary Education (1st and 2nd Cycles)

Age: 6 to 13 years, 9 months	
General Linguistic Objective	• Foster gain of new communication competencies in LSCh and apply them in learning content matter and socialization.
Specific Linguistic Objectives	1. Create safe and comfortable spaces where interaction for academic or social reasons in LSCh can take place in a meaningful way as a weekly routine. 2. Reinforce eye gaze to a target area where signs take place and to face the person signing. 3. Enhance linguistic resources of children and motivate them to use those skills correctly. 4. Utilize LSCh as a meaningful and important tool to learn other curricular subjects and as a base to acquire Chilean Spanish in its written form.
Teaching/Learning Activities and/or Strategies	• Set up space for conversation and communication purposes, where anecdotes, joke sharing, presentation, storytelling, investigation, and research can take place. • Aid in the search for appropriate strategies in dialogue and discussion between signers. Help children understand and value each other's point of view. • Use and apply different visual resources with subject matter to illustrate main points. • Encourage participation of all students in different social and cultural contexts so they develop appropriate use of different communication registers and correct vocabulary. • Create room for spontaneous and coached discursive activities that favor the use of linguistic resources, such as mimic, gestures, gazing, role changes, and classifiers.

It is important that in the final cycle in secondary school, theory and practice become one. Deaf teachers challenge students to envision and articulate how they will insert themselves into a hearing society. Students expand their learning about the characteristics of both cultures and how to conduct themselves in each (Ladd & Gonçalves, 2012). Deaf adults become moral and intellectual guides for Deaf students on the path to becoming Deaf adults and Chilean citizens.

TABLE 4: Multiple Disabilities Level

Age: 3 to 24 years	
General Linguistic Objective	• Develop functional communicative and discursive strategies to enable interaction with those around in a variety of spaces: social and work related.
Specific Linguistic Objective	• Specific objectives are tailored to individual needs and strengths of each student.
Teaching/Learning Activities and/or Strategy	• Development of linguistic skills focus on enhancing visual, gestural, and body for expression and comprehension of LSCh communication mainly. Activities take into consideration challenges and individual potential as well as family expectations.

Multiple Disabilities Level

The school provides education and supportive services to Deaf children with disabilities such as visual, mental, and motor disabilities and autism. Support may be temporary or permanent depending on the needs and personal, familial, or educational characteristics of the student.

Goal setting in terms of language acquisition and development are strictly individual and are based on challenges and abilities as well as interests and expectations of the family. Expectations vary from the very functional to achieving a good use of LSCh, which may enable them to obtain employment and/or the ability to participate socially as Deaf adults. See Otárola (2014) for more detail regarding the school's work with Deaf students with disabilities.

CONCLUSIONS

As we have seen in this chapter, the role of Deaf educators within an intercultural–bilingual context has been transformed from the beginnings of the project. We have described the essential position of Deaf educators in an intercultural–bilingual educational program and how they are fundamental in the education of Deaf Chilean students while recognizing the role of Deaf educators continues to evolve.

TABLE 5: Middle and High School

Age: 14 to 18 years (approx.)	
General Linguistic Objective	• Foster use of LSCh to acquire and construct new academic knowledge; analyze student's own language; identify cultural elements in the Deaf community; and come up with projects that benefit the school and the community.
Specific Linguístic Objectives	1. Model appropriate manners to express an opinion in different scenarios and contexts and to attend to others' opinion. 2. Stress importance of sign-space, sign pace, and sign tone as well as the arguments presented in a debate. 3. Secure safe space for presentations, debates, free expression, and interchange of information, opinions, and ideas. 4. Contribute to the study and analysis of cultural and linguistic characteristics of the Deaf community. 5. Investigate with students roles they can assume as members of the Deaf community. 6. Encourage student participation in different contexts, social and academic so they can apply linguistic competencies. 7. Empower students so they volunteer and get involved with the community as potential leaders. 8. Challenge students routinely so they develop higher thinking skills.
Teaching/Learning Activities and/or Strategies 	• Guide students in the analysis of various statements using their own linguistic resources and their knowledge of LSCh. • Develop tasks that allow comparisons between LSCh and Chilean Spanish in the written form. • Foster study and analysis of current events as well as historical ones dealing with the Deaf community in Chile and abroad. • Create spaces where debate and analysis of the local Deaf community as well as the international Deaf community can be held.

The role of Deaf educators as classroom teachers and teacher assistants in our school has changed considerably from their initial incorporation in the school setting. This is due to a diverse set of variables, such as initial teacher training, complexity of pedagogical tasks, school expectations, expectations of Deaf adults regarding their formative role, and expanded visualization of the Deaf community in Chilean society. Most importantly, these Deaf educators have engaged in self-reflection and an analysis of their own roles in the formation of Deaf children and youth.

Therefore, the description of the role of Deaf educators as educators and cultural models in Chile, particularly at the Dr. Jorge Otte Gabler School, will not be the same in the years to come. Although the transmission of the language and culture seems to be the fundamental task, the manner in which that happens in the classroom and in a variety of scenarios is challenging and requires creativity and imagination. We hope that in the future any modifications consider the positive changes that we have described in this chapter. At the same time, consider the new challenges ahead, which we have not yet considered.

As years pass, the school has faced new challenges. One such challenge is the need for Deaf educators to increase their knowledge and understanding of their own language and culture. We believe this would strengthen the intercultural–bilingual project and the mission of preparing Deaf individuals who are active contributors to Chilean society.

At present, in Chile, as in many other countries, we estimate that a large number of Deaf educators work as partners in pedagogical activities planned by hearing teachers. We propose that their main responsibility include a number of activities such as: passing on the language and the culture to students, their parents and the school community, promoting cultural identity and self-awareness among students, and assisting students with academic subjects. However, there is a lack of professional development opportunities that would prepare Deaf educators to achieve autonomy in their role (i.e., function as classroom teachers, not only assistants). As mentioned earlier, lacking these opportunities for training, many Deaf educators develop specific skills intuitively within the educational context in which they work (McKee, 2003; Santini, 2001).

As previously described, one of the most important challenges is providing Deaf educators access to pedagogy and linguistics coursework that allows mastery of teaching strategies for each educational level (early intervention through secondary) that meet the academic needs of their students. Additionally, they should have access to knowledge about various dimensions of deafness and a reflective toward Deaf identity. Deaf educators in Latin America have made these recommendations based on their own experience as identity models (Skliar & Quadros, 2004).

A stronger linguistics background and knowledge of their own language would allow them to reflect on the language's distinctive characteristics and linguistic mechanisms.

Consequently, they would be able to impart and teach according to the levels of student competency and readiness. For Deaf educators to be more effective linguistic role models, they need competence in the written language so that they provide skillful guidance to their Deaf students. Deaf adults who are competent in both languages are the models of the aim of an intercultural–bilingual school. It is important to value and recognize the role of Deaf educators and the application of pedagogical practices they develop. Most importantly, Deaf educators need to position themselves where they can be seen and have a say in the decision-making process regarding the education of their own community (Skliar & Quadros, 2004).

Finally, we believe that in an intercultural–bilingual educational project, it is necessary to get to know, respect, and value not only the Deaf and hearing cultures but also other cultures that students may bring from their country of origin into the classroom. This is a situation schools in Chile are experiencing lately (due to economic prosperity) with a growing number of children from other countries enrolling in Chilean schools (Doña & Levinson, 2004).

References

Biblioteca del Congreso Nacional de Chile. (2010). *Establece normas sobre igualdad de oportunidades e inclusión social de personas con discapacidad* [Sets standards for equal opportunity and social inclusion for persons with disabilities]. Retrieved from http://www.leychile.cl/Navegar?idLey=20422

Caiceo, J. (1988). La educación especial en Chile: un esbozo de su historia [Special education in Chile: An outline of its history]. *Revista de Pedagogía, 306*, 47–50.

Carmona, J., Sauvalle, I., Ulloa, C., & Venegas, R. (2003). *Percepciones, creencias y valores referidos al área de crecimiento y autoafirmación personal de los objetivos fundamentales transversales de la comunidad educativa de la escuela Dr. Jorge Otte G.* [Perceptions, beliefs and values referring to the area of growth and personal affirmation of the fundamental and intersecting objectives of the educational community of the Dr. Jorge Otte School]. Undergraduate dissertation. Universidad Metropolitana de Ciencias de la Educación, Santiago, Chile.

de la Paz, M. V. (2012). *Hacia la búsqueda de la cultura sorda en Chile: propuesta educativa intercultural bilingüe para Sordos* [Searching for Deaf culture in Chile: Intercultural bilingual education proposal for the deaf]. España: Editorial Académica Española.

de la Paz, M.V., & Salamanca, M. (2014). Elementos de la cultura sorda: una base para el curriculum intercultural [Elements of the Deaf culture: A foundation for intercultural curriculum]. In INDESOR & UMCE (Eds.), *10 años de bilingüismo en Chile: Experiencias pedagógicas de la escuela Intercultural Bilingüe para estudiantes sordos.* Fondo Editorial UMCE: Santiago, Chile.

Decreto Supremo de Educación No. 40. (1996, January 24). *Diario Oficial de la República de Chile.*

Doña, C., & Levinson, A. (2004, Feb.1). *Chile: Moving toward a migration policy. Migration Policy Institute.* Retrieved from http://www.migrationpolicy.org/article/chile-moving-towards-migration-policy

Fondo Nacional de la Discapacidad. (2004). *Primer estudio Nacional de la discapacidad en Chile* [First national study on disabilities in Chile]. Santiago, Chile: Fondo Nacional de la Discapacidad and Instituto Nacional de Estadisticas.

Gonçalves, J. (2009). *The role of Gaucho culture and Deaf pedagogy in rethinking Deaf education.* Doctoral dissertation. University of Bristol, Bristol, UK.

González, M. (2014). *How do Chilean Deaf educators construct their role and pedagogies in Deaf schools?* Unpublished manuscript. University of Bristol, Bristol, United Kingdom.

González, M. (2015, July–August). *Intercultural bilingual education for Deaf students: The role of Deaf educators.* Paper presented at the XVII World Congress of the World Federation of de Deaf. Istanbul, Turkey.

Grosjean, F. (1982). *Life with two languages: An introduction to bilingualism.* Cambridge, MA: Harvard University Press.

Herrera, V., Alvarado, J., & Puente, A. (2010). Trends and developments in deafness in Chile. In D. Moores & M. Miller (Eds.), *Deaf people around the world: Educational and social perspectives.* Washington, DC: Gallaudet University Press.

INDESOR (Ed.). (2014). *10 años de bilingüismo en Chile: Experiencias pedagógicas de la Escuela Intercultural Bilingüe para estudiantes Sordos.* [Pedagogical experiences in an International Bilingual School for Deaf students]. Fondo Editorial UMCE: Santiago, Chile.

Instituto Nacional de Estadísticas (INE). (2012). *Síntesis de resultados Censo 2012* [Synthesis of 2012 Census results]. Retrieved from http://www.iab.cl/wp-content/themes/IAB/download.php?archivo=11803%7Cresumencenso_2012.pdf

Johnson, R., Liddell, S., & Erting, C. (1989). *Unlocking the curriculum: Principles for achieving access in deaf education.* Washington, DC: Gallaudet University, Gallaudet Research Institute.

Just Landed. (2015). Education. Retrieved from https://www.justlanded.com/

Ladd, P. (October, 2005). *Blows against the empire: Deaf cultures and education of the deaf.* Keynote address presented at the 20th International Congress on the Education of the Deaf (ICED). Maastricht, Holland.

Ladd, P. (October, 2013). A final frontier: Can Deafhood pedagogies revolutionize deaf education? California School for the Deaf, Fremont, CA.

Ladd, P., & Gonçalves, J. (2012). A final frontier? How Deaf cultures and Deaf pedagogies can revolutionize Deaf education. In L. Leeson & M. Vermeerbergen

(Eds.), *Working with the deaf community: Deaf education, mental health & interpreting* (pp. 9–33). Dublin, Ireland: Interesourcegroup Publishing.

Mahshie, S. N. (1995). *Educating deaf children bilingually: With insights and applications from Sweden and Denmark.* Washington, DC: Gallaudet University Press.

Marschark, M., Tang, G., & Knoors, H. (Eds.). (2014). *Bilingualism and bilingual deaf education.* Oxford, UK: Oxford University Press.

McKee, R. (2003). *Report on a survey of Deaf paraprofessionals' perspectives on mainstream learning contexts for Deaf students in New Zealand.* Victoria University of Wellington. Wellington, NZ: New Zealand.

MINEDUC. (2013). Unidad de educación especial 2013 [Special education unit 2013]. Retrieved from http://www.educacionespecial.mineduc.cl/

MINEDUC. (2015). Proyecto TIC y Diversidad [Project TIC and Diversity]. Retrieved from http://www.educacionespecial.mineduc.cl/index2.php?id_contenido=31135&id_seccion=5187&id_portal=20

Ortúzar, P. (April, 2015). *Rol del adulto Sordo en una escuela intercultural bilingüe* [The role of the Deaf adult in an intercultural bilingual school]. Paper presented at the Seminar Transmitir lengua, transmitir cultura. Santiago, Chile.

Otárola, F. (2014). Dando respuesta a los desafíos [Responding to the challenges]. In INDESOR & UMCE (Eds.), *10 años de bilingüismo en Chile: Experiencias pedagógicas de la escuela Intercultural Bilingüe para estudiantes Sordos* (pp. 283–314). Fondo Editorial UMCE: Santiago, Chile.

Sáez, R. (2008). La educación intercultural para una sociedad global [Intercultural education for a global society]. In C. García (Ed.), Hegemonía e interculturalidad. Poblaciones originarias y migrantes. La interculturalidad como uno de los desafíos del siglo XXI [Hegemony and intercultualism. Original populations and migrants. Interculturalism as one of the challenges of the 21st century] (pp.103–129). Buenos Aires, Argentina: Prometeo Libros.

Santini, J. (2001). *The role models: Multicultural politics at bilingual deaf Schools in Britain.* Master's thesis. University of Bristol, Bristol, UK.

Sierralta, V. (2010). *Comunidad y educación de las personas sordas en Chile* [Community and education of deaf people in Chile]. Retrieved from http://www.cultura-sorda.eu

Skliar, C., & Quadros, R. (2004). Bilingual Deaf education in the south of Brazil. *International Journal of Bilingual Education and Bilingualism, 7*(5), 368–380.

Skliar, C., & Quadros, R. (2005). La educación Bilingüe para sordos en el sur de Brasil: La experiencia de la sordera y el camino de la ciudadanía Sorda [Bilingual education of the Deaf in southern Brazil: The experience of deafness and the path to Deaf citizenship]. In E. Venteo & M. Viader (Eds.), *El valor de la mirada: sordera y educación* (pp. 279–292). Barcelona, Spain: Edicions Universitat.

Sutton-Spence, R., & Ramsey, C. (2010). What we should teach Deaf children: Deaf teachers' folk models in Britain, the U.S. and Mexico. *Deafness and Education International, 12,* 149–176.

Svartholm, K. (2010). Bilingual education for deaf children in Sweden. *International Journal of Bilingual Education and Bilingualism, 13*(2), 159–174.

Young, A., Ackerman, J., & Kyle, J. (1998). *Looking on: Deaf people and the organization of services.* The Policy Press, Joseph Rowntree Foundation: York.

Zúñiga, M., & Ansión, A. (1997). *Interculturalidad y educación en el Perú.* Lima: Editorial Foro Educativo. Retrieved from http://macareo.pucp.edu.pe/~jansion/Publicaciones/Intercul.htm

6

The Incredible and Sad Tale of Sign Language Interpretation: A Latin American Perspective

Alex Giovanny Barreto Muñoz
and José Ednilson Gomes de Souza, Jr.

This chapter has an intentional ethnographic "flavor" or "spice." Readers will note that we decided to break with the formal register of Anglo academic writing. We wanted the content, our approach, and presentation of information to reflect an experience, particular kinds of relationships, and a way of seeing the Deaf world and their interpreters. A look—always partial—at all possibilities. In the short novel *The Incredible and Sad Tale of Innocent Eréndira and Her Heartless Grandmother* (1978), García Márquez features three characters: Eréndira (a young prostitute), Grandmother (a pimp), and Ulises (a liberating lover). We offer these characters in García Márquez's novel as metaphors for rethinking the social representations of sign language interpreters in Latin America. Are Latin American sign language interpreters exploited youth, like Eréndira, waiting for developed countries to provide salvation? Are they heartless hearing people planning to exploit the Deaf community by making a living off the backs of Deaf people? Are interpreters liberators and agents of change and social paradigms in the region? We suggest that the answer to these questions is complex; roles constantly overlap. Through an interview with an experienced Latin American sign language interpreter, and a critical essay on the region, we hope to contribute to rethinking the ways of seeing the relationship between sign language interpreters and the Deaf community in Latin America.

This chapter is partly based on sections of the Spanish article "La increíble y triste historia de la interpretación de lengua de señas: reflexiones identitarias desde Colombia" published in the journal *Mutatis Mutandis* 8(2) of the University of Antioquia (http://aprendeenlinea .udea.edu.co/revistas/index.php/mutatismutandis/article/view/22185). We thank the editors for permission.

Overview

As in any population where the number of Deaf people is significantly high, in Latin America there is a considerable number of sign language interpreters emerging from traditional contexts, including families with Deaf members, teachers, and other professionals connected to deafness, and religious groups. The relationship among religion, gender, education, and artistic expression with the development of Deaf culture in Latin America is an area of broad interest to linguistics, anthropology, and the nascent field of Latin American sign language translation and interpretation (Pires Pereira, 2010; Rodrigues & Beer, 2015). There are no accurate official data on Latin American sign language interpreters. In the 39 countries of Latin America and the Caribbean, there are 12 national associations affiliated with the World Association of Sign Language Interpreters (WASLI). The number of sign language interpreter associations and sign language interpreters could be higher. For example, Chile and Uruguay closed their national interpreter associations. Colombia and Chile, for a time, each had two national associations, and countries like Brazil, Argentina, and Colombia have local associations at the state level.

If it sounds bold and ambitious to discuss the entire Pan-American continent, it is even bolder to talk in terms of the *Latin people*, who typically in Europe and the United States are considered a singular ethnicity. The concept of ethnicity has a different interpretation in Latin American studies, in particular, opposition to the idea of *mestizo*, hybridization, or syncretism (Garcia Canclini, 1990; García, López, & Makar, 2010). In Latin America, the vast majority of mestizo Latin Americans do not see themselves as an ethnic group. They believe that the only ethnic groups are indigenous, Black people, Romani people, and Creole speakers in the Caribbean. However, populations in the region have great historical and cultural differences.

Even the Spanish language varies from country to country. There are regional idiomatic expressions and dialects that other Latin American Spanish speakers don't understand. Thus, although sociologically speaking there is a Latin American "integration"—that is, globalization and markets require Latin American countries to reconcile their cultural and linguistic similarities and differences—it is necessary to make a clarification regarding the scope of this chapter. The comments presented here require us to consider Latinos from Brazil and the United States differently. There are two vast curtains that divide the experience in relation to these countries: the south and the north.

The Brazilian Portuguese Barrier

With regard to sign language translation and interpretation studies and professional development of these roles, there is a marked difference between Brazil and other Latin

American countries. Brazil is the largest country in the region (almost half of South America), so we cannot make a Latin American analysis that ignores the dynamics of this country. Free access to graduate education in public universities (with stringent entrance exams) and Brazilian laws have contributed to significant advances in just over 10 years that have been outstanding compared to other countries in the region (Quadros, Fleetwood, & Metzger, 2012).

A comparison between sign language interpretation in major cities of Brazil and smaller cities indicates continued social inequality. However, the status of sign language interpretation in the smaller cities of the Latin American giant is very similar to those of the rest of Latin America. The contrast in the development of resources in larger cities and smaller cities is characteristic of Latin America, but in Brazil is where it finds the greatest extremes. These facts, coupled with the ignorance and the limited ability to read works written in Portuguese in other Latin American countries, make it clear that a "Portuguese language curtain" exists.

The American English Barrier

There are many Latinos living in the United States and Canada. The analysis of their experiences also involves a different framework than the analysis used here. Due to the use of English, a lot of the information and knowledge related to the profession circulating in North America is not accessible to many sign language interpreters from Central and South America. However, the use of English also creates a specific relationship with the region, in the case of multilingual interpreters (varieties of English-Spanish-sign languages) (Quinto-Pozos, Casanova de Canales, & Trevino, 2010; Ramsey & Peña, 2010).

Many of the interpreters of Latin American descent who live in the United States and Canada develop very different relationships with professional practices and activism in the countries of Central and South America. Although there are several exceptions, you may find a number of "Latino" interpreters who know absolutely nothing about sign language interpretation in their countries of origin or ancestry. They are Latinos (i.e., of Latin American descent) who live in the United States and Canada but are not Latin Americans (i.e., people who *live* in Latin America). Latinos are members of an "imagined community" in the northern countries where they live. Additionally, sign language interpreters in regions such as Mexico, Panama, the Caribbean Islands and West Indies, Dominican Republic, and Puerto Rico, to name a few, and in close contact with English-speaking countries, are very different as well from interpreters working in the rest of Latin America. The development of sign language interpretation in these countries is beyond the scope of this chapter.

One Life and One Heart: Questions for Brieva

José Luis Brieva Padilla is an experienced Colombian sign language interpreter who was born in Barranquilla, a Caribbean city in the northern part of the country. He works as an educational interpreter of Colombian Sign Language, and he has worked as an interpreter in international signs. Through Brieva's responses, we have the opportunity to study a representation of the multiple experiences of sign language interpreters of Latin America.

How did you learn and train to become a sign language interpreter?

Although I had some contact with Deaf people since childhood, I learned sign language in the church of the Jehovah's Witnesses. The course was very basic, so it provided daily and constant contact with the Deaf community, which allowed me to acquire this beautiful language and get to know a world that captivated me and I fell in love with even to today. Over time, after a lot of contact with Deaf leaders of my Caribbean region and without realizing it, I became a communication bridge for Deaf friends providing access to services and rights in Colombia that were beginning to develop. That is how I came to become a sign language interpreter—in this practical way.

Learning Colombian Sign Language let me know worlds, cultures and countries that I never thought I would. My international experience began in 2005 with the establishment of the Asociación Nacional de Intérpretes de Lengua de Señas y Guías intérpretes de Colombia [National Association of Sign Language Interpreters and Interpreter Guides of Colombia; ANISCOL]. At that same time the WASLI was born.

In Colombia there was no formal or four-year professional training but only a course for interpreter certification between 1998 and 1999, and sign language courses were and still are controlled by the National Federation of the Deaf of Colombia (FENASCOL). In 2007, Colombian interpreting educator, Margarita Rodriguez and I were surprised when WASLI invited us to participate as speakers at the second Conference of the WASLI held in Segovia, Spain. At the same event, I was selected by Latin American delegates as the Latin American representative to the WASLI board, an honor for me and an experience that allowed me to visit several Latin American countries and have contact with others. The countries I visited were: Peru, Argentina, Panama, Dominican Republic and Brazil, first as regional representative for Latin America, and later as Vice President of WASLI. Also, I kept in close contact through my eight years of service with Mexico, Nicaragua, Honduras, El Salvador, Costa Rica, Cuba, Venezuela, Ecuador, Bolivia, Chile, Paraguay and Uruguay. Through these visits and contact by telephone, email and Skype, I had the opportunity to maintain contact with hundreds of sign language interpreters throughout Latin America.

You have traveled to several Latin American countries and throughout the world. What do you think is the biggest difference in the way the sign language interpreting is done in this region?

In my opinion and according to my experience, a large number of interpreters in Latin America have been performing their work with the guardian or benevolent approach, which considers the Deaf person in need of protection, because they are vulnerable in society. However, in recent years as training improved, there has been a paradigm shift. Already there are more interpreters focused on working as allies and seeking to work hand in hand with the Deaf community to achieve their rights, while leaving it to the Deaf, whose responsibility it is, to do so. This does not apply to all countries, but to those who have [interpreter] training programs which are still limited compared to other regions [of the world].

From your perspective, what are the tensions, contradictions, and opportunities in movements of sign language interpreters compared to the Deaf community movements?

Tensions have focused on power management, primarily in the economic sector in Latin America. Deaf Associations or Federations historically have made known the importance of the use of sign language and the need to employ interpreting services. This in turn has created the opportunity to provide services paid by governments or in some cases, though rare, receive financial support from governments. Some associations of Deaf feel threatened by the creation of interpreter associations, because they may jeopardize the economic control that the Deaf associations have had (related to sign language interpreters) for years.

The implementation of the Convention on Human Rights of Persons with Disabilities has provided opportunities in our country, as it obliges governments to implement measures to eliminate barriers to accessing information and communication. This is an opportunity for both associated movements [for interpreters and of the Deaf] to work together to achieve real social inclusion of Deaf people in Latin America. Another opportunity is the great interest being shown by some universities to research sign language, to create training programs for sign language instructors or programs to train sign interpreters, something to which both Deaf associations and interpreters can contribute due to their experience.

Among the contradictions identified is that most Deaf associations consider sign language to be their property and believe that hearing people should not teach courses in sign language. Nor should hearing people participate in the creation of new signs. This has generated some tensions between the Deaf associations and interpreter associations, but primarily among interpreters.

Overall some countries have been able to establish cordial relations between WFD and WASLI. But there remain a few things that still need to be worked out between organizations of the Deaf and interpreters in each country.

What is the role of religious organizations in the development of sign language interpreting in Latin America?

They play an important role, because many of the interpreters in most Latin American countries come from these contexts, evangelical churches or Jehovah's Witnesses, which have designed strategies to expand the use of sign language in Latin American countries. This has led to many hearing people learning sign language and becoming interpreters. In countries like Colombia, for example, my estimate is that out of 10 interpreters working in educational institutions, on average 7 or 8 are Jehovah's Witnesses.

Therefore we could say that religious groups have been converted into niche interpreters, arising in a spontaneous way, because most hearing people who learning sign language in these religious institutions do not do so with the intention of becoming interpreters. But every day the marketplace asks for more and more interpreters, which leads them into this work. Although this has been positive given the great need for sign language interpreters in Latin America, it is also true that we must separate the religious part from the professional part and see that there is ethical training to ensure that interpreters function in more appropriate and impartial ways with Deaf people, independent of religious contexts.

What do you think is the area where Latin American interpreters contribute more widely to improve the quality of life of Deaf people?

History has shown that in terms of access to education, interpreters have played a determining role, which has created an open door that allowed Deaf people access to knowledge and information leading to other roads and access to other fundamental rights. It is noteworthy that the Latin American interpreters without proper preparation, and with few economic resources, whose work remains invisible and considered less worthy, have worked with next to nothing, with the few resources they may have, to ensure that Deaf people can eliminate communication and isolation that for years have been barriers. The work of Latin American interpreters in most cases has been from the heart rather than the mind, with resulting errors, but also with eagerness to want to do things well for the inclusion of Deaf people. Today there are better times and winds of change for the inclusion of Deaf people in this region of the world, new laws, new approaches, new technological dynamics in which interpreters will remain an important but not the only part of mechanism of communication for Deaf people.

Such is the importance of religious groups that in the Global Survey Report by the WFD Regional Secretary for South America, *Global Education on Human Rights of*

Deaf People: Preliminary project compiled by Collin Allen (2008) included the following note:

> The Working Group noted, positively, that the interpretation services provided by religious organizations, including Jehovah's Witnesses They are of high quality; his mixed success capacity is excellent and even better than those interpreters who have obtained their degrees at university or are members of a Deaf family. (General Secretariat, 2008, p. 65)

An interpreter is not above or below the Deaf person, is not invisible because he/she is human, is only a person who facilitates communication between two or more worlds, and for this, has been and will be important in history.

Comedy and Martyrdom?

The testimony of Brieva reveals some of the many ways in which the role of the sign language interpreter in the region has emerged. The role represents a figure, with many similarities and many key differences in gender, religious affiliation, social class, and academic status. Also, it includes a way to be an interpreter revealing regularities and few deviations. Latin America has the "gift of inequality," the grace of liquid modernity. In the region, time frames overlap intense and sophisticated ideas about development, living with great delays and disconnections with the globalized world. This specific situation can be read through one of the most well-known critiques that has been written about sign language interpretation in Latin America: *Interpretation LS/LO: Comedy or martyrdom?* (Sánchez García, 2012).

Carlos Sánchez García is a pediatrician with extensive experience in the formulation and implementation of bilingual deaf education. His most controversial thesis is called "language disability" (Sánchez García, 2011a, 2011b), which pays more attention to mental activity than language socialization itself (Barreto, 2015). The main contribution of this essayist to the discussion of deaf education and sign language interpretation is his critique of the optimism and simplicity in the formulation of educational policy for Deaf people.

Critiques

With a very provocative title, Sánchez's essay begins by questioning the performance of interpreters. He confronts readers with the question: Is sign language interpretation in Latin America a farce, reckless, or an excruciating sacrifice? The state of affairs that Sánchez actually wants to address is much more particular and interesting, including his specific proposal on language:

> [The] interpreter must transmit information via signs to Deaf who do not have complete language development and a deficit cognitive organization; who use

> impoverished sign language, restricted by its own users; who do not have the cognitive schemata or prior knowledge required to understand the topic which is related to the hearing (world); and interpreters have to communicate this in a language in which they are not fluent. A Gordian Knot impossible to loosen unless it is cut with a single stroke. (Sánchez García, 2012, p. 7 § 3)

And even more explicitly, his criticism rhetorically states:

> If interpreters know this [that most of their Deaf audience is made up of the "language disabled"] (and presumably I suppose, they cannot ignore it, unless they are suffering a schizophrenic breakdown) why don't they denounce this situation? Are they, as Paulo Freire would say about reluctant teachers, just ignorant, hypocrites or demagogues? (Sánchez García, 2012, p. 7)

This essay enraged many interpreters in Latin America. Many of them, feeling humiliated, responded defensively, on social networks and in hallways. In an open letter, an interpreter, trying to evade the fundamental issues raised by Sánchez, focused on what for him was the problem, not *what* Sánchez said but *how* he said *it*:

> Throughout the text there are no fewer than 200 negatives in just eight pages, averaging would be about 24 denials per page indicated by six negatives per paragraph; in other words, *each paragraph (that which is put together to express an idea) denies six times. How do you express something that way, except to complain?* (Pérez, 2012; emphasis in original)

It is not the first time the essayist has gotten unreceptive responses. In fact, one of the strongest criticisms, which summarizes much of what we have heard from interpreters and professionals in the field, was published in an open letter he received because of two of his essays (Sánchez García, 2011a, 2011b):

> Let us suppose that [you] are also a supporter of Deaf purism [a socio-anthropological purist] and don't use artful audist discourse. And if you are an audist, so what? Nothing wrong. Then, as an audist, you have an [socio-anthropological] artful discourse. . . . It is not clear what your position is. It is ambiguous. It is both audist and socio-anthropological. . . . There are two positions (here). Nothing in between. What's yours? What gives you the most pleasure? (Gauthier, 2011)

These words are not just against Sánchez. We have seen how professionals in the field, Deaf individuals, and sign language interpreters have begun to attack. They call him *audist* (i.e., racist and colonialist), for sharing his reflections on school failure of Deaf people and the advancement of cochlear implant technology, which, incidentally, Sánchez points out are their areas of expertise, and of which he has also been a critic (personal communication, 2015). It is unfair to require a doctor to say that medicine is a failure and has no future. Such arguments are very weak and certainly visceral. The critics respond with romantic gut reactions and believe in a kind of "Deaf noble savage" and a black-and-white world.

Of course, not all reactions to Carlos Sánchez are in opposition. Viviana Burad, a renowned Argentinian essayist on sign language interpretation, published "Inefficiency in the interpretation of binominal spoken language—hearing culture/Sign language—Deaf culture" (Burad, 2012), an essay that appears to be a response to criticism of *Comedy or martyrdom* in which she is not opposed to Sánchez's comments.

Sánchez's essay reveals attitudes assumed by many professionals in deafness toward sign language interpretation on the continent. This perspective is also adopted by many professionals and sign language interpreters in North America and Europe. Latin American sign language interpreters are dispossessed beings without the tools to build solid careers. They are victims of the painful circumstances of their environment.

Foreignization or Domestication: The Bridge Problem

Certainly, conditions of sign language interpretation in Latin America reflects major challenges facing nations called "underdeveloped" or "developing." However, Sánchez's insights and non–Latin American professionals' perspectives about the region don't consider that social challenges and relationships overlap in complex ways. Latin American sign language interpreters propose ingenious practices to respond to these challenges. They are cultural agents, in anthropological terms, in that *they engage in actions in order to transform their environment.*

Researchers on sign language interpreting in Latin America have particular views of these Latin American phenomena where consumption, adaptation and interrogating theories, foreign academic products, and domestic products coexist. It is a metaphorical proposal of *cannibalism (antropofagia)* (Campos, 1987, as cited in Sales Salvador, 2004 p. 239; see Calzada Perez, 2007), as Latin American authors analyze the academic knowledge about the sign language interpreting imposed by dominant countries, devouring those countries' books and sign language interpreting models to produce their own. Not in the sense of the submissive and helpless "noble savage" but in the sense of the "depraved savage," staunch defenders of their territory and cannibalistic devourers of Whites.

The Bridge Metaphor

The main weakness in Sanchez's criticism is his assumed model of communication. His suspicions are unsupported in his observation:

> I doubt that the interpreters' representation or discourse is intelligible to the vast majority of the Deaf. And this is what bothers me, that no one says it nor

denounces it nor discusses it, and instead, they stay hidden under the table.
(Sánchez García, 2012, p. 3)

This statement should not surprise anyone. Sánchez uses the metaphor of the bridge. It is assumed that interpretation is a bridge between languages and communities. This is a gross exaggeration. If Deaf people cannot understand the interpreters, interpreters cannot understand Deaf people and we would add, if the interpreters cannot understand the input (e.g., what they are supposed to interpret) what type of bridge is one that no one can cross? It is an imaginary bridge, "a thin rope" (Sánchez García, 2012, p. 7 § 6). However, the problem with the bridge metaphor is some believe it is *real*, not a metaphor. It is a metaphor, a comparison. It is neither an accurate nor a realistic way to understand sign language interpretation and translation.

This kind of metaphor comes from a particular model of communication, which Sperber and Wilson (1986 [1994]) call the *code model*, a model of communication that is strictly linear. This model is based on a more basic conceptual metaphor, the *conduit metaphor* (Reddy, 1993).

We need to move from a model in sign language interpretation of being a "conduit" to that of being a cognitive model. A Latin American version of the model was proposed 10 years ago in the literature in the field but has not yet been integrated into practice and discussions in the region (Wilcox & Shaffer, 2005).

Sign Language Interpretation and Language Planning

However, most sign languages, particularly in Latin America, face emerging vigorous language planning processes, as has happened in other countries (Reagan, 2010). Often these processes are guided by government entities or sometimes by agents who hold some authority and power. This emergence of language planning processes leads to the realization that there are no clear guidelines regarding the selection of (standard) signs in many sign languages. Sánchez questions this:

> In my recent experience at the school for the deaf in Merida…an interpreter said she used two signs: "laugh" and "joke", one after another, to mean "sense of humor". In the "*Amigos de la Causa*" Facebook page I asked a postlingually deafened person, a competent user of written language, how to sign "linguistic minority". He said he made the sign "small" or "shrink" and then the sign "linguist". I couldn't imagine how the Deaf wouldn't misunderstand this as (meaning) a "toddler linguist" or "shrinking linguist".…In Venezuela, the signs for MIND, PSYCHOLOGY and PSYCHOLOGIST are the same. I wonder what "element", what linguistic markers the Deaf use—and obviously this is unknown by hearing people—to differentiate one sign from another, that is, to indicate the correct meaning, because such ambiguity is not very beneficial for any language. Or is it? (Sánchez García, 2012, ¿Qué dicen los intérpretes? 2, para.2).

These linguistic elements, probably, are at the level of non-manual features, which allow for indicating differences in morphological, prosodic, and semantic terms (Herrmann & Steinbach, 2013). Many sign languages use initialization, mouth gestures, and mouthing for indicating such differences between words. Also, you can create significant differences in the meaning of signs, through specific manual configurations (Oviedo, 2004). For example, there are several signs to convey the meaning "small" in Colombian Sign Language (LSC), which differ according the configuration of the hands. There is a sign for SHRINK which applies to groups of people, or in other words, a minority group (two hands in a C shape). That is different from describing an individual person that is or becomes small such as a dwarf (one hand in a B shape). At least in LSC, the sign for LINGUISTIC MINORITY cannot be misunderstood as a "toddler linguist."

Above all, this grammatical discussion should not distract from the main focus of critique under discussion, namely what happens in the interpretation of minority languages in contexts where specialized languages are used, such as schools, universities, businesses, factories, and other workplaces. The problem is not the supposed language disabilities of Deaf people. The problem is that educational and linguistic policies for Deaf people have not materialized, and as a result interpreters of minority languages, in this case sign language, improvise extemporaneously.

Finally, what if Deaf people have not participated in basic (primary), secondary, and higher education? What if Deaf people do not have graduate-level education? They cannot understand scientific or technical discourse in the same way that hearing people with higher education experience can, even those Deaf people who are literate (read and write Spanish) and have a university education. This situation has nothing to do with alleged language (or supposed cognitive) deficits. Socio-economic conditions of Deaf people prevent access to certain discourses and practices, an obvious form of class domination through language (Bourdieu, 1985).

Foreignization and Domestication: Cutting the Gordian Knot

Discursive types or "unplanned" neologisms generated by sign language interpreters need some additional attention. We suggest that terminological gaps are not related to language or cognitive abilities of the Deaf community but with their social disadvantage; through production and domination of knowledge and specialized languages, interpreters (in this case sign language interpreters) effectively become "actors in the scene of power" (Delisle & Woodsworth, 2005, pp.109–132).

Lawrence Venuti (1995) has looked at the historical relationship in translation studies and *foreignization* and *domestication*. Venuti analyzes how translators throughout history have adapted their writings and the way that the contemporary publishing market operates, proposing that translation is governed by a series of ideological tendencies depending on the approach to the culture of origin. In general, the rule of translation, in relation to the American market, has been domestication. Publishers in the American market, eager to produce and sell acceptable translations throughout the world, prefer to "decaffeinate" foreign languages and cultures in order to fit into the American style. Editors accept this type of (bland) translation because versions that try to "spice up" English, with styles, structures, and ways of exposing the culture of origin, are often not well received by readers of these works. However, this is a false illusion of American translation consumers. Texts are results not only of the language system in question but also of a particular culture, and the "decaffeinated" versions that abound in the translation market are simply a product of an elaborate manipulation by *unseen* agents in the process: the translators. Thus, Venuti proposes that we "rethink new ways of reading and writing translations" (Venuti, 1995). *Domestication* is the most widespread trend in historical terms, a practice that softens linguistic and cultural differences, gives an illusion of equivalence, and is an "abuse of fidelity" (Lewis, 1985). *Foreignization* is the reverse process in which translations reflect the dissonance and bittersweetness of the text's culture. Foreignized translations are those that reveal the actual denseness of languages and cultures that we yearn to see.

This Venutian perspective could shed light on what sign language interpreters do in community settings in Latin America, including the situations experienced in school and academic events. Interpreters engage in a *domestication of sign language.* This domestication would be extremely complex, as it would include the manipulation of interpretations by interpreters to create interpretations that produce little resistance and that presumably are better absorbed and "understood" by Deaf people. It also includes the so-called adaptations that interpreting suffers due to the limitations, philosophies, and lack of linguistic processes in sign language. In the same manner, interpreters also participate in a domestication of spoken Spanish. This domestication includes interpreters' manipulations when they voice for Deaf people, that is, translate the signed discourse of the Deaf person into spoken language, changing the words of the Deaf person to avoid perplexing *the hearing* audience, and to assure they are clearly understood, and presumably, to avoid rejection and prejudice against Deaf people by members of the majority culture.

At this point, we find it very problematic to apply the concept of *Venutian foreignization* to the translation of sign languages into Spanish; that is, considering the Spanish language as *foreignized*. Research by Feyne (2015) showed that interpreters, eager to replicate "fidelity" to the structure of the sign language of Deaf professionals exhibiting in museums in New York, "infantilized" them in front of hearing patrons. Sign language users in this situation, however, could view these same exhibitions as complex texts, with quality and academic rigor, but translations of the Deaf artist's voice does not "sound" equal.

What's going on? To Feyne (2005), the answer lies in the concept of *authenticity*, that is, the process through which interpreters construct and redefine the situated identities of Deaf professionals. Interpreters are the only agents who can do it effectively. However, the case would be very different in a psychiatric consultation facilitated with a sign language interpreter. The psychologist or psychiatrist would be very interested in receiving a "foreignized" version of the sign language. If the professional comes from a Lacanian tradition, regardless of whether the "voice" sounds strange, he or she would be interested in revealing deep repression of the subconscious of the Deaf person, through what he/she says, avoiding filtering by the interpreter as much as possible.

This is feasible in the Latin American context where there are very few psychologists and psychiatrists who specialize in working with Deaf people. Finally, *foreignization* of Spanish in the context of sign language should be addressed. Specifically in universities, Deaf students need to approximate the way in which knowledge is expressed in the majority language. In these situations, the interpreter *needs foreignized sign language.* They should use varieties that express precise Spanish (the *foreign*) vocabulary in signs, which could include fingerspelled words using the manual alphabet, mouthing, and semantic and syntactic calques (loanwords) among other things.

In closing, we want to suggest that the only way to provide new avenues and understandings to rework this intricate situation of sign language interpreters is by looking at their *actions* rather than abstract models. It is necessary to "cut the Gordian Knot" with a single stroke, and it is necessary to question the role and ethics of the interpreter. The idea that interpreters are neutral is a myth (Metzger, 2002). This myth of interpreter neutrality has quickly taken root in many parts of Latin America. Interpreters in history have also been agents of change. Instead of continuing with *codes of ethics* disconnected from complex and profuse social practices (Burad, 2008), we must move towards new ethics based on *teleological models* (Dean & Pollard, 2011) that call for not only interpreting languages but also the cultural situations experienced by the interpreter and their huge responsibility in social change of the Deaf community.

AND HEARTLESS GRANDMOTHER?

Sign language interpreters in Latin America face a huge challenge in the future. There are conditions that lead us to think it is an "incredible and sad tale." Nonetheless, sign language interpreters face these challenges every day with realism and intelligence.

It's amazing that such a complex linguistic and cultural activity requiring specific skills and knowledge that only a few develop after overcoming enormous difficulties, remains relegated to being considered as *instrument*. Interpreting is seen as peripheral, as "reasonable accommodation" in the integral development of Deaf communities in many parts of Latin America. Startlingly, in many Latin American countries' recognition of the interpreting profession is precarious. There are few sites devoted to research and innovation related to sign language interpreting (or even research on sign language). It is upsetting that dozens of interpreters in Latin America are exposed to physical (ergonomic) and psychological complaints because they work many hours at one or more jobs. We do not know at this time the possible effects of this dizzying "line of psychological and occupational risk" (Dean & Pollard, 2001). And it is distressing that many interpreters are "selling" their bodies to interpret with unfair and ridiculous contracts imposed on them. As a result, they endure lonely hours of interpreting faced with impenetrable and invasive academic discourse with no alternative but to stoically accept their job or their fate.

We don't mean to say that there are not things to celebrate about sign language interpretation. We have not intended to ignore the work and effort that many interpreters have put forth in this job. We attempt to suggest that the scenario of practices around interpreting in Latin America is fractal. Before us we have possibilities to live and build sign language interpreting in contradictory and overlapping scenarios.

Of course, this situation leads us to look for the wrongdoers. In this regard, the example of *The Incredible and Sad Tale of Innocent Eréndira and Her Heartless Grandmother* (García Márquez, 1978) offers stimulating proposals to imagine. Eréndira, a 14-year-old girl who is prostituted by her grandmother to pay the price of an unintentional error, and who, by means of the bloody murder of Ulises, manages to escape and is forever lost in the desert. There are great paradoxes: the grandmother who was rescued from a brothel by a sailor with knives; Ulises, the son of a traveling salesman; and a native woman, Eréndira, a grandmother, surrounded by Indians. Multiple accounts appear resulting from different views of the same story. The Grandmother would be a fatal version of Eréndira freed from a brothel. Ulises' mother seems to be a happy version of Eréndira with her beloved. Eréndira could be any of these versions. She may be just herself and exit a vicious cycle to run to the sea, in the style of Nemo in the science fiction film *Mr. Nobody* (Godeau, 2009).

Sign language interpreting in Latin America has become, simultaneously, a young prostitute, a heartless grandmother, and a courageous lover. These roles co-exist in different times and spaces. Many interpreters live dedicated to the service of the Deaf community under conditions that undeniably violate their labor rights. They are economically exploited because of the absence of laws or regulations regarding the occupational health of sign language interpreters. Many interpreters live off interpreting as a lucrative business at the expense of those Deaf people who have taught them sign language and without making significant contributions to the movements associated with these minorities. Other interpreters are great heroes, fighting with passion every day to help improve the quality of life of Deaf people through manifold practices. And so the status of sign language interpretation in the region is an incredible and sad tale, a scenario we struggle every day to transform.

References

Barreto, A. G. (2015). La increible y triste historia de la interpretación de lengua de señas: Reflexiones sobre la identidad [The incredible and sad history of sign language interpretation: Reflections on identity]. *Mutatis Mutandi, 8*(2), 299–330.

Bourdieu, P. (1985). ¿Qué significa hablar?: Economía de los intercambios lingüísticos [What does it mean to speak: Economy of linguistic interchanges]. Madrid, Spain: Akal.

Burad, V. (2008). *Ética y procedimiento profesional para intérpretes de lengua de señas* [Ethics and professionals procedures for sign language interpreters]. Mendoza, Argentina: Universidad Nacional de Cuyo.

Burad, V. (2012). ¿Ineficacia en la interpretación del binomio lengua hablada*: cultura oyente/Lengua de señas-cultura sorda?* [Inefficiency in the interpretation of binominal spoken language: Hearing culture/Sign language- Deaf culture]. Retrieved from http://www.cultura-sorda.eu/resources/Burad_Viviana_Ineficacia_interpretacion_binomio_LSCS_LHLECO_2012.pdf

Calzada Perez, M. (2007). *El espejo traductológico: Teorías y didácticas para la formación del traductor* [The translatological mirror: Theories and educational techniques for interpreter training]. Barcelona, Spain: Octaedro.

Dean, R. K., & Pollard, R. Q. (2001). Application of demand-control theory to sign language interpreting: Implications for stress and interpreter training. *Journal of Deaf studies and Deaf Education, 6*(1), 1–14.

Dean, R. K., & Pollard, R. Q. (2011). Context-based ethical reasoning in interpreting: A demand control schema perspective. *The Interpreter and Translator Trainer, 5*(1), 155–182.

Delisle, J., & Woodsworth, J. (2005). Los traductores en la historia [Translators in history]. Íkala, *Revista de Lenguaje y Cultura, 10*(6), 343–346. Retrieved from http://www.redalyc.org/pdf/2550/255020409013.pdf

Feyne, S. (2015). Interpreting identity: Impact of interpreter-mediated discourse on perceptions of the identity of deaf professionals. In B. Nicodemus & K. Cagle (Eds.), *Signed Language interpretation and translation research: Selected papers from the First International Symposium*. Washington, DC: Gallaudet University Press.

García, O., López, D., & Makar, C. (2010). Latin America. In J. Fishman & O. García (Eds.), *Handbook of language and ethnic identity* (pp. 353–373). Oxford, UK: Oxford University Press.

Garcia Canclini, N. (1990). *Culturas Híbridas: Estrategias para entrar y salir de la modernidad* [Cultural hybrids: Strategies for entering and exiting modernity]. Madrid, Spain: DeBolsillo.

García Márquez, G. (1978/2010). *La increíble y triste historia de la cándida Eréndira y de su abuela desalmada* [The incredible and sad tale of innocent Eréndira and her heartless grandmother]. New York, NY: Vintage en español.

Gauthier, G. (2011). No dirigida a Carlos Sanchez. Retrieved from http://www.cultura-sorda.org.

General Secretariat. (2008). Global Survey Report. WFD Regional Secretariat for Mexico, Central America and the Caribbean. Global Education Pre-Planning Project on the Human Rights of Deaf People. Helsinki, Finland: World Federation of the Deaf and Swedish National Association of the Deaf.

Godeau, P. (Producer), Dormael, J. V. (Writer), & Dormael, J. V. (Director). (2009). *Las vidas posibles de Mr. Nobody* [Mr. Nobody] [Film]. France: Pathé; France: Wild Bunch; Spain: WandaFilms.

Herrmann, A., & Steinbach, M. (Eds.). (2013). Nonmanuals in Sign Languages. Amsterdam, Netherlands: John Benjamins.

Lewis, P. (1985). The measure of translation effects. In J. Graham (Ed.), *Difference in translation* (pp. 31–62). Ithaca, NY: Cornell University Press.

Metzger, M. (2002). *Sign language interpreting: Deconstructing the myth of neutrality.* Washington, DC: Gallaudet University Press.

Oviedo, A. (2004). *Classifiers in Venezuelan Sign Language* (Vol. 44). Hamburg: Signum Verlag.

Perez, R. (2012). *En respuesta a "La Interpretación LS/LO: ¿Comedia or martirio?* Retrieved from http://www.cultura-sorda.org

Pires Pereira, M. C. (2010). Produções acadêmicas sobre interpretação de língua de sinais: Dissertações e teses como vestígios histórico [Academic productions in sign language: Dissertations and theses as historical vestiges]. *Cadernos de Tradução, 2*(26), 99–117.

Quadros, R. M., Fleetwood, E., & Metzger, M. (Eds.). (2012). *Signed language interpreting in Brazil.* Washington, DC: Gallaudet University Press.

Quinto-Pozos, D., Casanova de Canales, K., & Treviño, R. (2010). Trilingual Video Relay Service (VRS) Interpreting in the United States. In R. L. McKee & J. E. Davis (Eds.), *Interpreting in multilingual, multicultural contexts* (pp. 28–54). Washington, DC: Gallaudet University Press.

Ramsey, C., & Peña, S. (2010). Sign language interpreting at the border of the two Californias. In R. L. McKee & J. E. Davis (Eds.), *Interpreting in multilingual, multicultural contexts* (pp. 3–27). Washington, DC: Gallaudet University Press.

Rcagan, T. (2010). *Language policy and planning for sign languages.* Washington, DC: Gallaudet University Press.

Reddy, M. (1993). The conduit metaphor: A case of frame conflict in our language about language. In A. Ortony (Ed.), *Metaphor and thought* (pp. 284–310). Cambridge, England: Cambridge University Press.

Rodrigues, C., & Beer, H. (2015). Os Estudos da Tradução e da interpretação de Línguas de Sinais: novo campo disciplinar emergente? [Translation studies and sign language interpretation: A new emerging disciplinary field?] *Cadernos de Tradução, 35*(especial 2), 17–45.

Sales Salvador, D. (2004). *Puentes sobre el mundo: Cultura, traducción y forma literaria en al narrativas de transculturación de José Maria Arguedas y Vikram Chandra.* New York, NY: Peter Lang.

Sánchez García, C. (2011a). *Los sordos: personas con discapacidad (…¡ Y con una discapacidad severa!) Parte 1.* Retrieved from http://www.cultura-sorda.eu/resources/Sanchez_C_Sordos_personas_discapacidad_2011.pdf

Sánchez García, C. (2011b). *Los sordos: personas con discapacidad (… ¡ Y con una discapacidad severa!) Parte II.* Retrieved from http://www.cultura-sorda.eu/resources/Sanchez_C_sordos_personas_discapacidad_Parte_II_2011.pdf

Sánchez García, C. (2012). *Interpretación LS/LO: ¿Comedia o martírio?* Retrieved from http://www.cultura-sorda.eu/resources/Sanchez_Interpretacion-comedia-o-martirio-2012.pdf

Sperber, D., & Wilson, D. (1986 [1994]). *La relevancia: Comunicación y procesos cognitivos. [Relevance: Communication and cognitive processes].* (E. Leonetti, Trans.) Madrid, Spain: Visor.

Venuti, L. (1995). *The translator's invisibility.* London, England : Routledge.

Wilcox, S., & Shaffer, B. (2005). Towards a cognitive model of interpreting. In T. Janzen (Ed.), *Topics in signed language interpreting: Theory and practice* (pp. 27–51). London, England: John Benjamins.

7

Middle School Deaf Education in Mexico: A Postponed Issue

Miroslava Cruz-Aldrete and Miguel Ángel Villa-Rodríguez

Mexico's National Education System is divided into three levels: basic, middle, and high. Basic Education includes Kindergarten, Preschool, Primary, and Middle (Secondary I) Schools; Middle Education includes High School (Secondary II, Technical or Commercial Degrees taken after Secondary School, and Basic Teacher Training); finally, Higher Education includes Advanced Teacher Training, Advanced Technical or Technological Degrees, Bachelors Degree, Professional, and Graduate Studies (INEGI, 2011). It is important to note that the Mexican State made completion of Basic Education mandatory several decades ago, and, that as of June 10, 2013, the State included Middle Education as well, with the publication of the decree in the Federal Official Newspaper (DOF, 2013).

Thus, access to these levels of education is guaranteed to all citizens in a judicial framework. The goal is to reach a universal coverage of these levels by the year 2022 (SEP, 2013). This disposition responds to the information provided by the Organization for Economic Collaboration and Development (OECD, 2013) regarding Mexico's education panorama of which three dire facts are worth noticing: first, 64% of Mexicans only have a diploma for Basic Education; second, the lowest enrollment rates are for people ages 15 to 19; and third, only six out of every 10 young people attend school.

Data set forth by the Organización de Estados Iberoamericanos para la Educación, la Ciencia y la Cultura (Organization of Iberoamerican States for Education, Science, and Culture) (OEI, 2010) states that this situation of education inequality dramatically impacting the welfare of this age group is shared by some Latin American countries, but that the problem increases among members of very poor communities, users

The authors wish to thank the educational institution that participated in the research.

of a minority language, or people with a sensory, mobility, or cognitive disability. Unfortunately, there are groups that present more than one of these conditions, such as the deaf population.

According to the National Institute of Statistics and Geography's (INEGI) 2010 census (INEGI, 2012, 2013), the numbers regarding deaf people in minority communities state that 35% do not have any education, and only 5.4% and 4.1% attended any Middle or Higher education level, respectively. These overwhelming figures lead us to urgently ask ourselves if we can continue to ignore the future of deaf youth who are users of Mexican Sign Language (LSM). The immediate response to this question would be "no," but then we should start by understanding the reasons behind this educational lag and find possible solutions.

The purpose of this chapter is to start a discussion on access to and retention in Middle Education by deaf users of LSM. First, we will consider the learning conditions of the deaf community on the Basic Level of education, particularly related to the implementation of the bilingual deaf education model, which considers their social and linguistic background, the incorporation of deaf teachers, and the training of hearing teachers in the education of the deaf student. Then, we will analyze the learning experience of deaf students in Middle Level education, the participation of an LSM interpreter in the regular classroom, and the deaf students' competence in written language.

Learning Conditions of Deaf Users of LSM in Basic Education

At the beginning of this chapter, we mentioned that Basic Education is compulsory for all Mexicans, with or without disabilities. One of this level's objectives is command of the written language. Deaf students' education also seeks this goal, therefore, all deaf students who attended Basic Education (nine to 12 years), were systematically taught Spanish in its written form using an oral focus or by the bilingual model. However, neither of these approaches has had a meaningful result regarding the students' competence in the written language (Cruz-Aldrete, 2009). This low level of reading and writing competence is made evident, especially when they attempt to continue on to Middle Education.

The requirement for adequate reading and writing proficiency (in Spanish) is high for all students, especially when the educational opportunities (i.e., supply) are insufficient to meet the demand of young people (both deaf and hearing) who wish to continue with their studies. Written exams are the first filter for selecting candidates, and it puts students whose native language is not Spanish in a disadvantageous position, as competence in the written language is required in order to understand the test questions.

Standard admission exams for public institutions offering this level of education, such as Instituto Politécnico Nacional or Universidad Autónoma de México, are the same for all candidates, deaf or hearing. There are no interpreters or translators for these exams, and there no additional time to complete the exam. On the other hand, in the case of private institutions, the criteria might vary, as most are self-governing in the selection of their students.

We acknowledge written competence in Spanish as a second language is difficult for both deaf and hearing students. However, deaf users of LSM have to adopt rules and conventions for written language that, though not an exact copy of the dominant language it represents, requires knowledge of the organizing rules of the spoken language. Thus, a deaf student is confronted with three levels for competence in a natural language simultaneously: oral, visual-gestural, and written.

In addition, there are other issues, such as the complete lack of government linguistic policies, meaning there are very few bilingual teachers (Spanish–LSM), inadequate teaching methods, lack of teaching resources, and late acquisition of LSM by deaf children, due to prejudice surrounding LSM (signs and gestures) as a real language. All of the above impact education the development of every deaf Mexican citizen as an individual, and the growth of the deaf community.

We must pay special attention to the vast socio-linguistic situations deaf Mexicans come from because of its great impact in the classrooms, clearly seen in Basic Education classes (see Cruz-Aldrete & Sanabria, 2008; Cruz-Aldrete, Sanabri, & Villa-Rodríguez, 2010, 2014; Cruz-Aldrete & Serrano Morales, 2014). Likewise, we observed that in Secondary School, the last three years of Basic Education for youth aged 13 to 16, different levels of competence can be found. These include: deaf students monolingual in LSM; students not competent in LSM who use home signs; students who have gone through an oral education and converse using both oral Spanish and LSM but cannot write; deaf students fluent in Spanish only; and the smallest group, those who are bilingual in LSM and written Spanish. In order to understand this linguistic situation, we must recognize two elements: the profound linguistic diversity deaf people are immersed in, and the very different forms of education they have received throughout their childhood.

These two elements require careful study within the framework of the Bilingual Model, introduced in Mexico more than 15 years ago. However, in this chapter we will focus on the following points: (a) the late introduction of deaf teachers into special education schools, also known as Multiple Attention Centers (CAM); (b) the training of special education teachers in the teaching of deaf students; and (c) the Public Education Department's special needs education coverage.

The relevance of the deaf adult—native signer—within the bilingual teaching model of LSM for deaf children, who typically come from hearing families, is very important. It is the deaf teacher who introduces deaf children and youth to the deaf community, its culture and sense of belonging. Nonetheless, due to administrative and teaching training setbacks, the integration of deaf teachers into the classrooms has been difficult.

There are very few deaf native users of LSM working in schools who could serve as linguistic models for deaf students. There is also the concern that, because most deaf teachers do not have a higher education degree or *Licenciatura* (Bachelor's Degree), the education system does not allow for them to be hired as teachers and consequently they are paid less. The result is a vicious cycle in which national education policy has not offered enough education opportunities for deaf people and the actual responsibility of acquiring pertinent education and degrees is left to the deaf community alone.

We do not wish to minimize this issue. Deaf teachers must not only be proficient in LSM but also have training in teaching in order to support and facilitate the acquisition of LSM. We recognize that the school context does not provide a natural environment for the acquisition of sign language, but it is a bilingual context due to the presence of Spanish (written and oral) that makes the school a bilingual bicultural community. However, deaf teachers often travel to several schools in order to satisfy the needs for deaf teachers. Due to the lack of trained deaf teachers, their presence as linguistic models in special education schools or CAMs is sometimes limited to as little as four hours a week.

This situation implies that deaf teachers must prepare an efficient and effective class for all ages in order to provide a "linguistic bath" of LSM helpful to students at all levels of Basic Education. Sadly, this is usually not enough for all children to learn LSM, since most of them do not have other LSM users, deaf or hearing, in their families to help provide opportunities to acquire LSM. Therefore, deaf teachers must be able to reflect upon a metalinguistic approach to their own language and prepare a systematic, well-organized class with very specific objectives to favor the learning of LSM by students who come from very diverse circumstances.

The bilingual method requires the participation of a deaf adult functioning as a linguistic model. Special education (deaf and hearing) teachers should undergo training with emphasis on recognizing deaf people as members of a minority community and not as a person with a disability. Teachers should all possess a thorough knowledge of not only LSM but also history and culture of the deaf community. Considering all of the above, a revision of the actual curriculum for the training of teachers is necessary.

It is important to note that special education teachers undergo training oriented towards special education's needs and the special attention required by people with a disability (of the senses, cognitive or of mobility). In the area for teaching deaf students, special education teachers attend several courses on deafness from a sociocultural point of view, as well as others on how to use various methods and systems, which support the communication competence of the deaf student. The bilingual method is also included, recognizing the importance of teaching deaf students in their native language, LSM, and Spanish (both written and oral) as a second language.

The benefits of bilingual and intercultural education are highlighted in the Communication Learning and Development of Deaf Students I and II courses from the Study Plan of the *Licenciatura* (Bachelor's degree) in Special Education (Auditory and Language Specialization). The management and financial difficulty of these programs are also explained: "the advisability of having a bilingual linguistic model for deaf students is analysed, considering that this option is administratively difficult to implement in most cases" (SEP, 2007a, 9). This view, along with the concept that deafness is a disability that must be cured, shows up in the content of Communication Learning and Development of Deaf Students II. This part of the training focuses on the rehabilitation and integration of deaf people through the learning of the oral language as a means to learn the written language (SEP, 2007b). It is contradictory. On the one hand, the benefits of the bilingual model, the use and study of LSM by hearing teachers, and the acquisition of this language by deaf students are recognized; on the other hand, the oral language is praised more than LSM as it is considered a prerequisite for the learning of the written language.

An analysis of the content of these courses demonstrates that the important role of LSM in the integral development of the deaf student is not clearly understood by those writing teacher training curricula. Their lack of research on the teaching and learning of the written language by deaf users of LSM is also apparent. This discrepancy between the training of new teachers and the ongoing training teachers already receive in the classrooms, which has already adopted the bilingual model, is very problematic. This can be seen in the informational text published by the National Education System *Orientaciones para la atención educativa de alumnos sordos que cursan la Educación Básica desde el modelo bilingüe bicultural* (Guidelines for providing education of deaf students enrolled in Basic Education from the bilingual bicultural model) (SEP, 2010), where a clear emphasis on the use of LSM as the primary language in the formal education process is stated.

Regarding the education options for deaf students offered by the Office of Special Education within the Public Education Ministry (SEP), it is important to note that most CAMs only teach the first levels of Basic Education, specifically, kindergarten and primary schools. There are very few CAMs that provide the secondary school level. Thus, when deaf students exit from primary school at 11 or 12 years of age, it is difficult for them to continue their mandatory remaining years of Basic Education (e.g., secondary I or Middle Education). This lack of educational options results in high levels of school desertion by deaf students.

The role and initiative of all CAM directors to encourage their students to continue with their education is very important. Some have established links with regular Secondary Schools in order to allow for deaf students to take an admission exam so they can continue their studies. This is only a small step in the path of guaranteeing Basic Education for deaf students so that they can continue onto Middle Education.

After deaf students have passed the admission exam (just like regular hearing students), CAM directors must produce the necessary paperwork in order for one of the center's teachers to accompany deaf students to the Secondary School to which they have been admitted. This puts the teacher between two education systems, regular and special, having to establish new relationships with hearing teachers and students who know little about deaf students' needs.

Thus, special education teachers have many roles: they function as interpreters of LSM; they are the communication bridge between deaf students, regular teachers, and hearing students; they have to build links between all members of the school community; and they promote the learning of LSM. Special education teachers must do all of the above, along with teaching and tutoring deaf students in their classes.

It is important to note that the organization and definition of this kind of special education teacher depends, most of the time, on the experience and dynamics of each CAM and their link to the Secondary School. The special–regular education pairing still requires major administrative and academic adjustments, especially regarding the inclusion of the deaf student to a school system planned for users of the spoken language. Regular education not only has a tradition in its teaching and evaluating methods but also possesses an organizational hierarchy that which becomes disrupted by the teacher–interpreter figure. This new situation complicates relations within the group not only because of the language but also because of culture (deaf and hearing) and the mediation required by the teaching–learning process.

Given these circumstances surrounding the support given to deaf students in Basic Education, we must reflect upon data reported by INEGI (2013) in a different light. Even though they state the need to expand educational opportunities for the deaf population, from our point of view, this should concern not only access to regular schools but also attention to their needs as LSM users. A redesign of educational and linguistic policies is urgent. Such changes should promote: (a) the acquisition of LSM as the first language; (b) a course in university and other institutions' training programs for learning LSM as a second language for Basic Education teachers; (c) research on new forms of education and cognitive processes involved in the teaching of reading and writing in Spanish for deaf students; (d) training of educational interpreters; and (e) bilingual specialization for teachers of deaf users of LSM.

Many of these suggestions can be related with the bilingual intercultural model used for the education of speakers of indigenous languages in Mexico, such as the training of bilingual teachers, studying and documenting grammars of indigenous languages, and the creation of teaching materials. However, it is hard to compare speakers of an indigenous language and deaf users of LSM, particularly related with proficiency in written Spanish. LSM continues to lack a written form, and there has not been enough discussion regarding the teaching of written Spanish to deaf people who haven't heard and spoken the language. Therefore, teaching methods used for hearing users of the majority language are still being replicated.

We have not addressed the gaps in the formation of signing deaf students on their own language. Unlike other minority linguistic groups who receive a bilingual education (native language and Spanish) and study their mother tongue, deaf students do not have a curriculum that includes teaching of LSM. As a result, deaf students have opportunities for metalinguistic reflection of their own language, which is indispensable for the formation of every individual.

In short, the problem of deaf education lies in the conception of language. Discrimination against LSM downgrades the importance of its early acquisition by deaf children. Likewise, teachers' ignorance of LSM indicates a lack of respect for this language and its users. Furthermore, by not following the structure of the language, the teaching–learning process of deaf students is hindered. This shows us that even in the "collective imagination," LSM does not have the same status as a language like Spanish.

Therefore, if we establish a hierarchy of the guiding principles for deaf education, we would establish LSM as the main point of intersection from which pertinent actions should develop, such as teacher and interpreter training, and research on the psycholinguistic processes of deaf users of LSM. Furthermore, with LSM at the center, these guiding principles would define teaching goals and objectives for Basic Education and subsequent level of education.

Education for Deaf Students in Middle School: The Role of Interpreters

Educators and other professionals, parents, and the general public often ask where they can learn LSM. While there are a number of Deaf associations and organizations (both deaf and hearing), offering LSM, there is no well-defined curriculum for teaching LSM. Classes are given based on the teacher's experience (deaf, hearing, or coda) and their own beliefs or attitudes towards the language and its users. The result is a lack of uniformity in the competencies expected from students at each level of language instruction. There are no established outcomes for students learning LSM, whether their goal is simply to be able to communicate in the language, teach deaf students, or become an interpreter of the language.

The ignorance surrounding LSM, especially regarding its grammar, affects not only hearing and deaf teachers (we do not deny their competence as LSM native users, but they lack linguistic knowledge of its grammar) but also sign language interpreters. Teachers are essential in Basic Education schools, but interpreters become important in Middle and High Education (Secondary I and II).

Thus, due to the lack of bilingual secondary schools (LSM–Spanish) with teachers fluent in LSM, the interpreter has become a fundamental component for deaf students to be able to continue their education beyond the primary level. Their role is not limited to interpreting classes, but they also provide academic tutoring to deaf students. However, in Mexico, teachers and interpreters are unable to fulfill these tasks due to their own lack of training. There are no courses or institutions dedicated to training Spanish–LSM bilingual interpreters, although there are for training interpreters of spoken languages.

Even though there have been efforts to develop specialization courses in public universities or BA programs for sign language interpreters, they have not flourished due to lack of state policy and finances and for academic reasons. Working sign language interpreters are in dire need of professionalization. Their work in the various public settings requires specific subject knowledge (e.g., health, justice, education), knowledge of relevant terminology, syntax, and grammar of both languages (Spanish and LSM), and knowledge of deaf culture. Additionally, and more importantly, educational interpreters must be valued and value themselves for their vital role in the education of the deaf community.

Against this background we recognize the work of both public and private institutions of higher education that have already adopted the bilingual method through the many Centros de Atención para Estudiantes con Discapacidad (Attention Centers for Students with Disabilities, CAED) existing within some institutions, such as:

1. Instituto Tecnológico de Tijuana (Technology Institute of Tijuana);
2. Universidad Tecnológica de Santa Catarina,Nuevo León (Technological University of Santa Catarina, Nuevo Leon);
3. Educación Incluyente A.C (Inclusive Education, A.C.);
4. Asociación Deportiva Cultural y Recreativa Silente de Jalisco A.C. (Silent Sport, Cultural and Recreation Association, Jalisco, A.C.);
5. Asociación de Sordos de Jalisco (Jalisco Association of the Deaf);
6. Colegio Nacional de Educación Profesional Técnica (CONALEP) Morelos (National College of Professional Technical Education, Morelos);
7. Colegio de Bachilleres del Estado de Querétaro (COBAQ) (Secondary State School of Querétaro, an inclusive high school);
8. Centro de Estudios Tecnológicos Industrial y de Servicios (CETIS) (Center for Technological Studies and Services); and
9. Centro de Bachillerato Tecnológico Industrial y de Servicios (CBTIS) (Technology Industrial Secondary Center for Services).

This small group of secondary and higher education institutions offering bilingual (LSM–Spanish) courses do so using various methods. Some, like Instituto Tecnológico de Tijuana, CONALEP Morelos, Educación Incluyente A.C., and Universidad Tecnológica de Santa Catarina, rely on the presence of a sign language interpreter within regular classes, where most students are not deaf. Others, like CETIS and CBTIS, which are supported by SEP's Undersecretariat of Middle Education, have recently launched an out-of-school program with the support of CAEDs. The structure of this program provides the training for teachers and tutors who are able to provide classes and advice to others that enables them to work with people of different abilities. This enables deaf secondary graduates to continue their secondary education in this out-of-school or open-school model.

There is no doubt many deaf students can continue with their education because of this program. Nonetheless, it is important to state that not all of these institutions have a CAED, not all teachers and tutors know LSM, and a sign language interpreter is not always available. Among the forms of communication between faculty and deaf students we have encountered are signed, Spanish, and writing, which denotes a communication problem with signing deaf students and makes teaching classes difficult. It seems that federal government policy regarding access to Middle Education for deaf students has focused on expanding its coverage. Regardless of its intention, the out-of-school secondary program does not consider the fundamental principle that in order for deaf students to achieve linguistic competence, teachers and tutors should know LSM.

Another example of this situation is the online High School program for deaf students, formally launched in 2009 by the Ministry of Education (SEDF, 2009). It was established by two reading comprehension professionals, three math teachers, a deaf computer studies teacher, and an interpreter. Aspiring students were evaluated in math, mathematical thinking, reading comprehension, and writing. As a result, the need for a remedial course in math, reading comprehension, and computer studies became evident. Specific objectives for this course were to: increase vocabulary, improve writing skills, and expand the student's ability to concentrate and formulate abstract thoughts.

The need for a remedial course before beginning secondary education is evidence of the deaf students' lack of competence in written Spanish. But it shows also a prejudiced view of the deaf students regarding their lack of vocabulary and deficiency of abstract thought. It was never considered this was a reflection of the learning of a second language and an education gap that has kept most members of the deaf community in an uninformed and marginalized position. The problem was focused on the deaf student's competence and not on the education system they have experienced.

Thus, one of the goals established from the beginning of the bilingual model promoted by SEP's Office of Special Education in Mexico City (Dirección de Educación Especial de la Secretaría de Educación Pública en el Distrito Federal) was for deaf students to acquire LSM as a first language and Spanish in its written form as a second one. Regarding this goal, we have to consider that the implementation of the bilingual system has not been uniform throughout the country. We have detected substantial differences in the development of this model at the Basic Education level within different states. There are some states that have moved forward in the implementation of the program, as in the development of educational strategies that favor the entry and retention of deaf students who use of LSM at the different levels of education of the National Education System. But there are other states that have just began their awareness program for teachers of the Basic level, regarding the needs and characteristics of the signing deaf students.

Even though each school has its own history, tradition, and dynamics defining the actions of each member of the educational community, certain key points regarding circumstances, expectations, and needs for Middle School deaf education are shared by different educational agents in Mexico City, Cuernavaca, Guadalajara, Monterrey, Tijuana, and Mérida. They all concur concerning the importance of sign language interpreters, students' competence in the written Spanish (both reading and writing), the formation of a support network between hearing and deaf students through tutoring, an awareness program for the hearing school community (teachers, administrative personnel, and students) before deaf students join a school whose main mode of communication is spoken language, and the participation of parents regarding the expectations they have of their deaf children.

As we can see, the role of the sign language interpreter is of vital importance throughout this education level. But as we have stated before, there are neither guidelines for the teaching of LSM as a second language nor an institution for the training of LSM interpreters. The result is that most people working as sign language interpreters do not have the cultural knowledge nor the training required for adequate interpretation of the content of the classes corresponding to this level of education. Most of those working as interpreters come from deaf families or are interpreters primarily in religious contexts, as in the case of interpreters who are Jehovah's Witnesses, but are not from professional backgrounds. Thus, their interpretation of the subject matter does not correspond to the actual level of the class or the detriment of the deaf students' learning experiences.

The low level of education of interpreters also affects their relationship with other faculty members. Interpreters are not considered part of academic discussion spaces, where they can ask for clarification of the class content they will have to interpret. Equally important is the fact that there is no explanation of the interpreter's role at the beginning of the school year. The lack of distinction between the roles of the hearing teachers, sign language interpreters, and deaf and hearing students, may result in difficulties in the teaching–learning process and the retention of deaf students.

Deaf Students' Competence in Written Language in Middle Education

We have observed that deaf secondary students demonstrate an alarming underdevelopment in reading comprehension and writing, resulting in the implementation of workshops by many school centers in order to compensate for this difficulty.

Nonetheless, these courses still employ the methods used for teaching hearing students and their knowledge of Spanish (often supported by the reading experiences they have had at home) without considering that many deaf students are not even fluent in LSM.

Even though the difficulty of reading and writing affects hearing and deaf students, we must emphasize the deaf students' disadvantages, as they are learning literacy in a language that is not their own. Learning a written language requires understanding phonology, which allows readers and writers access to phonetic information about words either directly through a mental lexicon containing images of written words or indirectly through the translation of written words into sounds. As we can see, both processes involve experience and knowledge of Spanish. Additionally, the identification of canonical patterns of syllables used in Spanish, and the frequent combinations that appear in words is also required. In order to understand that all of the elements of a linguistic system operate simultaneously and in parallel, it is not enough to identify the components of written words. A syntactic and semantic process is required in order to integrate meanings at higher levels, particularly at the sentence level.

We have identified certain reading and writing patterns in deaf students involved in this study. For one, we noticed many deaf students have difficulties grasping the meaning—denotative and connotative—of words while reading. We also found many had problems with the forming of words, phrases, and sentences while writing in Spanish. This is because they have not been taught enough about the actual graphic patterns composing each letter and characteristic elements of the morphology of words. They also don't comprehend the "role" of a word in various forms in sentences as they don't fully understand parts of speech (e.g., noun, verb, adjective, etc.).

We also carried out an evaluation in Morelos in June 2012 with deaf high school and technical degree students who used LSM in which we considered another variable in addition to fluency in LSM and Spanish. The group in Morelos at the Temixco National College of Technical Education (CONALEP) included 30 first-year students, 11 deaf and 19 hearing. We introduced several common tests used internationally in neuropsychological evaluations to test basic cognitive abilities through visual attention in order to compare deaf and hearing student results. These included: processing speed, working memory, short- and long-term visual memory, incidental learning, perception, access to visual and lexical semantics, and executive functions. The tests used were: Corsi Cubes (Milner, 1971), The Complex Shape Test (Osterrieth, 1944; Rey, 1941), Test of the Pyramids and Palm Trees (Howard & Patterson, 1992), and Digits and Key Symbols from the Barcelona Test (Peña-Casanova, 1991). The results showed no significant differences between the average scores obtained by both groups, except on two tasks: reverse order of Corsi Cubes, and in the second part of the Pyramids and Palm Trees Test in which they had to perform the semantic work using written words instead of images used in the first part of the test.

We were able to recognize a significant difference between the deaf and hearing students' results in *working memory,* a cognitive function that could be a component of the basic difficulties in learning to read. In Baddeley's (2000) model, two separate brain storage areas are proposed: one for phonological and the other for visual or spatial information. However, this second area has not been studied as much. It is likely that the formation of both storage areas is deeply related (Morey, 2009), which could explain the reduced development of the deaf students.

While one would think given the visual nature of gestural sign languages, users should have a greater development of spatial skills, our data do not confirm this assumption and indicate clear differences in the online cognitive processing of spatial information. It is likely that the root of the marked difficulties presented by deaf students at learning this skill are significant differences in the cognitive processing of visual information related with working memory.

We consider that curriculum for the education of the deaf community should include opportunities to develop metalinguistic reflection on LSM as well as teaching grammar in order to be able to explain the structure of the Spanish language. In addition, there is need for varied instructional materials that employ different communication situations, which require the use of written language, giving it a value that goes beyond the classroom. Changes should be based on the explicit development of the visual and spatial components of working memory to form a visual and spatial awareness of written language as a counterpart for phonological awareness.

It is necessary to test this hypothesis and to continue with the investigation of the learning of the written language by deaf students who use LSM. It is through systematic research with a solid theoretical base and methodologies that answers will be found regarding this complex situation.

Conclusion

We reaffirm that at the center of the debate on deaf education in Mexico, we find the lack of a linguistic policy and of evaluation mechanisms that could allow us to identify what is happening with the implementation of the Bilingual Model for deaf people. The problem we face will not be solved by only focusing on the education of this community using LSM but must include discussion of the training of bilingual teachers and educational interpreters. Additionally, we must investigate why deaf students, even after completing all levels of Basic Education, still have difficulties reading and writing.

On one hand, a critical analysis of the education deaf students have received in Basic Education—referencing the approach detailed by the Secondary School Reform (SEP, 2006), which put emphasis on the written language—should lead us to search for strategies that allow deaf students to continue onto the Middle Education school level with appropriate skills and competencies in written language. On the other hand, substantial steps we are making allow us to recognize that there are language mechanisms that organize a visual and spatial language and impact the learning process of its users. Thus, being deaf allows an individual to adapt in some other way in order to interact with a mainly hearing world, and strategies must be designed with satisfactory learning in mind. We insist the problem is not deafness itself; the problem is an education system that does not respond to the fact that LSM is a fundamental element for the development of deaf people and an indispensable tool in the education of deaf students.

It is not enough to expand education or to implement remedial courses. What is needed is to go to the root of the problem: acquisition and fluency in LSM as the primary language for deaf people in Mexico; lack of competence in written Spanish; and, equally important, lack of infrastructure (human and organizational resources) that would transform the training of teachers and interpreters in the adequate use of LSM corresponding to the needs in Middle School education.

The role of the sign language interpreter is vital to guarantee access and the retention of deaf students in secondary school. Nonetheless, we cannot place all responsibility for deaf students' success or failure on their shoulders. Nowadays, interpreters are evaluated not only on their abilities to perform their work but also on their teaching skills. Sign language interpreters working in education have intuitively developed strategies that allow them to attend to deaf students' needs in the classrooms. For example, they study alongside the deaf students to answer their questions, help with homework and administrative paperwork, and, in many cases, become the tutor of the group they interpret for. Their actual duties surpass those of an interpreter, and this issue should be addressed, formalizing the expectations that the education system has of sign language interpreters.

There is no question of the interpreter's importance in the classroom and in other public spaces, and thus the need for their professionalization. We must recognize the lack of institutions or universities providing LSM interpreting degrees that would allow them to perform better and be taken more seriously in the different settings in which they work. We also must not overlook the training of hearing teachers and the need to modify curriculum for teacher education regarding the competences needed to teach to signing deaf students.

Likewise, the early acquisition of LSM and developing competency in the language must be a main objective in the curriculum for deaf students. The study of LSM grammar throughout Primary and Secondary Schools (Basic Education) and the study of Spanish grammar in order to acquire fluency in written Spanish must also be priorities.

Summing up, we know what the problems are, but we have not taken on the challenge. Thus, if we believe that education is the best instrument to overcome social development difficulties, we must urgently respond to the educational needs of deaf youth. Their education has been very limited compared with that of their hearing peers due to the lack of clearly delineated linguistic and education policies. The complexity involved in deaf education demands the participation of members from different disciplines, but mainly, it demands a change in attitude towards deaf people themselves, as they must be recognized as users of another language with their own culture, different from that of the majority.

If Mexico sees itself as a multicultural and multilingual nation, it is urgent that the needs of the deaf population be met. Their members constitute an essential part of the nation, just like indigenous people. It is only in this way that identification of strategies for an appropriate deaf education proposal can be achieved. And in this way, the recognition of the right all Mexicans citizens who are linguistic minorities to education have will be made evident.

References

Baddeley, A. D. (2000). Short-term and working memory. In E. Tulving & F. I. M. Craik (Eds.), *The Oxford handbook of memory* (pp. 77–92). Oxford, UK: Oxford University Press.

Cruz-Aldrete, M. (2009). Reflexiones sobre la Educación bilingüe Intercultural para el sordo en México [Reflections on intercultural bilingual education for the Deaf in México]. *Revista Latinoamericana de Educación Inclusiva, 3*(1) 133–145. Universidad Central de Chile y Red Iberoamericana de Investigación sobre Cambio y Eficacia Escolar.

Cruz-Aldrete, M., & Sanabria, E. (2008). Algunos aspectos sociolingüísticos de la comunidad silente en México [Some sociolinguistic aspects of the silent community in México]. In R. M. Ortiz Ciscomani (Ed.), *Memorias del IX Encuentro Internacional de Lingüística en el Noroeste*. Universidad de Sonora. Hermosillo, Sonora. México. 2, 347–366.

Cruz-Aldrete, M., Sanabria E., & Villa-Rodríguez, M. (2010). Educación intercultural bilingüe: Actas del Primer Congreso en la Red sobre Interculturalidad y Educación. [Intercultural bilingual education: Acts of the First Congress of the Interculturalism and Education Network] La comunidad sorda mexicana y la educación bilingüe intercultural: un problema sin voz [The Mexican deaf community and intercultural bilingual education: A problem without a voice]. In F. Villalba & J. Villatoro (Eds.), *Prácticas en educación* (pp. 113–120).

Cruz-Aldrete, M., & Serrano Morales, J. (2014). Elementos alfabéticos en la Lengua de Señas Mexicana: un acercamiento sociolingüístico [Alphabetic elements in Mexican Sign Language: a sociolinguistic approach]. In P. M. Butragueño & L. Orozco (Eds.), *Argumentos cuantitativos y cualitativos en sociolingüística. Segundo*

120   Miroslava Cruz-Aldrete and Miguel Ángel Villa-Rodríguez

coloquio de cambio y variación lingüística (pp. 249–265). México City, México: El Colegio de México.

Diario Oficial de la Federación. (2005). Ley General de las Personas con Discapacidad [General Law of Persons with Disabilities]. Retrieved from http://www.dof.gob.mx/

Diario Oficial de la Federación. (2013). Decree reforming articles 3o., 4o., 9o., 37, 65 y 66; adding articles 12 and 13 of the Ley General de Educación. Retrieved from http://www.dof.gob.mx/

Howard, D., & Patterson, K. E. (1992). *The pyramids and palm trees test.* Bury St Edmunds, Thames, UK: Valley Test Company.

INEGI. (2011). *Marco conceptual del Censo de Población y Vivienda 2010* [Conceptual framework of the Population and Housing Census 2010]. México City, México: INEGI.

INEGI. (2012). *Anuario estadístico de los Estados Unidos Mexicanos 2011* [Statistical Yearbook of the United Mexican States 2011]. México City, México: INEGI.

INEGI. (2013). *Las personas con discapacidad en México. Una visión al 2010* [People with disabilities in México. A vision to 2010]. México City, México: México Instituto Nacional de Estadística, Geografía e Informática.

Milner, B. (1971). Interhemispheric differences in the localization of psychological processes in man. *British Medical Bulletin, 27,* 272–277.

Morey, C. C. (2009). Integrated cross-domain object storage in working memory: Evidence from verbal-spatial memory tasks. *The Quarterly Journal of Experimental Psychology,* 62, 2235–2251.

OCDE. (2013). *Education at a glance. Indicators.* Retrieved from http://www.oecd -ilibrary.org/education/education-at-a-glance-2013_eag-2013-en

OEI. (2010). 2021 *Metas educativas: la educación que queremos para la generación de los bicentenarios* [Educational goals: The education we want for the bicentennial generation]. Retrieved from http://www.oei.es/metas2021/libro.htm

Osterrieth, P. A. (1944). Le Test de Copie d'une Figure Complexe [The Copy a Complex Figure Test]. *Archives de Psychologie, 30,* 206–356.

Peña-Casanova, J. (1991). *Programa integrado de exploración neuropsicologica: Test Barcelona.* [Integrated neuropsychological examination program: Barcelona Test]. Barcelona, Spain: Masson.

Rey, A. (1941). L'examen psychologique dans les cas d'encephalopathy traumatique [The psychological examination in cases of traumatic encephalopathy]. *Archives de Psycholigie, 28,* 286–340.

SEDF. (2009). Avances de los alumnos sordos al Bachillerato a distancia de la SEDF [Progress of deaf students in the distance education Baccalaureate SEDF]. Retrieved from http:// www.eadf.df.gob.mx/portal/articles/entry/Avances-del-Bachillerato -para-alumnos-Sordos

SEP. (2007a). *Aprendizaje y desarrollo comunicativo de los alumnos sordos I. Programa y materiales de apoyo para el estudio. Licenciatura en Educación Especial.* [Learning and communicative development of deaf students I. Agenda and supporting materials for the degree in Special Education]. México City, México: Secretaría de Educación Pública.

SEP. (2007b). *Aprendizaje y desarrollo comunicativo de los alumnos sordos II. Programa y materiales de apoyo para el estudio. Licenciatura en Educación Especial.* [Learning and communicative development of deaf students II. Program and support materials for the study for a degree in Special Education]. México City, México: Secretaría de Educación Pública.

SEP. (2010). *Orientaciones desde el enfoque bilingüe para la atención educativa de alumnos sordos que cursan la educación básica.* [Guidelines from the bilingual approach to education and care of deaf students enrolled in Basic Education]. México City, México: Secretaría de Educación Pública.

8

Inclusive Education in Mexico: De Facto Segregation of the Signing Deaf

Boris Fridman-Mintz

In Mexico, so much is said about educational integration or inclusion of persons with disabilities that it may seem as if the main challenge of deaf education is simply that of access to schooling. Although this may be the case in some remote or isolated regions of the country, it is not the case for young Deaf people in urban settings, for whom the real problem is the quality of the schooling modalities that are available to them. In this chapter, I offer an encompassing review of such modalities and document the state of affairs they present.

I undertake this exposition of the specific circumstances of Deaf school children in Mexico for two reasons. The first is to attract attention to the needs of those who stand at the lower level of the educational institutional hierarchy, although in institutional discourse they constitute their own raison d'être. The second is to illuminate the ways in which current discourse on the topic justifies neglecting the specific needs of each of the subjects participating in the educational process through the application of generic discourses about persons with disabilities and with abstract defenses of diversity. For the same reason, before addressing the characterization of the schooling modalities of Deaf students in Mexico, it is necessary to briefly reflect on the nature of Deaf people, as well as on the variety of Deaf individuals that do exist (Fridman-Mintz, 2006).

In conventional wisdom, a Deaf person is thought of as a one with a significant degree of hearing loss. This is the complement to the assumption that a normal person has a reasonably good level of hearing. However, every concept of normality is dependent upon the perceptions of the one who holds it. Therefore, conceptions of the normalcy of deafness will be different for people who have always been Deaf. Specifically, for a signing member of the Mexican Deaf community, not hearing is a natural condition of existence and, as such, defines normalcy. Taking this perspective into account, I propose a generic definition of deafness, as follows:

This chapter is dedicated to Robert E. Johnson, who readily commented and corrected this chapter and who, therefore, will share with me the pride of being irreverent.

> A *Deaf person* is any person whose possibilities of linguistic ascription is conditioned by his or her limited or null hearing, by making it difficult to participate in certain linguistic communities, facilitating participation in others, and completely impeding it in some social circumstances. (Fridman-Mintz, 2009, p. 95)

This approach suggests that, to the extent that it is a biological condition, deafness determines the socialization possibilities of a given subject within diverse linguistic communities. Therefore, being Deaf becomes a positive condition for diversified social identity, depending on the available alternatives in the socio-historical context of each individual. Therefore, it is neither a permanent disability nor a negatively defined condition.

Schematically, Mexican Deaf people tend to fall into one of three fundamental Deaf identities: Spanish-speaking Deaf individuals (who I will identify as the speaking Deaf), Deaf persons who remain socially isolated and linguistically undefined (the semilingual Deaf), and members of the Mexican Deaf community (the signing Deaf). This characterization should not be taken to mean that speaking Deaf people do not sign nor that signing Deaf people do not speak. It is a statement of identity rather than one of restrictive practice.[1]

Because each of these categories interacts with and within formal education depending on its own linguistic and cultural identity, they must be considered in evaluating the educational situation of Deaf people in Mexico.

> The "Speaking Deaf" are those Deaf individuals who assume a spoken language as their first and preferred language, regardless of how or when they became Deaf. Although because of their limited hearing they are often unable to sustain a natural dialog in spoken language. Nonetheless, they may keep on speaking it in order to keep their life and sociocultural identity within what they consider to be their native community. (Fridman-Mintz, 2009, p. 103)

Often these are persons who became Deaf during adulthood, but the category also includes children and youth who became Deaf during childhood and/or who may have had some degree of success at acquiring Spanish with the help of therapies or speech-based educational strategies. Their social life often becomes restricted or

---

1. The use of the noun "Deaf" in this text is only to be understood as it is here defined. As explained further on and by Fridman-Mintz (2006), terminology such as "hearing disabled" or "hard of hearing" have introduced a number of ambiguities and misguided practices. That is why they were completely avoided in the *Ley General de las Personas con Discapacidad* (2011).

altered when their interpersonal links can no longer flow through spoken conversations, but they are characterized by determinedly holding on to their pre-established family, educational, working, and fraternal environments. In Mexico these things are mostly circumscribed to the Spanish-speaking (hearing) world. In order to maintain this identity, they may undertake any form of rehabilitation or assisted communication, under the assumption that their particular condition as persons with a linguistic disability is unavoidable and that it needs to be repaired for them to function as a whole person.

In Mexico the presence of the second type of Deaf is regrettably abundant and persistent. These are a group I call semilingual Deaf. They haven't fully developed any language because they are prelingually Deaf and haven't had any access to a natural sign language (Fridman-Mintz, 2009).

Their existence is due to two facts: first that the absence or loss of hearing by infants can be neither completely prevented nor cured, and second, that the Spanish-speaking (hearing) majority (to which some 95% of the parents of Deaf children belong) (Fridman-Mintz, 1998) persists in preventing their children from acquiring LSM (*Lengua de Señas Mexicana*, i.e., Mexican Sign Language) and contacting those who use it, namely the Mexican Deaf community or CSM (*Comunidad de Sordos Mexicana*).

It should be noted that the earlier a person becomes Deaf, the fuzzier the boundary between a Deaf person who believes himself to be a speaker and to have command of Spanish as a first language and the Deaf person who refers to himself as a Spanish-speaker but is actually semilingual. Regardless of the subtle differences that may exist between speaking and semilingual Deaf children, 90% of them become signing Deaf (Fridman-Mintz, 1999). The most fluent Spanish speakers become balanced bilinguals of LSM and Spanish, and those who are clearly semilingual become fundamentally monolingual in LSM. Between these extremes exists various level of biliguality.

Finally, I must define the group known as the signing Deaf, whose linguistic and cultural rights have just begun to be recognized by national and international legislation. These are the Deaf people whose essential forms of communication and social identity center on the culture of a Deaf community and its sign language (Fridman-Mintz, 1999).

Given their quite different communicative and cultural needs, public and private Mexican education should offer differentiated access to school socialization for each of these types of Deaf people in order that they might fully develop their respective capabilities and effectively participate in formal education and society.

I propose the following schematic design. First of all, the speaking Deaf could be schooled inclusively in general education, schools where spoken Spanish is the language of instruction (or spoken language of their families in the case of indigenous languages). Of course, the necessary accommodations must be put in place beforehand, so that these Deaf students may have visual access to the surrounding linguistic interaction. This access would include:

1. providing copies of classroom notes;
2. interlocutors whose faces remain visible;
3. allowing the Deaf students to watch either the blackboard or the person speaking;
4. projected texts;
5. visual signals to alert them to bells and spoken announcements;
6. acoustically appropriate environments for the use of hearing aids; and
7. technical support for cochlear implant devices, etc.

In the case of signing Deaf students, they should be inclusively schooled in bilingual schools where LSM is used for face-to-face interactions and Spanish is introduced as a second language for written communication. This should be the setting minimally for preschool, kindergarten, and the primary grades in order to foster their collective identity and self-esteem, as well as a dignified and gradual approach to the Spanish or indigenous cultures of their hearing surroundings.

Semilingual Deaf students should be provided access to schooling as soon as possible, with signing Deaf children, in bilingual schools where LSM is the language of face-to-face interactions. The acquisition of LSM is the only proven way of improving the odds that they will leave behind their semilingual condition. However, such conditions for these Deaf students are not widely available in Mexico.

Below, I will enumerate the six schooling options available for Deaf people in Mexico, not without first stating how, and in what context this classification was achieved. As a result of an organized social mobilization that began in 1997, LSM was legally recognized as a national language (Secretaría General, 2011, p. 7). As a part of this process, it was legally declared that Mexico has the obligation of, among other things, "Granting access to public, obligatory and bilingual education to Deaf population, including the teaching of Spanish language and LSM" (Secretaría General, 2011, p. 6). Since the Federal Department of Education or SEP (*Secretaría de Educación Pública*) has not had the necessary political will to comply with this mandate, a complaint was filed at the Mexican National Commission for Human Rights or CNDH (Comisión Nacional de los Derechos Humanos, 2011–2015).

In the course of presenting arguments at the CNDH, and in the absence of official or trustworthy quantitative data, I developed the schooling categories that follow. They are based on information from the input of numerous Deaf persons, parents of Deaf children, and other hearing people, mainly interpreters and teachers of Deaf students. Similarly, to try to avoid omissions, the synthesis was elaborated in collaboration with some of the more knowledgeable advocates of the complaint, in meetings organized in Mexico City by *Enséñame A.C.*, through February and March 2008.

Only 16 of 32 states in the country replied to the complaint. In the replies to the complaint that were sent by the SEP to the CNDH, besides omitting any reference to the public school spaces that operate as bilingual schools, de facto, none of the ensuing categories were invalidated. Furthermore, in spite of its poorness, the quantitative data afforded by the SEP in its defense confirmed the following interpretations.

Spanish-speaking CAM with Segregated Deaf

A signing or semilingual Deaf child may attend a CAM (*Centro de Atención Múltiple*, i.e., Multiple Attention Center), which serves persons with various disabilities and where a Deaf child is unable to socialize with the Spanish-speaking majority. LSM is absent and the children are treated simply as disabled children without regard to their linguistic needs (Fridman-Mintz, 2008).

The Deaf children assigned to this CAM are usually semilingual and remain so for as long as they stay there. In most cases they are offered speech therapies focused on isolated words, which in the end allow them to command 100 to 200 words or conventional phrases, which limits them to the most basic conversations and certainly does not convert them to speaking Deaf people.

Signing Deaf children who have been Deaf since birth or early childhood probably have signing Deaf parents who are usually reluctant to send their children to a CAM without children from other LSM signing families. They know that there their children will have no access to the content of an education program, will not be able to properly socialize with anyone, and will be treated as persons with an intellectual disability, which they do not have. Speaking Deaf children are almost never schooled in a CAM.

Regular Schools of Spanish Speakers with Segregated Deaf

All speaking Deaf children, some signing children, and a few semilingual children may attend a primary education school with the assistance of Units of Service and Support for Regular Education (USAER, Unidades de Servicio y Apoyo a la Educación Regular). Here, "they likewise cannot socialize with the Spanish-speaking majority. LSM is noticeably absent. The very few that can gain access to the regular curriculum always rely on a classmate or a family member that functions as an interpreter, translator, or auxiliary teacher, in an improvised manner and on their own initiative" (Fridman-Mintz, 2008).

The bulk of Deaf children who are schooled in regular Spanish-speaking educational institutions are speaking Deaf children. Usually, there is only one enrolled Deaf child. Occasionally there might be one or two more. Those who exert influence on the schooling of Deaf children generally feel empathy for those who can vocalize Spanish to some degree and consider them to be—or to have the necessary potential to become—speaking Deaf people (designated as *hipoacúsicos*, hard of hearing, in the SEP statistics and pseudo medical jargon of special education). If one adds to this circumstance the pressure exerted by the SEP to offer increasing statistics of inclusive education, one can understand why, without hesitation, the speaking Deaf are assigned to regular schools.

It is generally assumed that speaking Deaf children will develop without major problems in their neighborhood school, even if that school has not been prepared to receive them. Although it is assumed that these Deaf students and their teachers will be assisted by the USAER teams, in reality, the material and interactional accommodations that are set in motion to facilitate their participation in school life are scarce. Therefore, their school socialization turns out to be plagued by inequitable practices. For example, the professor speaks and the hearing students listen and write at the same time (not a possibility for Deaf children), everyone speaks without regard for whether the Deaf child can see their face, and projected written material is never available at public events. Though their academic and social achievements are quantitatively and qualitatively low, the possibility of integrating them in bilingual schools for the Deaf, using Spanish and LSM, is not even considered. In fact, such schools do not officially exist.

As for the assignment of semilingual Deaf children to a Spanish-speaking regular school (a *normo-oyentes,* normal-hearing, environment in the clinical jargon of special education), the official guidelines state that they must be included provided that they behave or "integrate" in an acceptable manner, as shown by their psycho-pedagogic evaluation. However, these evaluations are intrinsically subjective and may be biased. Therefore, on one hand, it is not surprising that many officials are reluctant to apply such vague criteria, since they correctly judge that a minimal command of the majority language at school is indispensable to achieve the aforementioned acceptable behavior and integration. On the other hand, semilingual Deaf children who are nevertheless assigned to regular monolingual schools remain semilingual, without exception, because although they may have been physically present in the classroom ("integrated" or "included" in the jargon of special education), they remain socially and linguistically segregated and are seldom included in any meaningful educational or social interaction.

Finally, the signing Deaf children who are individually enrolled in Spanish-speaking schools receive the same denomination as the semilingual Deaf, as statistically integrated "regular Deaf," unless they are partially bilingual and somewhat able to vocalize Spanish in which case they will be classified as integrated hard of hearing (hence lumping them together with monolingual Spanish-speaking Deaf). Thus, although signing Deaf children may be physically within a regular school, they are all excluded from face-to-face socialization and are linguistically segregated. Any equitable participation in linguistically articulated processes of formal education remains inaccessible to them. The gathered testimonies show that what they can learn depends on the friends and family with whom they maintain some capacity of dialogue, always in the context of marginal or extracurricular school activities.

Spanish-speaking CAM with Marginally Congregated Signing Deaf

Some semilingual and signing Deaf attend CAMs, which are schools for children with a range of disabilities. Here they can socialize informally in LSM with a few other Deaf children but never in the classroom. The teachers neither sign LSM fluently nor are they required to learn it (Fridman-Mintz, 2008).

The semilingual children who go to these CAMs are fortunate to be exposed to the LSM of their signing peers. This allows them to leave semilingualism behind and to assume their identity as signing Deaf individuals. However, the school and its Spanish-speaking teachers neither recognize nor take advantage of the positive nature of this process in social and linguistic maturation. The teachers generally focus on the Spanish vocalizations of their pupils with rather mechanical and repetitive oral rehabilitation exercises. Very few teachers are aware that they could use LSM to explain instruction to these Deaf students. In order to do so they would have to be willing to learn LSM from the Deaf students themselves. What is worse, teachers often forbid any LSM conversation within the classroom because they do not understand such conversations, cannot participate in them, and hence, their authority is threatened. Many also believe that signing is harmful to the development of speech, which is highly valued.

Although signing Deaf children lack an adult model of LSM in these schools, they nevertheless have a proficiency in their language, which is far better than that of their teachers. Yet, paradoxically, teachers in these institutions tend to consider their Deaf students as language disabled, as semilingual Deaf, and often assume for themselves a normative authority over LSM, using the questionable argument of being specialists in Hearing and Language, although this generally implies that they have been educated to believe that the use and command of LSM is undesirable.

Spanish-speaking Regular Schools with Marginally Congregated Signing Deaf

In Mexico City, other semilingual children and a few signing Deaf children attend general (regular) education schools where Spanish is the language of the classroom and environment. This type of integration is known as CAM: Integrated Groups. Here they can socialize in LSM among themselves but never in the classroom because, in general, the teachers don't sign (Fridman-Mintz, 2008).

As in the case of CAM with marginal Deaf students, most of those who attend these Spanish-speaking schools are semilingual Deaf. Until just a few years ago, for a semilingual Deaf student to be accepted in these programs it was required that they be able to vocalize some Spanish reasonably well. What this meant was a subjective interpretation on the part of the official conducting the evaluation. Since such Deaf children are integrated as a group into the Spanish-speaking school, they are able interact amongst themselves. For the same reason, the presence of a single signing Deaf in these groups triggers the immediate spreading of LSM among them all, a circumstance that makes it possible for all of the semilingual children to become signing. However, as is the case of CAMs with groups of Deaf children, the use of LSM between the students is excluded from the formal educational process: The functions of LSM are restricted to social mingling, and, more rarely, to some less prestigious academic activities (such as physical education or manual labor workshops), but Spanish is imposed on most of the formal teaching, even if the students do not understand it.

The signing Deaf children who are accepted in these integrated groups must be evaluated by an official who judges their Spanish vocalizations as "acceptable." By virtue of this attributed capability, signing and semilingual Deaf are classified by their teachers as hard of hearing. As in the case of the CAM, the actual presence of the CSM within the Spanish-speaking school community is not formally recognized, although it exists as a de facto bilingual and bicultural community. This lack of recognition impedes access to quality bilingual education, as needed by Deaf students. Miscommunication persists and, even though all Deaf students become signing on their own, educators generally remain steadily loyal to their proselytism of a pure Hispanic *normo-oyente* (normal and hearing) goal for their pupils.

CAM with Congregated Signing Deaf

There are several CAMs that offer bilingual education—Morelos (2), Quintana Roo (1), Querétaro (1), Sonora (1), and Mexico City (1). Some semilingual and signing Deaf children are fortunate to attend these CAMs in which the teachers attempt to establish bilingual education. Teachers have done this work despite continuous harassment by federal administrators from the National Program for the Strengthening of Special Education and Educational Integration (PNFEEIE; *Programa Nacional para el Fortalecimiento de la Educación Especial y la Integración Educativa*). They have also done so without the human or financial resources that regular programs of education take for granted (Fridman-Mintz, 2008).

In these special education schools in which Deaf children have historically gathered, conditions of true bilingualism have emerged. Such circumstance has made it easier for some hearing teachers to accept and formally recognize that LSM must be used in the classroom as part of the formal process of education. There is significant variation among the views of these teachers, ranging from those who conceive LSM as a mere communication instrument and bilingual education as a pedagogical method to those who acknowledge that LSM is part of the cultural identity in which the students commune and that bilingual education consists of a school manifestation of what ought to be a more equitable relationship between the CSM and the national Spanish-speaking majority.

The semilingual Deaf children who arrive at these schools quickly acquire signing and, together with those who already sign, are gradually introduced to Spanish as a second language, primarily in its written form. In the process, they all undergo a process of maturation and enhancement of self-esteem, which make it possible for them to strive for a quality integration in the Spanish-speaking world, including that of their own parents and siblings.

Having said this, Deaf children need to have teachers who are, like them, bilingual and signing Deaf. They need to witness that, as a representation of society as a whole, their school has a positive perception of its signing Deaf teachers. They need to perceive that their school is as valuable as the regular schools. However, SEP does not formally recognize that these educational centers are regular bilingual schools. Thus, it does not give them the resources or consideration given bilingual schools nor does it take responsibility for setting up programs specifically addressed to the education and certification of signing Deaf teachers. The few signing Deaf teachers working in these CAMs are merely tolerated by the authorities. They are neither recognized nor paid as proper teachers in charge of a group. In other words, SEP authorities keep these Deaf students attending CAMs in a legal and administrative limbo, which, in addition to generating uncertainty for the whole community, takes on the presence of a constantly threatening power that hammers into the pupils an awareness that to the SEP federal educational authorities they are nothing more than a disabled population among many others.

It is important to notice that, likewise in private and public schools that maintain a de facto bilingual approach, the speaking Deaf are systematically excluded under the assumption that they do not require special education. However, no Deaf child deserves to be segregated to the domains of special education by virtue of being Deaf. Once this grave distortion is corrected, many speaking Deaf children who are now inadequately integrated in regular Spanish-speaking schools could very well be included in a bilingual Deaf school. This would not make them less speaking but certainly would make them more bilingual. It would stimulate bilinguality among their signing Deaf peers, and it would allow them to live a more pleasant, less anxious, and less lonely infancy, childhood, and puberty.

PRIVATE SPECIAL EDUCATION FOR CONGREGATED SIGNING DEAF

Thanks to the restlessness and nonconformity of some parents of Deaf children with respect to the public system of education, some semilingual and signing Deaf children have the fortune to be educated in a private bilingual school. These non-profit organizations, some privately financed through donors, were established to provide bilingual deaf education programs (e.g., IPPLIAP and Tessera, both in Mexico City). However, their certificates of study are supplied by the National Institute for the Education of Adults and don't have the formal recognition of the SEP (Fridman-Mintz, 2008).

Some of these institutions, like IPPLIAP, were originally created to assist semilingual and signing Deaf children (they accepted neither hard of hearing nor fluent speakers of Spanish). As was true of some CAMs with a predominantly Deaf population, having accumulated experience and frequent interaction with signing Deaf persons, they abandoned the clinical approach to deafness, and as they realized the cultural diversity of their pupils, they favored a bilingual approach to their education. Others, like Tessera, explicitly emerged to set up spaces for bilingual education, given the reluctance of the federal institutions to create them. As in the CAMs that intend to follow a bilingual approach, their teachers and authorities oscillate between those who think of LSM as a mere instrument of communication and bilingual education as a pedagogical method and those who recognize the collective identity of the signing Deaf and conceive the school experience as existing in the intercultural borderlands between the CSM and the national Spanish-speaking majority.

As in the case of the de facto bilingual CAMs, the semilingual Deaf that attend these private institutions quickly acquire signing and are immediately introduced to Spanish as a second language. A characteristic feature of the private bilingual schools for the Deaf has been that they have made significant efforts to promote the participation of the parents and guardians of the minors in the bilingual integration of their children, from setting up LSM courses to fostering their social interaction with adult members of the signing Deaf community.

Likewise, depending on their financial capability, these private schools have assumed the task of preparing and hiring signing Deaf teachers alongside hearing competent bilingual teachers. However, these schools have not been recognized by the SEP, the abilities and knowledge of their signing Deaf teacher have not necessarily been recognized by the SEP, and these teachers are systematically paid less than their hearing colleagues. These circumstances have created an uncertain and inequitable environment, which undoubtedly will be reflected in the pupils as a fertile ground for hopefully more critical and demanding generations of signing Deaf people.

Monolingual Immersion Is Now Disguised as Bilingual Education

The Mexican Deaf community has fought for and won for themselves and for the semilingual Deaf the legal right to have access to bilingual education in Spanish and LSM. Beyond preexisting health and rehabilitation public policies, the Mexican Deaf community also fought for and won the addition of the cultural and communicative needs of the speaking Deaf to the new legislation, emphasizing the role played by vision and literacy in the form of projected text, closed captioning, or subtitles (Secretaría General, 2011, p. 6).

Nevertheless, for these legally established rights to be complied with in educational institutions, the federal authorities would have to execute a number of actions, in various institutions. The professionalization of teachers specialized in deaf education should be diversified and profoundly reformed. The colleges that prepare teachers nationwide in the Hearing and Language specialties (*Escuelas Normales*) would be the more affected ones. If their curriculum remains solely focused on the needs of the speaking Deaf children who are integrated in monolingual Spanish-speaking schools, then other colleges or university schools should focus on the needs of bilingual education of the signing and semilingual Deaf. Among other things, the new careers for teachers of Deaf students would have to formally recognize the value of LSM and Spanish proficiency in the profiles of their applicants and in the profiles of those who are about to finish their studies. The professionalization of signing Deaf teachers should be promoted. Likewise, all the schools that, to some extent, practice bilingual education should be transformed into regular bilingual schools, fully recognized as such, and new ones should be opened, at least where the signing and semilingual Deaf population need them the most.

Undertaking these measures would require confronting several preexisting interests. The staff and the goals of the Hearing and Language careers would have to be modified, and the structure of the careers on indigenous education would also have to be expanded and adjusted to include the bilingual education of Deaf students. The staff and workloads of the CAMs transformed into regular bilingual schools would also have to correspond to their new formal status. Finally, the newly created schools would require new financial and human resources as well as reassignments of preexisting ones.

Regrettably, the SEP has decided to do nothing of the sort, although in doing so it violates the law by not complying with Articles 10 (in particular the paragraphs referring to LSM) and 12 of the General Law for Disabled with a Disability (Secretaría General, 2011, p. 6). Beyond the suggested financial and labor costs, there seems to be a more profound reason for the rigid rejection of the SEP to comply with the law. According to the institutional interpretations of the policies of Inclusive Education, people with a hearing disability should receive the same schooling options as any other person (with or without a disability), systematically ignoring the fact that signing and semilingual Deaf children have collective identities and linguistic needs that are incompatible with the common monolingual (or bilingual in spoken languages) schools of compulsory education.

In the current argumentation of the SEP, for the purpose of schooling, all Deaf people are alike. Not even the traditional distinction of hard of hearing versus Deaf is pertinent:

The integration of children with a hearing disability implies that within regular schools they have access to the same type of experiences that the rest of the educational community; their participation in all the spaces (family, society, school, and work) is aimed, and with it, the elimination of marginalization and segregation.… To opt *exclusively* for special schools for Deaf children could encourage an effect contrary to the spirit of educational, family, and social integration. (Martinez, 2008)

Certainly, as implied by "exclusively" of the second paragraph of this official statement, it would be discriminatory to force speaking Deaf to attend bilingual schools in LSM and Spanish, whose population is necessarily and predominantly composed of signing Deaf, specifically if this would be done against their own will or that of their parents or legal guardians. However, the use of "exclusively" reflects the restrictive nature of a monolithic educational policy that does not originate in those of us who strive for the foundation and formal recognition of schools for the Deaf. Rather it comes from the norms of the special education federal authorities (PNFEEIE), which treat Deaf people as if they were all speaking Deaf. The authorities systematically omit any reference to the Spanish monolingual identity of the regular schools in which they intend to include all Deaf people, without distinction. The only option left for those that happen not to resist the Spanish whip is seclusion in a CAM (Martinez, 2008).

Furthermore, circumstances have forced the SEP to pretend that their policy of inclusive education also complies with their legal duty of offering bilingual deaf education, in LSM and Spanish. To that effect, in the report presented by the SEP to the CNDH, it is stated that the following measures are being taken (Martinez, 2008):

1. Reduce bilingual education to individualized teaching by offering the formation of Spanish-speaking teachers as specialists in LSM, in the short term, so that these very same teachers (in charge of a group of hearing, Spanish-speaking students) may be encouraged to function as interpreters for the single Deaf student included in their classrooms, in the long term. All of these with the intermittent support of the LSM specialist of the special education system (USAER teams) functioning as interpreters and auxiliary professors of LSM.
2. Offer workshops and courses in LSM to prepare specialized staff, specifically targeted at the hearing teachers in the CAMs, and those regular schools to which individual Deaf pupils are assigned. With the same purpose, introductory courses in LSM have been included in the programs of the Hearing and Language specialists.
3. The CAMs and the colleges with a specialization on Hearing and Language will become normative authorities on LSM, specifically aiming at giving them the power to prepare and certify their specialists as bilingual professors and interpreters without requiring full proficiency in LSM.

It should be pointed out that these actions are accompanied by an official discourse in favor of the inclusion of persons with disabilities, including the persons with hearing disabilities that use "signs" but avoiding systematically any mention of LSM or the CSM and omitting any reference to their role within the linguistic and cultural diversity of the nation.

Overall, the measures taken by the SEP are intended to give the appearance of change but prevent anything from really changing. Signing Deaf adults remain excluded from the "bilingual" teaching profession, because the same Spanish-speaking (hearing) specialists will now be LSM certified. The schooling of signing and semilingual Deaf children in bilingual schools remains forbidden but is marginally tolerated. The socialization of semilingual and signing Deaf children continues to be procrastinated among themselves and with respect to the signing Deaf adults who could function as their accessible linguistic and social role models. The CSM is still not allowed to participate in the education of Deaf children, who will ultimately become its members. Inclusive education that is labeled as bilingual in LSM and Spanish is offered, yet the proscription and persecution of the gathering of semilingual and signing Deaf in school spaces goes on.

References

Comisión Nacional de los Derechos Humanos. (2011–2015). Retrieved from http://www.cndh.org.mx/

Fridman-Mintz, B. (1998, March). Sociedad y naturaleza: encuentros y desencuentros en el cuerpo de cada cual [Society and nature: Meetings and disagreements in the body of each]. *Géneros, 13,* 1–19. Universidad de Colima, Mexico.

Fridman-Mintz, B. (1999, March). La comunidad silente [The silent community]. *Viento del Sur, 14.* Mexico City, Mexico.

Fridman-Mintz, B. (2006). Los ropajes de la sordera: foro resistencia y alternativas [The robes of deafness: Resistance and alternatives forum]. *Festival Internacional Ollín Kan.* Tlalpan, México. Retrieved from http://homepage.mac.com/chido/Cultura_de_Sordos.html

Fridman-Mintz, B. (2008, June). First extended complaint. *CNDH/2/2008/1840/Q,* p.3. Retrieved from http://www.sordos.org.mx/RespuestaCNDH.pdf

Fridman-Mintz, B. F. (2009). De sordos hablantes, semilingües y señantes [About speaking, semilingual and signing Deaf]. *Lynx: Panorámica de estudios lingüísticos,* 8, 93–126

Martínez, J. M. (2008). Desarrollo de la Gestión e Innovación Educativa, Subsecretaria de Educación Básica. Informe sobre las políticas y acciones que la Secretaría de Educación Pública (SEP) desarrolla en torno a atención de los derechos humanos de los ciudadanos sordos. [Report on the policies and actions that the Secretary of Public Education (SEP) developed for attention to the human rights of Deaf citizens]. *Expediente. CNDH/2008/1840/Q, Oficio No. V2/23827*. México, City, Mexico.

Secretaría General. (2011). Ley General de las Personas con Discapacidad. [General law on persons with disabilities]. Retrieved from http://www.diputados.gob.mx/ LeyesBiblio/abro/lgpd/LGPD_abro.pdf

9

Deaf Communities in Portuguese-Speaking African Countries: The Particular Case of Guinea-Bissau

Mariana Martins and Marta Morgado

The largest school for the Deaf in Portugal, Instituto Jacob Rodrigues Pereira (Education and Development Center, Institute for the Deaf [CED JRP]), has always admitted Deaf children and youth from the Portuguese-speaking African countries (Países Africanos de Língua Oficial Portuguesa) or PALOP so they could be educated. In the 1970s, it received mainly students from Angola and Mozambique. From the 1990s onwards, admissions from the other three PALOPs—Cape Verde, Guinea-Bissau, and São Tomé and Príncipe—became more noticeable. As schools were established in their respective countries of origin, there was a noticeably decreasing number of these students. Currently, the children of São Tomé and Príncipe are undoubtedly the largest number in the school. To portray this reality, see the children's book *Mamadu, o herói surdo* [*Mamadu, the Deaf Hero*] (Morgado, 2007) in which is illustrated by many real children's accounts and includes a DVD showing authentic cases of Deaf people who had to leave their families to access schooling and sign language.

The Portuguese Deaf Association has been a pioneer, since the 1980s, in teaching Portuguese Sign Language (LGP) to society, in general, and to teachers of Deaf students, in particular, and in training Deaf teachers and interpreters of LGP. It is in this institutional and professional context that a close collaboration began with Deaf communities of PALOP or Lusophone Africa, enabling descriptions of those communities, always with a deep respect for linguistic and cultural traits endogenous to those communities.

DEAF EDUCATION IN PORTUGUESE-SPEAKING AFRICAN COUNTRIES

Africa is the poorest continent in the world. The needs are immense, especially at economic and educational levels. Developed countries have supported several African countries, in particular in regards to the establishment of the necessary structures that promote the autonomous development of national Deaf communities. Deaf communities of

PALOP have been, unfortunately, back to back, as if they had never known each other or shared a history and a written language.

Mozambique

Of all of PALOP, Mozambique is the country that presents a more structured situation. In this country of southeast Africa it is not known for certain when sign language was born, but it may have developed in some of the schools for the Deaf.

In 1995, the Finnish Deaf Association initiated a project in Mozambique to help structure the local Deaf community, in collaboration with the Ministry of Women and Social Action. One of their goals was to empower and build a network of local support for Deaf people in the 11 provinces, giving special emphasis to the involvement of Deaf women.

In 1999, the National Association of the Deaf of Mozambique (ASUMO) was established to which the Finnish Association continued to provide organizational support until 2006. From 2001 onwards, together with the Ministry of Education, they focused on the development of deaf education by training Deaf people—sign language instructors and classroom assistants—for the existing schools for the Deaf, one in Maputo and another in Beira. They also promoted bilingual education by raising awareness among hearing teachers to use sign language with Deaf students, on the one hand, and by including sign language courses in the training of specialized teachers, on the other hand.

While activating the teaching of Mozambican Sign Language, the Ministry for the Coordination of Social Action supported the development of a first volume of the dictionary in 1995 (Rytkonen, Magumbe, & Muianga, 1995), and ASUMO produced a second volume in 2002 (Fernando & Bertrand, 2002). The immediate goal of this initiative was to improve understanding and communication for Deaf people in society. At the same time, they attempted, with the university, to plan the professional training of sign language interpreters. However, despite all efforts, there is still no uniform sign language throughout the country. In a vast area of over 800,000 km^2, it is estimated that, unfortunately, the percentage of educated Deaf people is less than 1%. Thus, there are very few who are in school communities. Moreover, the association movement can hardly organize in such a vast territory and with very limited infrastructure.

Angola

In Angola, the number of Deaf people is quite high primarily due to lack of medical care, mostly during pregnancy. Deaf people have their own sign language but with an influence of Brazilian Sign Language (Libras) and LGP. This occurred because both

Brazilian and Portuguese people gave training in their own sign languages, which eventually caused a mixture of those two languages with the indigenous signs.

Another constraint is the fact that, in school, Deaf students are still mixed with disabled students, as there are still no schools for the deaf. Deaf students are still not provided a space where they can freely join and develop their own language. Nonetheless, the National Association of the Deaf of Angola (ANSA) was founded in 1999 to serve the community of an estimated half a million Deaf Angolans.

In 2006, the National Institute for Special Education of the Ministry of Education, in partnership with the United Nations Educational, Scientific and Cultural (UNESCO), released a CD with 500 signs in order to facilitate communication of Deaf people in society and help standardize Angolan Sign Language. Later this project was consolidated with the publication of a new dictionary in 2012 (Valdez & Manuel, 2012).

Cape Verde

Cape Verde's 2000 population census identified 400 Deaf school-age children and 1,550 adults. However, the contact between the Deaf has been difficult because there are many islands with no easy connections between them, and the Deaf rely on sign language and face-to-face communication. Moreover, Deaf school-age children are inadequately mainstreamed and have little contact with their Deaf peers.

In Praia, the Association for Development and Integration Support of Disabled Children (AADICD), established in 1996, has been the only institution in the country trying to meet the needs of Deaf school-age children. From 1997 to 2003, every day, in its small office, it supported a group of about 30 Deaf children and adolescents. With the support of a Deaf assistant, who had done his schooling in Portugal, it pursued the development of communication with children in LGP, while it gave them support in school learning. In 2003, four employees of AADICD conducted a six-month internship in CED JRP in Lisbon, Portugal. This experience was repeated in 2015 with four other teachers.

At this time, their sign language is still under development, with influences from LGP, but it is still far from being a national language. There are already schools referred to for deaf education where they are gathering groups of Deaf students (e.g., in Praia, Sal, São Vicente, and Fogo. For Deaf students from first to sixth grade, the school in Praia also has a Deaf sign language teacher who did her training at the Portuguese Association of the Deaf between 2005 and 2009. The secondary school, in turn, has the support of three sign language interpreters, two of whom translate the daily newscast on national television.

To support literacy for Deaf people, the authors edited a version of the bilingual guide *A turma do Dinis: 1º ano* [*The class of Dinis: 1st year*] (Morgado, 2015) in which they adapted the cultural references and the type of exercises according to the reality observed, entitled *A turma do Jonas: 1* [*The class of Jonas: 1*] (Morgado, 2015).

São Tomé and Príncipe

In São Tomé and Príncipe, the first school for the Deaf was established in 2013 by the Education and Development Foundation. This institution also promoted the creation of the first national association of Deaf people. Previously, there was the Association for the Support of Advocacy of the Deaf from Príncipe Island, founded in 1994, which unfortunately did not last.

In a country whose geography presents constraints in terms of dislocation and the two islands barely interacting with each other, the newly created school operates as the only place where Deaf people can develop a language together. Thus, the sign language of the country is still in an embryonic state. Due to limitations that are slow to provide adequate education for Deaf people, many have come to Portugal to be educated in LGP.

THE EDUCATIONAL MODEL ADVOCATED FOR THE DEAF COMMUNITY IN PORTUGAL

In Portugal, the course of the Deaf community resembles much that of other Western countries. A Swedish educator, Per Aron Borg, brought with him the sign alphabet of his country, and founded the first school in 1823.

Over the years, deaf education went through various methods pursued to oralize the Deaf community, and to improve their overall communicative abilities. In 1998 the Portuguese educational system finally started bilingual education for Deaf students after the recognition of LGP in the constitution. In 2008, bilingual education was consolidated with a new legal framework and the approval by the Ministry of Education of LGP curricula as the first language (LGP-L1) (Cavaca, 2008a, 2008b) and Portuguese as the second language (LP-L2) for Deaf students (Baptista, 2011). The new Law 3/2008 (Law No. 21, 2008) established a network of schools for bilingual education for Deaf students suggesting the development of LGP-L1 as early as possible. Throughout their school life, Deaf students have LGP-L1 and LP-L2 courses for an equal number of hours per week. In order to promote a consistent bilingualism, teachers competent in LGP and classes made up only of Deaf students are preferred for all subjects.

In addition to working with LGP in its own curricular space, developing interactive, metalinguistic, literacy and cultural skills, it is assumed that LGP-L1 plays a key role in the development of intersecting skills, establishing itself as a language of access to the entire curriculum. It is also through LGP that Deaf students access LP-L2 and other oral/written languages in a more facilitative way. This multifunctionality of LGP-L1 is illustrated in Figure 1.

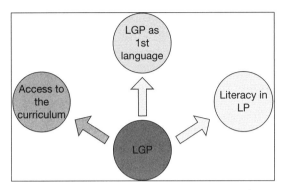

FIGURE 1 LGP functions of the bilingual education of deaf students.

In this context, bilingual education should be seen as not only necessary for Deaf students but also a right, based always on the assumptions that sign languages are a form of human patrimony and that they express the culture of the Deaf community.

In order to acquire and develop a language, it is vital to use it in real situations and contexts. Therefore, more extensive involvement in sign language will allow the Deaf student to become a fluent and confident speaker. The Deaf student should experience sign language as the language "spoken" by the entire school population, where the presence of Deaf professionals in different sectors of educational activity should be preferred, and LGP proficiency should be an essential condition for hearing professionals. Furthermore, the functions of each professional should be well clarified assuming everyone should master LGP as the primary language of the bilingual deaf education system, whereas only the LGP teacher teaches it as a course subject.

The ultimate goal of bilingual education around the world is to make Deaf students fully proficient in both languages: their native language and the official language of their country. It is this skill that will ensure the learning of all curricula subjects, as well as a wide range of knowledge that can be accessed in society throughout their lives.

To the extent that we cannot speak a language without detaching it from its culture, it is common to refer to bilingual–bicultural education as a teaching system shared by two languages and two cultures, while maintaining the predominance of the mother tongue over the second language. Being an essential survival value to the Deaf community, one must not forget that culture is transmitted from generation to generation, from older to younger through sign language. The fact that the Deaf community is not limited to the boundaries of a school, a city, or even a country should be stressed. Deaf people feel they are members of a global community, with its own institutions and a well-defined hierarchical structure, easily finding common forms of communication between each other. Therefore, bilingual and bicultural education must promote contact between schools for the Deaf and Deaf associations, between different schools for the deaf, between schools in different cities, and even between different countries as a way to enhance the sociocultural identity of Deaf students.

The Particular Case of Guinea-Bissau

Guinea-Bissau became independent from Portugal in 1973. It is an extremely poor country where infant mortality is high and life expectancy is only 49 years. The political situation was never stable, having undergone several civil wars.

Besides the diversity of religious beliefs—42% traditional African, 44.7% Muslim, 12.3% Christian, and 1% other (Association of Religious Data Archives, n.d.), the population is divided into several ethnic groups, each with its own language. Balanta (25%), Mandiga (10.8%), Fula (16.3%), Manjaco (11.3%), and Papel (8.8%), among others, are indigenous languages spoken in the country (Guinée-Bissau, 2015). Although the official language is Portuguese, only half of the population is literate and only 13% of the population speak it. However, the national language is Guinean Creole in which 80% of its vocabulary is derived from the Portuguese language. Creole is used by about 60% of the population as a lingua franca. Of these, 40% have it as a second language and 11% as a first language (Ethnologue, 2016).

The Deaf community in Guinea-Bissau reflects the ethnic, linguistic, and religious diversity of the country. However, by 2003, Deaf people were simply ignored, leaving most without access to language, education, or even consciousness of their identity. Since 2003, when Deaf children and youth began to gather in the same school, they quickly developed their own language: Guinean Sign Language (LGG). The fact is that a sign language arises whenever Deaf people get together. The larger their number and the more diverse their age range, the faster the sign communication used by Deaf people naturally develops, becoming more complex until it achieves the grammatical structure of an authentic language.

Usually sign languages emerge in a school context, where there is a higher concentration of Deaf people. But when Deaf people do not have access to a school or to education, they end up creating basic sign codes to communicate with people around them, which, in general, are hearing people. So before there was a school in the capital, Bissau, Deaf people were isolated in their families and villages. Fortunately, because there is such a linguistic diversity in the country, hearing people in Guinea-Bissau automatically use a sign communication among themselves so that communication with Deaf people was never a problem, so much so that some signs are commonly used throughout the society.

Even before the school was established, both in Bissau and elsewhere in the country, small groups of Deaf people naturally got together in their villages to share a common system of specific manual codes, called traditional signs based on mime, which also served as the basic communication between Deaf and hearing people. However, these groups turned out to be insufficient for the complex construction of a language. In Guinea-Bissau, Deaf people were able to get together for the first time in greater numbers in 2003 at the Bengala Branca School. The Guinean Association for the Rehabilitation and Integration of the Blind (AGRICE) ran the school, and at that time, it was the only possible alternative for their schooling.

AGRICE fought for many years for equal rights for disabled people in general. In 2002, it founded a school for the blind, the Bengala Branca School, but the next year Deaf people also began attending, quickly overtaking the number of blind students. In the beginning there were 50 children and Deaf students, which quickly doubled to twice that number. In 2005, AGRICE realized it was not able to teach Deaf students and asked the Portuguese Association of the Deaf (APS) for help. APS did not have financial support available, so they offered the school the book of LGP, *Gestuário* (Ferreira, 1991), and a poster of the Portuguese manual alphabet.

Furthermore, as part of this support, the authors, that same year, gave training to teachers and made an assessment of the communication used by the Deaf students. As a result, they found that the signs used by the Deaf students already allowed documentation of an essentially concrete vocabulary and showed significant influence of the national culture that was shared by that group of Deaf students. In 2006, the Deaf Association of Guinea-Bissau (AS-GB) decided to undertake the teaching of almost 200 Deaf students through the establishment of the National School for the Deaf.

Despite the positive development of the language of the Guinean Deaf community, many Deaf people remained excluded from schooling. There was no room for more students because there was still no dormitory for Deaf students living outside the capital city of Bissau. To overcome this marginalization, the Portuguese Cooperation financed the construction of new facilities for the National School for the Deaf, enabling it to accept 500 students, half of them in residency.

In the context of such a poor country with so few resources, Deaf people do not have access to any hearing or oral rehabilitation. However, in communicating with hearing people, besides the social signs that are generally used by everyone, they also use a few words of oral Creole and/or native languages. When necessary, they resort to writing and sometimes oral Portuguese. The country does not have sign language interpreters but some teachers, friends, and family members of Deaf students perform as interpreters as needed.

The Birth of Guinean Sign Language

In addition to sign languages that emerge naturally within Deaf communities, there are very rich experiences of sign languages that are born outside of school, involving groups of both Deaf and hearing people. Of these bilingual communities, the most famous is undoubtedly Martha's Vineyard, from the eighteenth century onward

(Groce, 1985). In the following century, there are some examples to be mentioned, such as the one of Adamorobe Sign Language in Ghana (Nyst, 2007) and the sign language of the Brazilian Indians, Urubu-Kaapor (Ferreira Brito, 1995). In the twentieth century, this phenomenon was observed in Kata Kolok in Bali (Branson, Miller, Marsaja, & Negara, 1996) and in Al Sayyid Bedouin Sign Language in Israel (Meir, Sandler, Padden, & Aronoff, 2010).

There are several studies showing the natural emergence of sign languages. Overall, we know that they are born from the moment a school for the Deaf is established. The oldest one would be *Langue des Signes Française* (French Sign Language, LSF) since 1760. Most sign languages in Europe and North America have emerged during the nineteenth century. It is worth mentioning, as the earliest examples, Libras and *Lengua de Señas Mexicana* (Mexican Sign Language) in Latin America; South African Sign Language in Africa; and *Zhōngguó Shǒuyǔ* (Chinese Sign Language) in Asia.

Nonetheless, in the second half of the twentieth century, many sign languages were still unborn, as many Deaf people were still uneducated, particularly in Africa. Examples include Uganda's, since 1962, and Kenya's, since 1980, but also in Latin America, as we can see from the important description of *Idioma de Señas de Nicaragua*, since 1977 (Kegl, Senghas, & Coppola, 1999).

In PALOP, the example of LGG is a highlight, as its evolution happened virtually without any external intervention from the moment Deaf students started attending school. In fact, there is almost no influence of LGP in LGG. The only noticeable manipulation is observed with the manual alphabet and with the sign for "sign name." The first was due to the use of a poster of the APS in the beginning of deaf education. As mentioned earlier, when asked for help in 2004, the APS took the LGP manual alphabet poster to the school for the Deaf in the capital, Bissau. There the teachers, who at the time had not yet realized that the Deaf students were developing a communication system, resorted to using the manual alphabet in class, establishing its use among Deaf people. The sign for "sign name" was adopted during 2005's training, where it was very obvious that the students were using sign names among themselves but did not explicitly designated them as such. This sign was adopted because of the need to identify the concept of "sign name" and to employ it with great frequency. However, being a very common sign, it eventually did evolve in its phonological characteristics and did go through slight modifications.

At the same time, in addition to the manual alphabet, that team also brought Bissau's school, a copy of the LGP book *Gestuário*, containing about 800 basic LGP signs. Teachers, eager to communicate with students, used the signs taken from the *Gestuário*, which, being visually static, were executed with little or no movement. However, at the time of 2005's training it was noticed that students used LGP signs with the teachers, but the use seemed to be limited to those teachers. They used other signs, more iconic and mimetic when communicating freely between each other at recess. It was from these conversations and informal play we noticed that they were developing their own sign language based on native signs without any influence of LGP, and, even though it was on a basic level, it was already possible to glimpse a visual codified system.

Educational Guinean Sign Language Dictionary

Sign language is naturally acquired and used by Deaf people everywhere in the world. The motivation to create signs and sign language is strongly dependent on a particular visual culture and on aspects related to day-to-day life of and environments surrounding Deaf people. Thus, the way of living, being, and thinking in a particular community will influence the lexicon of its language. What is common to every Deaf person is the spontaneous use of handshapes with various orientations, different locations in sign space, and a wide variety of movements and facial expressions.

When it was realized that Guinean Deaf people had created indigenous signs, the importance of recording this early stage of communication became essential. In 2005, just two years after Deaf students came together in the same school space, the authors initiated the first cataloguing of signs. In the beginning, about 10 Deaf people were selected, from five to 25 years old, based on their participation in this micro Deaf community. In the short period of time available for this task, we sought to stimulate the group to discuss specific concepts, primarily by presenting images. From here, the group chose the most appropriate codification, not interfering with the decisions on the choice of signs. The manner chosen for the linguistic representation of concepts had to concisely represent the sign by segmenting it for recording photographically. The signs agreed upon by Deaf participants were all photographed, resulting in the first collection of signs. In only two days, it was possible to document more than 200 signs covering various topics, such as food, school, nature, health, society, and clothing.

The following year, in 2006, the work with the Deaf community focused primarily on the lexical recording of Guinean Sign Language now undergoing expressive evolution. The discussion was extended to a much larger group of Deaf people of various ages and topics covered were naturally elicited. The work on the dictionary was divided in two distinct times: mornings consisted of free participation, open to all Deaf people who wished to contribute and afternoons were directed only to more fluent Deaf people. The afternoon sessions aimed to deepen the topics discussed during the mornings, to confirm modifications of signs over time, and to add related vocabulary. Five hundred and twenty signs were identified on these video recordings. All the work that followed in preparing the dictionary—selecting signs, designing the most appropriate format, organizing content, processing images, and editing graphics—took about two years.

In 2008, in order to document signs using photography, two Deaf Guinean children, nine and twelve years old, were chosen as models. The youngest child, who had moved to Lisbon to attend the school for the deaf, hadn't seen his mother for four years. He was offered the chance to spend time with his family in Bissau when the dictionary was launched. The eldest child, who had been attending the school for the deaf in Bissau since its beginning, was given the chance to spend four months in Lisbon, since he was particularly communicative and participative.

The structure of this dictionary was designed mainly based on the student textbooks for natural and social sciences *My Environment*, for first and second grades, and *Our Life,* for third and fourth classes. These textbooks reflect, with all its cultural manifestations, learning content for children in Guinea-Bissau during the early years of schooling.

The dictionary is organized by topics, presenting suggestions of exercises to be worked by students, as shown in Figure 2.

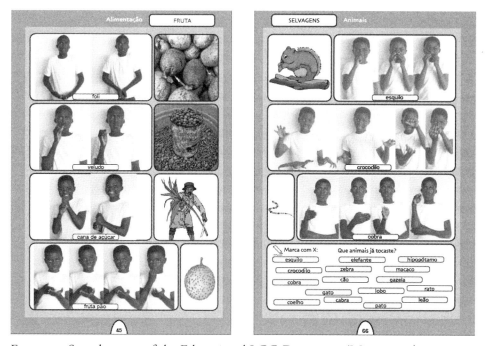

FIGURE 2 Sample pages of the Educational LGG Dictionary (Martini and Morgado, 2008).

One should remember here the importance of always developing an understanding of concepts through sign language, and only after internalizing them can students move on, when appropriate, to writing or other forms of demonstrating knowledge, such as drawing, games, and so forth. In the dictionary, all signs are identified by the word in Portuguese and are, generally, illustrated. The words in Guinean Creole were put on at the end of the book, because on the pilot version, Deaf students were confused when the words in Portuguese and Creole appeared together.

At the end of this work, an illustrated and trilingual LGG dictionary was the result. This was an educational project directed mainly at schoolchildren but available to be used by the entire school community, families, and associated milieus. The dictionary was edited by Surd'Universo and funded by the Portuguese Cooperation. The aim was primarily to support the establishment of a developing language, documenting it in its beginning, a point when there was still enough fluidity in sign productions. Another important purpose was to promote bilingual education through a specific school resource that could serve to guide and encourage teachers to develop their own strategies. Finally, the importance of permanently raising awareness in society and public institutions to the Guinean Deaf community's sign language and the vital need for the Deaf community to have a bilingual education was taken into consideration.

Of course, being that Guinean sign language was such a new language and therefore somewhat unstable and in rapid evolution, it is possible that some signs quickly ceased to be used. The hope is that some signs might be replaced by other more discernible signs or that they will become more economical and less iconic sign forms.

In order to understand the evolution collected signs were going through, the different sign documentation periods were compared (Figure 3). That is, the two dictionaries, the informal one from 2005 and the dictionary published in 2008 (Morgado & Martini, 2008), and the current state of LGG in 2013 were compared. It was found that, between 2005 and 2013, 61% of signs had changed. The most changes, corresponding to 43% of signs, occurred between 2005 and 2008. Between 2008

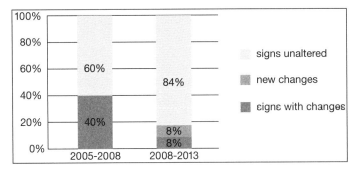

FIGURE 3 Evolution of LGG signs.

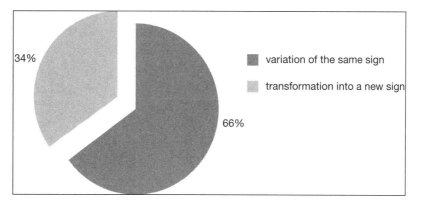

FIGURE 4 Types of changes in LGG signs.

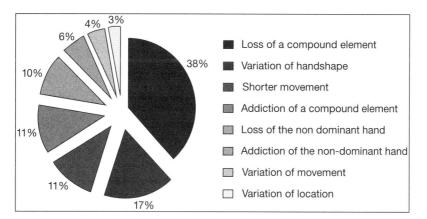

FIGURE 5 Types of variations on the same signs.

and 2013, 9% of signs that had already changed underwent new transformations and another 9% were modified for the first time.

From the 61% of the signs that changed, we tried to understand what kind of modifications were happening (Figure 4). We observed that 66% of those changes consisted of variations of the same sign and 34% were transformations onto entirely new signs.

Taking into consideration signs that presented minor variations in their evolutionary process, it was found that 66% of the changes were due to various elements that interfered with the combination of active phonological parameters (Figure 5). Although we noticed a general trend for sign economy, this was not the overall motivation. Altogether, we concluded that, in sign evolution, Deaf people seek to adjust signs to produce greater semantic clarity and more comfortable articulation.

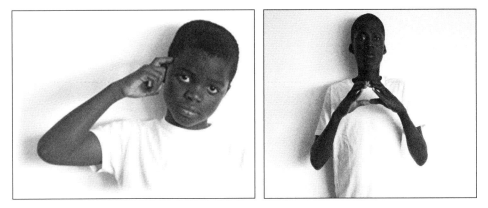

FIGURE 6 Sign for "TO KNOW"—*Loss of a compound element ("GOOD")*

FIGURE 7 Sign for "POTATO"—*Addition of a compound element ("TO PEEL")*

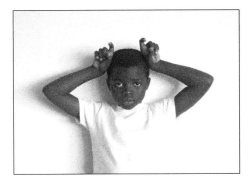

FIGURE 8 Sign for "GAZELLE"—*Variation of handshape*

FIGURE 9 Sign for "MUSLIM"—*Reduction of sign movement*

In variations of the same sign, it was found that the largest percentage (38%) show, in fact, a movement towards economizing by losing a compound element, while 11% consisted of exactly the opposite process by adding a compounding element. See examples of signs in Figures 6 and 7.

In addition to these, there was the change of handshape in 17% and reduction of sign movement in 11%, as illustrated by Figures 8 and 9.

Even though the loss of the non-dominant hand has been observed in 10% of signs, the reverse, that is the addition of the secondary hand, was noted to occur less often (6%). See the Figures 10 and 11.

FIGURE 10 Sign for "TO CRY"—*Loss of the non-dominant hand*

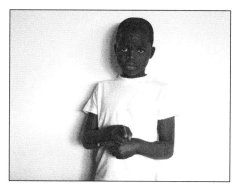

FIGURE 11 Sign for "TO PEE"—*Addition of the non-dominant hand*

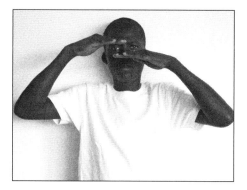

FIGURE 12 Sign for "NIGHT"—*Variation of movement*

FIGURE 13 Sign for "TO GO AWAY"—*Variation of location*

Even though they occurred in a small number of cases, the variation of movement was also verified in 4% of the signs and the variation of location in 3%, as shown in Figures 12 and 13.

Of the 34% of signs that became completely different signs, it was observed that there was a general preference for semantic adequacy. The remaining variables underwent adjustments at the level of handshape, a more economic perspective of the sign (see Figure 14).

In modifications that consisted of changes to new signs it was observed that 83% of Deaf people chose to make a new association to represent certain concepts. See, for example, Figure 15.

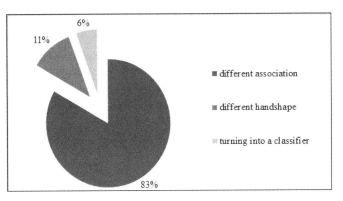

FIGURE 14 Types of motivations in changes to new signs.

FIGURE 15 Sign for "AWAY"—*Different association*

In far smaller percentages, there was the choice for a different handshape (11%) and the transformation into a classifier (6%), as illustrated by Figures 16 and 17.

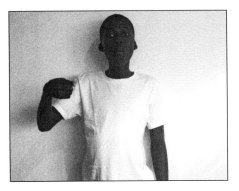

IMAGE 16: Sign for "TOMORROW"—*Different handshape*

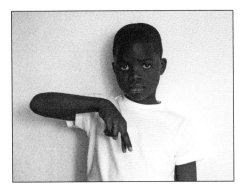

IMAGE 17: Sign for "TO WALK"—*Transformation into a classifier*

In spite of being aware of the complex grammatical structure involving vocabulary, the authors did not explore the grammar during their contact with the Guinean Deaf community. However, it was very clear that grammatical structure was evolving quickly and becoming increasingly stable and complex.

Deaf Education in Guinea-Bissau

The 2005 training provided a general awareness on issues related to Deafness; the Deaf community and its structure, history, identity, and culture; sign language, including grammatical aspects, its acquisition, and development; and bilingual deaf education. At that time, there was only one classroom for over 100 students. Because of the school's poor conditions, students were divided into three age groups and three different shifts. There was no contact between the groups, an important condition for language evolution. It was then important to make the educators aware of the need to enable the Deaf students to converge in the same space at the same time. Moreover the creation of a Deaf association would be fundamental for Deaf adults to gather and for Deaf children to access identity and linguistic reference models.

As a result of that first training, a young adult was selected to participate in a professional sign language teachers' course at APS, between 2005 and 2009, together with another Deaf person who was later chosen from Cape Verde. In addition to these two, a three-month internship was provided to two hearing teachers in the Education and Development Centre (CED) Jacob Rodrigues Pereira of Casa Pia de Lisboa.

In 2006, the influx of Deaf students to school had become so unbearable that the newly created Association of the Deaf of Guinea-Bissau (AS-GB), based in the same location as the school, decided to take over the teaching of the Deaf children. Aware that a space separate from the blind students was needed, where they could develop sign language, the National School for the Deaf was created. The new school, making multiple use of classrooms, managed to bring Deaf classes in shifts together to develop greater contact. At the same time, AS-GB began to promote weekly activities with the school, where children, youth, and adults got together. In 2006, the conditions for the development of LGG, used by nearly 200 Deaf students, were quite favorable. It created a valuable context for carrying out a second sign language recording project. This work exclusively focused on the video recording of LGG. The aim was also to engage teachers and other school staff, elements of AS-GB and family members of Deaf students, so that they could understand the richness of LGG and learn signs.

In 2008, training was mainly focused on teaching practices, closely monitoring teachers in classroom context. It aimed at structural aspects of bilingualism, the development of concepts in Deaf students, the learning of writing and reading by Deaf people, curriculum for sign language as a first language, bilingual teaching strategies, and the adequacy of the LGG dictionary for educational use with students. The goal has always been to guide teachers of the National School for the Deaf into bilingual education of these students, doing so by clarifying ways to teach reading and writing through LGG, improving the methods at various school levels and helping them deal with difficulties students had.

Conclusion

With the work carried out in Guinea-Bissau it was possible to demonstrate, once again, that the larger the Deaf community, the more productive it becomes in the evolution of its sign language. It was also shown that, without the interference from any other sign language, the communication between Deaf people develops in an equally complex manner according to their surrounding cultural context and motivation. As a living and dynamic entity, it is expected that the regular use of the language by speakers progressively consolidate its structure and enhance the fundamental representation of the surrounding world.

This description of the Deaf communities of PALOP, included the brief history of their education and the urgency they have experienced related to developing their sign languages. It is intended to compare them not only to each other but also to the remaining Portuguese-speaking countries. Although their sign languages have evolved to be quite different due to different educational and cultural influences over time, the written language and a common collective history is undoubtedly a strong motivation to seek each other.

References

Association of Religious Data Archives (n.d.) Guinea-Bissau. Retrieved from http://www.thearda.com/internationalData/countries/Country_100_1.asp

Baptista, J. A. (Ed.). (2011). *Programa de Português L2 para Alunos Surdos* [L2 Portuguese program for Deaf Students]. Direcção-Geral de Inovação e Desenvolvimento Curricular. Lisbon, Portugal: Ministério de Educação.

Branson, J., Miller, D., Marsala, I. G., & Negara, I. W. (1996). Everyone here speaks sign language too: A Deaf village in Bali, Indonesia. In C. Lucas (Ed.), *Multicultural aspects of sociolinguistics in Deaf communities* (pp. 39–57). Washington, DC: Gallaudet University Press.

Cavaca, F. (Ed.). (2008a). *Programa curricular de Língua Gestual Portuguesa: Educação pré-escolar e ensino básico* [Program curriculum of Portuguese Sign Language: Preschool education and basic education]. Direcção-Geral de Inovação e Desenvolvimento Curricular. Lisbon, Portugal: Ministério de Educação.

Cavaca, F. (Ed.) (Coord.). (2008b). *Programa curricular de Língua Gestual Portuguesa: ensino secundário* [Program curriculum of Portuguese Sign Language: High education]. Direcção-Geral de Inovação e Desenvolvimento Curricular. Lisbon, Portugal: Ministério de Educação.

Ethnologue (2016). Crioulo: Upper Guinea. Retrieved from http://www.ethnologue .com/language/pov

Fernando, J., & Bernandeo, A. F. (2002). *Dicionário da Língua de Sinais de Moçambique, volume 2* [Dictionary of Sign Language of Mozambique, Volume 2]. Maputo, Mozambique: Associação dos Surdos de Moçambique.

Ferreira, A.V. (1991). *Gestuário de Língua Gestual Portuguesa* [Signs of Portuguese Sign Language]. Lisboa, Portugal: Secretariado Nacional para a Reabilitação e Integração das Pessoas com Deficiência.

Ferreira Brito, L. (1995). *Por uma gramática de Língua de Sinais* [For a grammar of sign language]. Rio de Janeiro, Brazil: Tempo Brasileiro.

Groce, N. E. (1985). *Everyone here spoke sign language*. Cambridge, MA: Harvard University Press.

Guinée-Bissau (2015). L'aménagement linguistique dans le monde: Guinée-Bissau. Retrieved from http://www.axl.cefan.ulaval.ca/afrique/Guinee-Bissau.htm

Kegl, J., Senghas, A., & Coppola, M. (1999). *Creation through contact: Sign language emergence and sign language change in Nicaragua*. In Degraff, M. (Ed.), Language contact and language change: The intersection of language acquisition, creole genesis, and diachronic syntax (pp. 179–237). Cambridge, MA: MIT Press.

Law No. 21/2008. (2008, May 12). Define os apoios especializados na educação pré-escolar e nos ensinos básico e secundário (altera o Decreto-Lei n.º 3/2008, de 7 de Janeiro, do Ministério da Educação) [Defines the specialized support in pre-school education and primary and secondary schools (amending Decree-Law No. 3/2008 of 7 January)]. *Diário da República, 1*(91). Assembleia da República. Lisbon, Portugal.

Martini, M., & Morgado, M. (2008). *Dicionário Escolar de Língua Gestual Guineense* [Dictionary School of Guinea-Bissau Sign Language]. Lisbon, Portugal: Surd'Universo.

Meir, I., Sandler, W., Padden, C., & Aronoff, M. (2010). Emerging sign languages. In M. Marschark & P. Spencer (Eds.), *Oxford handbook of Deaf studies, language, and education*, Vol. 2 (267–280). Oxford, UK: Oxford University Press.

Morgado, M. (2007). *Mamadu, o herói surdo* [Mamadu, the Deaf hero]. Lisbon, Portugal: Surd'Universo.

Morgado, M., & Martini, M. (2015). *A turma do Dinis: 1º ano* [The class of Dinis: 1st year]. Lisbon, Portugal: Surd'Universe.

Morgado, M., & Martini, M. (2015). *A turma do Jonas: 1* [The class of Jonas: 1]. Lisbon, Portugal: Surd'Universe.

Nyst, V. (2007). *A descriptive analysis of Adamorobe Sign Language.* Doctoral dissertation. University of Amsterdam.

Rytokonen, P., Magumbe, C. P., & Muianga, T. P. (1995). *Dicionário da Língua Moçambicana de Sinais, volume 1* [Dictionary of Mozambican Sign Language, Volume 1]. Maputo, Mozambique: Ministério da Coordenação da Acção Social.

Valdez, C. M., & Manuel, M. D. F. (2012). *Dicionário da Língua Gestual Angolana* [Dictionary of Angolan Sign Language]. Porto, Portugal: Lusoimpress.

10

The Uruguayan Deaf Community: Strategic Collective Activism through Education and Media

Elizabeth M. Lockwood

In Latin America and the Caribbean, Deaf persons continue to encounter barriers to most sectors of society. This largely stems from the limited availability of trained and qualified sign language interpreters; ineffective or unenforced deaf-related programs, policies, and laws; lack of accessible telecommunication services; the absence of bilingual education in sign language; inadequate employment opportunities; no recognition of a distinct sign language and Deaf culture; and the widespread lack of awareness about Deaf people. Despite the critical need for global assistance, Latin America and the Caribbean are by and large overlooked regarding disability issues, especially Deaf communities. Moreover, there is a dearth of research, literature, and particularly rigorous studies of Deaf communities in the region. Therefore, this chapter provides a new perspective by exploring the process of community empowerment and development from the use of strategic tools for access by the Deaf community in Uruguay. Specifically analyzed are the strategic methods in which the community utilized access to education and media to increasingly engage in hearing society and consequently achieve community objectives.

BACKGROUND

Less than 1% of the total Uruguayan population comprises deaf and hard of hearing individuals, which makes it the third largest national disability group (Calvo, 2003). A report from *Instituto Nacional de Estadística* (National Institute of Statistics) estimates that 30,193 deaf and hard of hearing persons reside in Uruguay (La lengua, 2001), but some community members believe that the number is closer to 38,000 individuals. The precise number of sign language users is difficult to ascertain, although the main concentration of signers resides in metropolitan areas (Administración Nacional De Educación Pública & Consejo Directivo Central, 2008). The Deaf community estimates that throughout Uruguay, approximately

10,000 individuals use *Lengua de Señas Uruguaya* (Uruguayan Sign Language, LSU), 1,500 persons belong to the Deaf community in the capital city of Montevideo, and out of those, approximately 120 Deaf people are actively involved with the national Deaf association, *Asociación de Sordos del Uruguay* (Uruguayan Association of the Deaf, ASUR). Although they are named the national association, they primarily represent the Deaf community in and around the capital of Montevideo. Two other large Deaf associations are the *Asociación de Sordos de Salto* (ASS) and la Asociación de Sordos de Maldonado (ASOMA).

Despite making up less than 1% of the national population and being one of the smaller disability groups, the Uruguayan Deaf community has advocated effectively for several deaf-focused programs, policies, and laws. Achievements include: official recognition of bilingual education (LSU and Spanish) in the primary school for the Deaf in Montevideo in 1993; the implementation of interpreters at two Montevideo secondary schools in 1996 and 1999; the addition of relay operators by *Administración Nacional de Telecomunicaciones* (National Telecommunications Administration, ANTEL) in 1999; the recognition of LSU as the language of Deaf Uruguayans and of Uruguay[1] in national legislation in 2001 (Ley Nº 17.378, 2001); the enactment of a 75% discount on text messages from ANCEL, ANTEL's cellular phone service, in 2005; the state provision of sign language interpreters at the *Universidad de la República* (National University) and *Universidad del Trabajo del Uruguay* (Technical University of Uruguay, UTU, a trade school which is a secondary school) in Montevideo in 2007 (Cursos en UTU, 2008; Lima & Gallardo, 2007); the provision of interpreters at employment competitions in 2007; the creation of the first accessible national film in 2008; and the State-sponsored program to teach state employees LSU in 2009.[2]

Despite ubiquitous barriers, the Deaf community has mobilized to gain greater access into majority society and as a result has created more programs, policies, and laws for Deaf persons than most other Latin American and the Caribbean nations. Moreover, the Uruguayan Deaf community has achieved more objectives than other

---

1. Uruguayan laws do not designate any official language. However, LSU is the only language in Uruguay that has legal status as established by Civil Code, 2002 and the Disability Law, 2007. In 2008–2009, the General Education Law established three "mother tongues" in education, which are Spanish, Portuguese, and LSU (Peluso, 2009).
2. Recent developments in Uruguay include expansion of web-based videos in LSU for the Deaf community supported by la Univeridad de la República and FENASUR (Federación Nacional de Instituciones de la Comunidad Sorda de Uruguay). The Centros de Lengua Extranjera (CLE) (Centers for Foreign Languages) provide free LSU courses for secondary students and the Univeridad de la República (L. Peluso, personal communication, 2015).

national disability groups. The impressive development of the Deaf community is not simply from effective national disability legislation but rather from the combination of a supportive social structure and continual Deaf community advocacy efforts. Uruguay contains fewer disability laws and decrees than found in culturally, politically, and economically similar nations such as Costa Rica and Argentina, as well as in differently structured nations like the Dominican Republic and Honduras. Yet at the same time, Uruguay boasts more deaf-focused laws and decrees than any of these countries (Allen, 2008; Dudzik, Elwan, & Metts, 2007). Furthermore, deaf-related legislation and policies in Uruguay are not modeled after foreign systems but rather represent the first of its kind in the region (Michailakis, 1997).

Methods

The research in this chapter draws on an identity-based grassroots development and social movement framework to provide insight into the development and sustainability of the Deaf community in Uruguay. In particular, this chapter analyzes the ways in which the Deaf community has used education and media as tools to gain access into hearing society and consequently gain Deaf rights.

The findings are from doctoral fieldwork that took place in Uruguay from 2008 to 2009 from an in-depth case study of the Uruguayan Deaf community carried out by the author who was an Inter-American Foundation Grassroots Development Fellow. Qualitative data was gathered over a 12-month period through in-depth interviews with 14 community leaders and 12 community members, extensive participant observation, and document analysis. The majority of the observations were carried out at the three main Montevideo-based Deaf organizations: ASUR (Uruguayan Association of the Deaf), *Centro de Investigación y Desarrollo para la Persona Sorda* (Center for Research and Development for the Deaf, CINDE), and *Asociación de Padres y Amigos de Sordos del Uruguay* (Uruguayan Association of Parents and Friends of the Deaf, APASU). Observations also took place at *Organización Deportiva de Sordos del Uruguay* (Uruguayan Sports Organization for the Deaf, ODSU) and various deaf-related events throughout Montevideo.

All interviews were videotaped privately in LSU or in spoken Spanish. Fourteen Deaf community leaders, key informants, were interviewed to provide insight about their leadership roles and direct involvement in the process and sustainability of community collective action. In addition, a sub-sample of 12 community members was also interviewed to complement the leaders' perspectives and to provide ground level viewpoints. Both leader and member perspectives are highlighted throughout this chapter to illustrate the complementing standpoints. Each participant was interviewed approximately one to three times until saturation occurred.

All research participant names have been changed for anonymity, and at times, pseudonyms have been removed when the subject matter could indicate the identity of an interviewee. Since the Deaf community in Montevideo is few in number, names of signifying events also have been changed or eliminated to protect research participants. Almost all participants were Deaf persons who utilize LSU, but in a few cases hard of hearing, oral, and hearing people involved in the Deaf community were interviewed in spoken Spanish to provide additional perspectives. Since only a few hard of hearing, oral, and hearing people were interviewed; deaf/hard of hearing/oral/hearing status has been left out for confidentiality. Age was well represented with participants falling between the ages of 18 to 64, but age too has been left out to protect the identity of participants. Gender was evenly distributed between both leader and member groups and thus is indicated by the gender of the pseudonyms.

For this study "access" is defined as the freedom or ability to obtain or make use of something or gain entry into a system (Penchansky & Thomas, 1981). In particular, the Uruguayan Deaf community considers access to communication with Deaf and non-Deaf individuals and access to mainstream information vital in gaining human rights. As such, "information" in this context is defined as knowledge obtained from instruction and study, local and global news sources, facts and data, and social interaction and experiences.

Communication access is a key aspect in the success of grassroots organizations (Alinsky, 1971). The more grassroots organizations encourage open communication, the more the community discusses and resolves disputes and mitigates conflict, resentment, and dropout. Effective communication is also necessary to achieve goals and sustain a movement (Bettencourt, Dillmann, & Wollman, 1996). Throughout history, aspects of Deaf movements have evolved like other social movements, but unlike other identity movements, Deaf movements have particularly focused on the fundamental right to communicate (Jankowski, 1997).

Communication and language tend to play more significant roles in Deaf movements, because communication is often inaccessible to Deaf individuals (Berenz, 2003). Deaf movements, in contrast to other identity-based movements, have the disadvantage of being excluded from communicating demands in the dominant (spoken) language, posing an even larger barrier (Jankowski, 1997). When Deaf communities are denied access to communication, barriers can arise, such as lack of effective leadership (Bateman, 1996), lag in development (Stanley, 2006), and—arguably the most hindering—the inability to equally and fully participate in the public sphere (Jankowski, 1997). In the case of the Uruguayan Deaf community, lack of communication is regarded as the most significant barrier to gaining access to equal participation in society, and consequently, a key area for which the community advocates the most (Leader Interviews, Felipe, 2008).

Access to diverse sources of information can add understanding of the surrounding environment and increase opportunities for individuals and groups, especially in receiving more timely and relevant information about forthcoming opportunities (Dey & Westendorff, 1996; Sandefur & Laumann, 1998). For the Deaf community, having access to information *through sign language* is essential for obtaining literacy skills and thus highly important. In addition, increased information access assists Deaf leaders and communities to become empowered and encourages political activism (Alinsky, 1971; Bateman, 1996; Freire, 1993; Leal, 2009).

When group members increase their sense of belonging to a community and become empowered, they believe they can mobilize (Alinsky, 1971; Freire, 1993). Empowerment is integral for successful community mobilization because it takes place when communities gain mastery over issues of concern to them (Bolland & McCallum, 2002). Empowerment occurs in small groups at the local level when individuals organize for social change in order to accomplish goals they cannot achieve as separate individuals. An empowered community is more politically active and collectively uses skills and efforts to reach goals and can influence decisions and changes in the larger social system (Israel, Checkoway, Schulz, & Zimmerman 1994; Marschall, 2001). Michele Andrisin Wittig (1996) argues that an individual's sense of group consciousness and empowerment, as well as understanding of what is fair, might affect her or his willingness to become involved in collective action. As a result, perceptions of self-esteem and self-efficacy might improve, new social identities form, attitudes toward the political system might change, and skills and resources might be acquired.

Increased international contact with politically empowered Deaf people and changing consciousness in Deaf communities largely affects the empowerment of Deaf people (Breivik, 2005; Goodstein, 2006; Jankowski, 1997; Monaghan, Schmaling, Nakamura, & Turner, 2003). Similarly, when Deaf people come in contact with Deaf cultural rhetoric, it leads them to deconstruct and then reconstruct their lives, creating a more cohesive Deaf identity, moving toward activism (De Clerk, 2007). Additional studies indicate that the first generation of graduates of secondary schools for the Deaf became future leaders with examples from Kenya (Kakiri & Wilson, 2005) and Nicaragua (Polich, 2005). Sign language, too, can be used as a vehicle for empowerment that transpired in the Deaf movement in New Zealand (Smiler & McKee, 2007).

Education and the Deaf Community in Uruguay

> Now things are better for Deaf people because the community is growing and sign language is being used in the liceos (high schools). Communication occurs more at the liceos now than at ASUR (Uruguayan Association of the Deaf). ASUR is beautiful, has a building, visitors, but the liceos are really progressing more and it is an interesting process. (Alejandro, Member)

On July 25, 1910, the Uruguayan government opened the first school for the Deaf in Montevideo run by an educator, Ana Bruzzone de Scarone. Bruzzone de Scarone had spent time learning about deaf education practices from María Ana McCotter de Madrazo, a Uruguayan who worked at an Argentine school for the Deaf in Buenos Aires (Member Interviews, Anabel, 2009). Uruguay's primary school differed from those in Argentina and much of the region by being a public and State-run facility as opposed to a religious institution (Druetta, 2009). The Montevideo school for the Deaf was considered advanced in the region and educated Deaf students from Paraguay since at this time Paraguay had no school for the Deaf (Leader Interviews, Anabel, 2009).

The Uruguayan primary school for the Deaf provided the space for the formation of early community mobilization similar to other Deaf communities (Buchanan, 1999; Monaghan, et al., 2003) and also provided the place where long-lasting friendships were fostered and some sign language was learned (Jankowski, 1997). Yet, distinct from other Deaf communities, Uruguayans have fewer ties with the deaf primary school and instead place ASUR at the center of the community.

Similar to many nations, Deaf Uruguayans were denied access to full communication and information in educational settings from pervasive oral deaf education methods (Peters & Chimedza, 2000). For many years hearing instructors rejected LSU practices and hence forced.

Deaf students were to communicate orally in an attempt to conceal the student's "disability." Instructors went as far as telling students that when they signed they looked like monkeys (Bolla, 1998). Even worse, the word used was in fact not *mono,* the general term for monkey, but rather *macaca,* which conveys racist and pejorative connotations (Leader Interviews, Santiago, 2009). Despite severe criticism of and lack of access to sign language in the classroom, Deaf students found ways to communicate in LSU, such as during recess. These moments allowed sign language literacy to emerge and spread among Deaf students.

Since the deaf education system did not provide an ideal space to gain Spanish literacy, the Deaf community took this task into their own hands by teaching Spanish writing and vocational skills at the Deaf Association in 1932, thus exhibiting an early example of community activism to gain access to hearing society. This is similar to the US Deaf community in the early nineteenth century that unified, not so much through sign language but by learning written English (Krentz, 2007). Emphasis on literacy in the United States also occurred outside the traditional primary school system with the creation of Gallaudet University in Washington, DC, in 1864. This monumental event also parallels key moments of the birth of the earliest mass social movements in Western Europe and the United States in which print (literacy), association, and coalition campaigns built connective structures among larger numbers and laid the foundation for collective action (Tarrow, 1998).

Later, after learning that Deaf Argentines and Europeans worked in post offices and did archival work, Deaf leaders in Uruguay established a literacy program for the Deaf community. Deaf leaders, primarily Cayetano DiLuca, organized the literacy program at the Deaf Association called *Primeras Letras* (First Letters or Basic Writing). These classes were taught only by Deaf teachers with the primary goal of increasing Spanish literacy and vocational skills for Deaf adults, which was necessary in obtaining State employment. This Deaf community program was especially important since public deaf education ended at the primary school at the age of 14 with no educational opportunities for Deaf students beyond this point.

The Deaf Association continued to provide educational courses to the community until 1986 when vocational education was transferred to the primary school for the Deaf and continues to be housed there. Consequently, the quality of instruction decreased with less-focused classes with non-signing instructors and no formal diploma. With the transition, literacy classes were dropped entirely leaving no place for Deaf adolescents and adults to gain these valuable skills. This left a learning gap for many Deaf adults, and as a result, the emphasis on literacy skills shifted from Spanish literacy to LSU literacy. A community member describes how this is viewed today.

> Oral deaf and hard of hearing people have better written and spoken Spanish skills, which are more highly valued in hearing society, but less so in Deaf society. They have more access to words and hearing culture. But, often signing Deaf people don't encounter those words and don't understand them. Yes, we use the Spanish language, but this is not as important as using LSU because our customs are different. (Gabriel, Member)

When vocational education was removed from the Deaf Association, LSU literacy became even more important within the Deaf community. Strategies to gain greater access to majority society then shifted from focusing on written Spanish literacy to training Deaf adults to become LSU professors. In 1986, the informal training of Deaf LSU professors began, and in 2006, a three-year program was officially established at CINDE (Leader Interviews, 2009). The LSU professorship not only provides opportunities for Deaf adults to gain employment, fully accessible at that, but also creates important linkages to Deaf individuals in the countryside, who are often isolated due to lack of information, awareness, and resources.

It was not until March 1996 that secondary education became accessible for Deaf students through LSU, a key moment in the community's development. This achievement was the outcome of a project advocated by leaders from APASU (parents) and CINDE to the *Consejo de Educación Secundaria* (Secondary Education Council), which eventually approved the project (Consejo de Educación Secundaria, 1997). The first cohort consisted of 13 Deaf students who attended Liceo 32, a public middle school located in central Montevideo. Students were placed in deaf-only classrooms and taught by non-signing hearing instructors with the assistance of interpreters (the original CINDE graduates). Although hearing students also attended Liceo 32, interaction between deaf and hearing students only occurred outside of the classroom. Liceo 32 was chosen to house Deaf students because of its central location for all Montevideo residents. When the first class graduated three years later, APASU parents again fought for their deaf sons and daughters to continue their secondary education with interpreters. Resultantly, in March 1999 interpreters were placed at a prestigious high school directly behind the National University, Liceo 35, widely known as IAVA (Leader Interviews, Teresa, 2009).

Since the start of accessible secondary education, literacy and empowerment appear to have increased among Deaf youth, thus prompting activism within the Deaf community. Information is now more readily circulated throughout the deaf educational system, creating a cyclical effect described by a member.

> Language and empowerment have increased from accessible secondary education. For example, I was in the first class that had interpreters at Liceo 32 in 1996. At that time there were 13 of us. We didn't have information and didn't know what some of the words meant. We used new signs and it was very difficult, but we slowly got through the system. Then more and more Deaf students attended the program. As a result, the school for the Deaf became more aware from interpreters at the liceos and consequently more Deaf students attended the liceos. From this, LSU developed more as a language and empowerment grew in the community, and thus the community began to expand. (Pseudonym not used for confidentiality reasons)

> Deaf youth mostly benefit from the newly accessible learning environments, but the entire community is impacted from a new empowered generation of young leaders who provide and share information. Moreover, this process has assisted many Deaf people of various ages in gaining employment. (Leader Interviews, Jorge, 2009)

Although access to secondary education improves the lives of Deaf people, barriers remain. Interpreters are appreciated, but since it has been more than 10 years that Deaf students have attended the liceos, younger Deaf leaders are now pushing to phase out interpreters and implement signing instructors to create a fully accessible environment (ASUR Observations, 2008). This is a difficult task since deaf education does not yet exist as a university discipline in Uruguay, and even when individuals with teaching degrees can sign, they are not provided with any assistance in getting hired at either secondary school setting for Deaf students.

As a result of advocacy efforts by APASU, CINDE, and other Deaf community leaders, the first interpreters were hired in 2007 at the public and free National University and the Technical University of Uruguay. Interpreters are funded by the State-run University Welfare Department ("Cursos en UTU," 2008). Accessible and free university education for Deaf persons sets Uruguay apart from its neighbors and is indeed a strong factor contributing to the recent development and increased cohesion of the Deaf community (Allen, 2008). Consequently, more options are available to Deaf Uruguayans, especially those graduating from secondary school and for older Deaf persons who return to school to take advantage of the new system. Even Deaf students not actively involved in the Deaf community, can take advantage of the policy and use interpreters in their classes and these students in turn become more involved in the Deaf community by participating in marches, CINDE courses, and community meetings.

Media

Access to media significantly assists Deaf individuals increase their independence, create better relationships with majority society, and provide better educational and employment opportunities (Federación Nacional de Sordos de Colombia, 2009). For this study, "media" is defined as agencies of mass communication providing information and news to the public through print in newspapers and magazines, broadcast in radio and television, and Internet on websites, blog, and vlogs. Deaf Uruguayans access information through television programs, notably news programs, online and print articles, and the Internet. These tools greatly assist the community by providing different avenues from where information can be attained and allowing different forms of communication, which resultantly increases group empowerment.

With an increasingly transnational world, media access, including television, radio, newspapers, and the Internet, has become a powerful tool through which local communities gain attention from potential advocates and the State (Almeida & Stearns, 1998). Collective action scholars have noted the increased exposure to media in the local and global context to be both empowering and disempowering for grassroots and social movements (Morris, 2000; Pilisuk, McAllister, & Rothman, 1996; Putnam, 2000; Tarrow, 1998; Woliver, 1996). Collective action researchers debate the effects of media on local communities. Sidney Tarrow (1998) writes that the increase of television access may have hurt volunteer organizations but not social movements. Putnam (2000) similarly suggests that the increase of television has hurt civic organizations in the United States. Morris (2000) and Almeida and Stearns (1998) argue that media coverage of grassroots and social movements are a powerful force eliciting the attention of both potential supporters and the state. Crossley (2008) writes that media can importantly link communities together to fight for collective goals.

Although this type of research is expanding, very little has examined media and its relationship with Deaf community activism.

Often, Deaf people have limited access to media and other information (Haualand & Allen, 2009). Historically, media have portrayed Deaf persons as defective or as objects of pity and Deaf rights and culture are often ignored, adversely impacting public attitudes and awareness about Deaf persons (Alker, 1994; Jankowski, 1997). Yet, this changed during the Deaf President Now protest in 1988 (DPN) when the media portrayed protesters as clean cut, attractive, and well behaved, placing deafness as a secondary characteristic, unlike previous media portrayals of persons with disabilities (Christiansen & Barnartt, 1995). Additionally, the media provided sympathetic exposure, creating outside public support for the cause. All of this assisted the community in becoming stronger and more cogent and leading to the ultimate success of the protest (Jankowski, 1997).

Similar to DPN, the Uruguayan Deaf community has benefitted from the media, albeit in a different manner. Examples of media access in Uruguay include accessible national and local news programs through LSU and closed captioning, accessible national and foreign films, and various online and print articles about and for the Deaf community. The Deaf community primarily uses media access to receive and share information inside and outside the community, leading to a more cohesive and active organization. Media have also assisted in the dissemination and exposure of LSU and Deaf culture to Uruguayan society as a whole. Uruguayan television and newspapers widely publicized the addition of LSU interpreters at the National University and the Technical University of Uruguay and the impact on Deaf students (Cursos en UTU, 2008; Igualdad de oportunidades, 2007; Lima & Gallardo, 2007). The media also documented the first accessible national movie and theatre event for Deaf Uruguayans in 2008.

> Previously Deaf and hearing persons were different and existed as very separate groups with tension between them. There was lack of communication and information about the Deaf community. Hearing people didn't know how to talk to Deaf people and Deaf people didn't have interpreters so hearing and Deaf people clashed. Now information about the Deaf community has been disseminated to society and hearing people are aware that Deaf people can communicate. Hearing people have also realized that Deaf and hearing people are equal. (María Laura, Leader)

Because of the increased media exposure, majority society has gained more awareness and sensitivity toward the Deaf community, and consequently, deaf-related discrimination has lessened, as described previously by the Deaf community leader. In recent years, LSU has gained higher visibility and more recognition, as noted earlier, thanks to the proliferation of courses (many free) available to the general public.

Accessible News

Traditionally in Latin America, the State was obligated to provide access to information to Deaf persons via State news programs, yet with the increase of privatization, no legal obligation remains, only the suggestion of providing access. Consequently, there is no enforcement of accessible news programs, which is becoming an increasingly important issue in the region (Astorga, 2009). Uruguay has strongly avoided the pervasive wave of privatization and much of the country remains State run. Much of this has to do with the democratic rights of Uruguayan citizens to overturn any law that has been implemented by the government to privatize a public institution (Stein, Tommasi, Echebarría, Lora, & Payne, 2006). Invariably, citizens overturn government pushes for privatization, keeping telephone, electric, and gas companies, and certain television stations public. Due to Uruguayan political structure and Deaf community activism, access to news programs is actually increasing. Two interpreted news programs are aired through public channels, but a private Montevideo-area channel also uses closed captioning on its news program (Member Interviews, 2009). At the time of the study, the interpreted programs are aired twice daily, and closed captioning was available for certain programs on one channel. There has been expansion of interpreting since that time, but it is still not universal. However, in recent political campaigns, most events included interpreters (Personal communication, L. Peluso, Oct. 25, 2015).

Uruguayan interpreters were first brought to the nationwide State news program on Canal 5 from 1986 until 1990 (Importancia, 1986; Isabel Pastor, 1989). The interpreters were removed due to a change in political parties and public complaint of having an interpreter on the nightly news as distracting. Interpreters only returned in 2004 when an interpreter was placed on the Montevideo municipal cable evening news program (Canal 24, TV Ciudad) through a project with ASUR. In January 2009, the status of TV Ciudad's interpreter Beatriz Olivera improved when she was hired as a municipal employee and paid directly for her services (Leader Interviews, 2009). This marked a significant achievement for the Deaf community because it illustrated that the State recognized the importance of interpreting services through broadcast television. In 2005, interpreter Isabel Pastor was reinstated on the public national midday news program, Canal 5 SODRE. This action occurred in part from actions by the Frente Amplio party that took office the same year. Since 2005, this left-of-center political party has been instrumental in upholding Law 17.378, which requires information access to the Deaf community (Leader Interviews, 2008). In 2007, Deaf community leaders from CINDE and APASU created a proposal to have closed captioning added to a news program. One local privately funded television station agreed, and thus the Canal 10 news program subsequently added closed captioning. Since 2007, Canal 10 has further added closed captioning to its programs, but much is still lacking.

Closed captioning is considered beneficial, but at the same time, many Deaf people cannot afford televisions with closed captioning devices. Also, for many members of the Deaf community, news through LSU is more accessible, particularly for those who have difficulty reading Spanish. Thus, providing both closed captioned and LSU-accessible news programs is highly valued in the Deaf community. The community finds that more accessible news contributes to an increased interest in and knowledge about the local and global world. Deaf people also increase their Spanish literacy skills from watching interpreted news programs (Leader Interviews, 2008/2009). Quite significant is the empowerment of the community through increased access to information, as this interviewee expresses.

> Now we receive news from interpreters on television and from the Internet. We can read about what is happening in the world so the isolated Deaf world of the past is now open. We weren't only deaf, but blind too and now we are finally seeing. The Deaf used to walk blindly, but now the blinders are off. (Felipe, Leader)

The Deaf community, as this leader states, uses media as a tool to empower its members and advocate for collective goals. This also has occurred with the increase of the Internet that provides more receiving, sharing, and sending of information and news.

In conclusion, the Deaf community in Uruguay strategically has used education and media as effective tools to gain access into majority society, which in turn has empowered the community. The Deaf community has utilized education as a tool to gain both Spanish and LSU literacy skills with and without the assistance of the State to empower the community when public resources have not met the needs of Deaf community members. This progressed into the organization of the Deaf community to implement its own training program for Deaf adults to become LSU professors, which in turn creates employment opportunities for the Deaf community and simultaneously provides valuable skills for future interpreters. Although, it is important to point out that the Deaf community also benefits from public services remaining in State hands, which provides the lion's share of funding for deaf-related services (e.g., interpreter salaries) and a reassurance that services will not be removed. This stability in public services, such as the provision of interpreters, allows for more consistent access to valuable information in which the community is aware and more easily able to engage in majority society. Finally, the use and increased availability of access to media connect Deaf community members with each other and create linkages with majority society. The increased sharing of information among community members, as well as with the Uruguayan society as a whole, has had a positive effect on the empowerment of the community, impacting its development of national Deaf rights.

References

Administración Nacional De Educación Pública & Consejo Directivo Central. (2008). *Documentos de la Comisión de Políticas lingüísticas en la Educación Pública* [Documents of the Commision of Linguistic Policies in Education]. Montevideo, Uruguay.

Alinsky, S. (1971). *Rules for radicals*. New York, NY: Random House.

Alker, D. (1994). Misconceptions of Deaf culture in the media and the arts. In C. J. Erting, R. C. Johnson, D. L. Smith, & B. D. Snider (Eds.), *The Deaf way: Perspectives from the international conference on Deaf culture* (pp. 722–725). Washington, DC: Gallaudet University Press.

Allen, C. (2008, June). *Global education pre-planning project on the human rights of deaf people*. Helsinki, Finland: World Federation of the Deaf and Swedish National Association of the Deaf.

Almeida, P., & Stearns, L. B. (1998, February). Political opportunities and local grassroots environmental movements: The case of Minamata. *Social Problems, 45*(1), 37–60.

Astorga, L. F. (2009). Desarrollo inclusivo [Inclusive development]. Paper presented at the VI Encuentro Latinoamericano de Sordos. Bogota, Colombia.

ASUR Observations. (2008/2009, August–July). Observations of the Deaf Community. Montevideo, Uruguay.

Bateman, G. C. (1996). Attitudes of the deaf community toward political activism. In I. Parasnis (Ed.), *Cultural and language diversity and the deaf experience* (pp. 146–159). Cambridge, UK: Cambridge University Press.

Berenz, N. (2003). Surdos venceremos: The rise of the Brazilian deaf community. In L. Monaghan, C. Schmaling, K. Nakamura, & G. Turner (Eds.), *Many ways to be deaf: International variation in deaf communities* (pp. 173–193). Washington, DC: Gallaudet University Press.

Bettencourt, B. A., Dillmann, G., & Wollman, N. (1996). The intragroup dynamics of maintaining a successful grassroots organization: A case study. *Journal of Social Issues, 52*(1), 169–186.

Bolla, V. (1998, September 27). Un mundo de silencio con su propio idioma [A world of silence with its own language]. *El Observador,* pp. 3–5.

Bolland, J. M., & McCallum, D. M. (2002). Neighboring and community mobilization in high-poverty inner-city neighborhoods. *Urban Affairs Review,* 38(1), 42–69.

Breivik, J. (2005). *Deaf identities in the making: Local lives, transnational connections.* Washington, DC: Gallaudet University Press.

Buchanan, R. M. (1999). *Illusions of equality: Deaf Americans in school and factory 1850–1950.* Washington, DC: Gallaudet University Press.

Calvo, C. (2003). *Demanda y uso de banco de datos sobre discapacidad.* 2DA reunión sobre estadísticas de discapacidad en el Cono Sur [Demand and use of the database on disability. 2nd meeting on statistics on disability in the Southern Cone]. Washington, DC: Inter-American Development Bank.

Christiansen, J. B., & Barnartt, S. N. (1995). *Deaf President Now!: The 1988 revolution at Gallaudet University.* Washington, DC: Gallaudet University Press.

Crossley, N. (2008, April). Small-world networks, complex systems and sociology. *Sociology, 42*(2), 261–277.

Cursos en UTU para sordos [Courses for the deaf in UTU]. (2008, March 4). *Sociedad Uruguay.* Retrieved from http://www.sociedaduruguaya.org/2008/03/cursos-en-utu-para-sordos.html

De Clerk, G. A. M. (2007). Meeting global deaf peers, visiting ideal deaf places: Deaf ways of education leading to empowerment, an exploratory case study. *American Annals of the Deaf, 152*(1), 5–19.

Dey, K., & Westendorff, D. (1996). Getting down to ground level: A community perspective on social development. *Development in Practice, 6*(3), 265–269.

Druetta, J. (2009). *El intérprete sordo* [Deaf interpreters]. Paper presented at the VI Encuentro Latinoamericano de Sordos. Bogota, Colombia.

Dudzik, P., Elwan, A., & Metts, R. (2007). *Disability policies, statistics, and strategies in Latin America and the Caribbean: A review.* Washington, DC: Inter-American Development Bank.

Federación Nacional de Sordos de Colombia. (2009). *La tecnología: un camino a la independencia* [Technology: A path to independence]. Bogotá, Colombia: FENASCOL: Federación Nacional de Sordos de Colombia.

Freire, P. (1993). *Pedagogy of the oppressed* (20th Anniversary Edition). New York, NY: Continuum.

Goodstein, H. (Ed.). (2006). *The Deaf way II reader: Perspectives from the Second International Conference on Deaf Culture.* Washington, DC: Gallaudet University Press.

Haualand, H., & Allen, C. (2009, January). *Deaf people and human rights.* Helsinki, Finland: World Federation of the Deaf and Swedish National Association of the Deaf.

Igualdad de oportunidades para sordos Uruguayos [Equal opportunities for the Deaf]. (2007, April 10). *Sociedad Uruguay.* Retrieved from http://www.sociedaduruguaya.org/2007/04/igualdad-de-oportunidades-para-sordos-uruguayos.html

Importancia de la traducción gestual en la televisión [The importance of gestural (sign language) translation on television]. (1986, September 12). *El Diario.*

Isabel Pastor, la mujer que informaba diariamente a 15 mil sordos Uruguayos [Isabel Pastor, the woman who informs 15 thousand Deaf Uruguayans daily]. (1989, August 26). *Cambio, 5.*

Israel, B. A., Checkoway, B., Schulz, A., & Zimmerman, M. (1994). Health education and community empowerment: Conceptualizing and measuring perceptions and individual, organizational, and community control. *Health Education Quarterly, 21*(2), 149–170.

Jankowski, K. A. (1997). *Deaf empowerment: Emergence, struggle, and rhetoric.* Washington, DC: Gallaudet University Press.

Kakiri, N. O., & Wilson, A. T. (2005). *Final report for the Kenyan Ministry of Education: A survey of the development assistance desired by deaf Kenyans.* Unpublished report. Washington, DC: Gallaudet University.

Krentz, C. (2007). *Writing deafness: The hearing line in nineteenth century American literature.* Chapel Hill, NC: The University of North Carolina Press.

La lengua de señas Uruguaya es casi oficial [Uruguayan sign language is almost oficial]. (2001, Sunday, May 20). *El Observador, 4.*

Leader Interviews. (2008/2009, August–July). Interviews with Deaf community leaders. ASUR, CINDE & APASU. Montevideo, Uruguay.

Leal, J. A. (2009). *El proceso de fortalecimiento de la comunidad sorda en el marco de la Convención de la ONU y el desarrollo inclusivo* [The process of strengthening the deaf community in the context of the UN Convention and inclusive development]. Paper presented at the VI Encuentro Latinoamericano de Sordos. Bogotá, Colombia.

Ley Nº 17.378. (2001). *Reconócese a todos los efectos a la Lengua de Señas Uruguaya como la lengua natural de las personas sordas y de sus comunidades en todo el territorio de la República* [Recognizing hereby for all purposes Uruguayan Sign Language as the natural language of Deaf people and their communities in the entire territory of the Republic]. Retrieved from http://www.parlamento.gub.uy/leyes/AccesoTextoLey .asp?Ley=17378&Anchor=

Lima, M. E., & Gallardo, M. (2007). *Los sordos podrán ir a la universidad en este 2007 Educación: La Udelar financiará intérpretes por 10 años* [The deaf can go to the university in 2007: Udelar finances interpreters for 10 years]. Retrieved from http:// www.sordos.com.uy/novedades/universidad.htm

Marschall, M. J. (2001). Does the shoe fit? Testing models of participation for African-American and Latino involvement in local politics. *Urban Affairs Review, 37*(2), 227–248.

Member Interviews. (2008/2009, August–July). Interviews with Deaf community members, ASUR, CINDE, and APASU. Montevideo, Uruguay.

Michailakis, D. (1997). Government action on disability policy: A global policy. Retrieved from http://www.independentliving.org/standardrules/UN_Answers/ UN.pdf

Monaghan, L., Schmaling, C., Nakamura, K., & Turner, G. H. (Ed.). (2003). *Many ways to be deaf: International variation in deaf communities.* Washington, DC: Gallaudet University Press.

Morris, A. (2000). Reflections on social movement theory: Criticisms and proposals. *Contemporary Sociology, 29*(2), 445–454.

Peluso, L. (2009). *Ley de reconocimiento de la LSU: ¿Política lingüística u ortopedia?* [Linguistic policies or orthopedics?] Paper presented at the IV Encuentro Internacional de Investigadores de Políticas Lingüísticas, Santa María, Brazil, Universidad Federal de Santa Maria. Retrieved from www.cultura-sorda.eu

Penchansky, R., & Thomas, J. W. (1981, February). The concept of access: Definition and relationship to consumer satisfaction. *Medical Care, 19*(2), 127–140.

Peters, S., & Chimedza, R. (2000, August). Conscientization and the cultural politics of education: A radical minority perspective. *Comparative Education Review, 44*(3), 245–271.

Pilisuk, M., McAllister, J., & Rothman, J. (1996). Coming together for action: The challenge of contemporary grassroots community organizing. *Journal of Social Issues, 52*(1), 15–37.

Polich, L. (2005). *The emergence of the deaf community in Nicaragua.* Washington, DC: Gallaudet University Press.

Putnam, R. D. (2000). *Bowling alone: The collapse and revival of American community.* New York, NY: Simon & Schuster.

Sandefur, R. L., & Laumann, E. O. (1998). A paradigm for social capital. *Rationality and Society, 10*(4), 481–501.

Smiler, K., & McKee, R. L. (2007). Perceptions of *Māori* deaf identity in New Zealand. *Journal of Deaf Studies and Deaf Education, 12*(1), 93–111.

Stanley, K. (2006). Partnership in the Irish deaf community. In H. Goodstein (Ed.), *The Deaf way II reader: Perspectives from the Second International Conference on Deaf culture* (pp. 38–41). Washington, DC: Gallaudet University Press.

Stein, E., Tommasi, M., Echebarría, K., Lora, E., & Payne, M. (Eds.). *The Politics of policies: Economic and social progress in Latin America 2006 report.* Cambridge, MA: David Rockefeller Center for Latin American Studies, Harvard University & Washington, DC: Inter-American Development Bank.

Tarrow, S. (1998). *Power in movement: Social movements and contentious politics.* Cambridge, UK: Cambridge University Press.

Wittig, M. A. (1996). An introduction to social psychological perspectives on grassroots organizing. *Journal of Social Issues, 52*(1), 3–14.

Woliver, L. R. (1996). Mobilizing and sustaining grassroots dissent. *Journal of Social Issues, 52*(1), 139–151.

11

Bilingual Education or Multiple Linguistic and Technological Channels Shaping a Plurilingual Education: The Uruguayan Experience

Juan Andrés Larrinaga and Leonardo Peluso

In this chapter we articulate five major theoretical developments concerning language within the field of Deaf studies:

1. a French structuralist linguistic tradition, heir to Saussure's proposal in the early twentieth century (de Saussure, 1916/1993);
2. a socio-cultural psychology tradition that also began in the early twentieth century and is heir to the work of Vygotski (1931/1995; 1934/2001) and later reformulations such as those made by Werstch (1988; 1993);
3. a tradition of studies on language and communication technologies, which in our view has two major lines: the one heir to the works of McLuhan (1964/1996) and Ong (1982), and followers such as Olson (1998) and Sampson (1996), mainly directed towards the study of relations between orality and literacy; and the one heir to the work of Auroux (1992), directed to the processes of grammatization of languages;
4. a tradition of studies in sociolinguistics that introduces the concepts of speech community (Gumperz, 1968) and standard language, with authors such as Garvin and Mathiot (1974) and Gallardo (1978); and
5. a tradition that is linked with language learning, plurilingualism, and bilingual and bicultural education (Council of Europe/Language Policy Division, 2001).

Preliminary Considerations

As we, the authors of this chapter, belong to a Latin American community that expresses traditions in a particular way, we provide clarification on the use of certain terms that will be used throughout this chapter.

171

We will clarify the following terms: oral/orality; speech community and the *speaking* of a sign language; plurilingualism as opposed to multi(bi)lingualism; standard language and intellectualization; and language technologies.

Other terms from various conceptual fields—such as deferred textuality, recorded texts, or grammatization—are defined in the respective sections in which they are introduced.

Oral Language and Orality

Following the Saussurian conception (Saussure, 1916/1993) of language and linguistic sign, by sign language we mean the language whose signifiers (the shape of the sign as opposed to the concept or signified) are represented visuo-spatially as opposed to oral language whose signifiers are structured acoustically.

In turn, it is important to distinguish this sense of *oral* (related to the organization of an acoustic representation) from another meaning of *oral,* also used in this work, which contrasts *oral* (e.g., spoken) with *writing* or *literacy* (Catach, 1996; Goody & Watt, 1996; Olson, 1998; Ong, 1982). Here the distinction is not specified by the characteristics of the material perception of each language (visually or auditorally) but by the possibility that the language can be channeled through writing, which gives the language a representation of certain structural and functional characteristics.

Speech Community

The notion of speech community has had different conceptualizations within linguistics. To Gumperz (1968, 462) a speech community is characterized by frequent and regular interaction of its members through a shared code, which produces strong identification processes and groupality. In this chapter we think of the Deaf community as a speech community with a repertoire composed basically by two languages with a certain functional and social distribution: sign language in which they feel like native speakers; and oral language, which functions as a second language and is the majority language, in which each member of the Deaf community has varying degrees of competence and identification.

Are Sign Languages Spoken?

This chapter uses the term to *speak* a sign language instead of using the term to *sign,* which is common in publications in English. There are academic and political arguments for doing so, although the use of *speak* applied to sign languages is normal in our Latin American culture.

In academic terms, we can say that *speak* refers to the functioning of the language—from the Saussurian (1916/1993) meaning of the word *parole* as realization or functioning of the system: the *langue*—even taking into account that a sign language is not spoken in an auditory sense. Also, as Deaf people make up a speech community wherein the main language of their linguistic repertoire is a sign language, it seems appropriate, within this other theoretical framework, to consider that they speak that language.

Politically, holding that Deaf people speak a sign language helps show clearly that sign languages are natural languages as much as oral languages are and that Deaf people are not mute; they speak a language.

Plurilingualism and Second Language Teaching

In the *Common European Framework of Reference for Languages* (Council of Europe/Language Policy Division, 2001) the concept of *multilingualism* is discussed, and its replacement by *plurilingualism* is proposed as a framework of education (and implicitly of use) of languages in the European Union. According to that document, *multilingualism* "is the knowledge of a number of languages or the co-existence of different languages in a given society" (Council of Europe Language Policy Division 2001, p. 4).

This perspective conceives that the knowledge and use of each language is not to be mixed with another and that, in all cases, the native speaker is the model. Teaching a second language or a foreign language, in this view, aims at teaching all the competencies a native speaker has in his language.

In opposition to this concept of *multilingualism*, and its implied kind of bilingualism, *plurilingualism* promotes the use of many linguistic varieties, with varying balance according to needs, places, and knowledge of the individuals of these varieties and of the strategies and technologies (reading and writing) in which they are handled. In turn, it strongly defends the individual's own variety (Council of Europe/Language Policy Division, 2001, p.4).

Taking this idea a little further, this should be not only a political defense but also a cognitive one. Accordingly, in oral or written production, the ideal that seeks native-like accuracy in the variety of languages an individual may use should be eased (Larrinaga, in press).

Standard Language and Intellectualization

The tradition of studies about standard language and linguistic standardization processes dates back to the Prague School (Havranek, 1964, as cited in Garvin & Mathiot, 1974). In the late seventies Garvin and Mathiot (1974) defined standard language as "the codified form of a language that is accepted and serves as a model for a relatively large community" (p. 303). Within this framework, this chapter proposes that a standard language is the one that has gone through the standardization processes, that is, processes by which it was technologized, basically through writing and descriptive grammars and lexicons, generating around these the idea of the correct ways of speaking.

One of the properties Garvin and Mathiot (1974) and Gallardo (1978) assign to the standard variety of a language is intellectualization: the process through which the language acquires lexical systems characterized by "clarity, accuracy and avoidance of ambiguity" (Gallardo, 1978: 89) and expands its grammatical structures.

Technologies and Mediation

Technology is understood as the set of knowledge, devices, and practices a human community develops to transform some aspect of the world. A key element of technology is its property of mediation (Silvestri & Blanck, 1993; Vygotsky, 1931/1995 and 1934/2001; Wertsch, 1993). Technology can be considered a mediational tool that expands possibilities for managing our world.

Language technologies are those that take languages and their units as objects to transform. They are writing systems, audio video recordings, descriptive grammars and lexicons, and computer technologies.

Language technologies introduce new forms of mediation, basically, in the relationships that human beings establish with respect to their languages and the way in which they can reflect on them and manipulate them. Thus, language technologies will change the languages on which they operate and the linguistic activity undertaken with such modified languages, which in turn will change their speakers.

RESEARCH CONTEXT

This work is based on research conducted in the framework of the project Deferred Textuality in Uruguayan Sign Language (TRELSU), at the University of the Republic in Uruguay, within the group for research on Uruguayan Sign Language (LSU)–Spanish interpreters (TUILSU).

The research line of TRELSU has three objectives. First, to develop a linguistics of LSU that does not rely on written Spanish for a description and analysis of LSU and, therefore, can contain monolingual devices of grammatization (e.g., grammars and dictionaries of LSU in LSU). Then, it aims to implement the use of videotapes as LSU written textuality, both for the production of texts in LSU and for the translation of texts written in Spanish into LSU. Finally, and from the developments of the objectives just mentioned, it intends to generate new methods of language teaching, given the language model being developed in the TRELSU program and the new language technologies proposed for the management of deferred textuality in LSU. It must be pointed out that this research is carried out at the University, together with the Deaf community, and with hearing teachers, Deaf teachers, and Deaf students who attend a bilingual public school for the Deaf (in the city of Salto).

Bilingual Education in Uruguay in the Public Education System

Overview

The bilingual and bicultural model has had a strong development in Uruguay since 1987, marking a shift in relation to the tradition of oralism (ANEP/CEP/Inspección Nacional de Educación Especial, 1987; Behares, 1989; Behares, Brovetto, & Peluso, 2012; Larrinaga & Peluso, 2007; Peluso, 2010; Skliar, 1999).

The situation of bilingualism has followed different paths in the different educational levels: Preschool and Primary (0–11 years), Secondary (Basic: 12 to 14 years and Higher: 15 to 17), and Tertiary (18 and over). Several educational institutions with bilingual Deaf programs have a long tradition in Uruguay. In Montevideo, the capital of Uruguay, we can find: LSU–Spanish School No. 197 Ana Bruzzone de Scarone (Preschool and Primary), Center for Deaf Adults (trade school), Secondary Basic No. 32 Guayabo, Secondary Higher IAVA, UTU (Technical School with trade [vocational] courses but also secondary education combined with technical education) and the University of the Republic. In the other 18 departments of Uruguay, there are three bilingual Deaf schools and Deaf classes in ordinary schools that follow a common program that includes LSU in the curriculum. Bilingual Deaf schools (called *Schools for the Deaf and the Speech and Language Impaired*) are: LSU–Spanish Bilingual School No. 116 (city of Salto), LSU–Spanish Bilingual School No. 84 (city of Maldonado), and LSU–Spanish Bilingual School No. 105 (city of Rivera). Additionally, in the cities of Salto, Rivera, Maldonado, and Tacuarembó there are Deaf students integrated in regular education high school classes with LSU–Spanish interpreters.

Preschool and Primary Level Bilingual Deaf Education

At the preschool and primary grades level, bilingual and bicultural education incorporates two languages and two cultures in the classroom in their educational approach. LSU serves as the first and native language and Spanish as the second language.

The School for the Deaf in Montevideo dates from the early twentieth century. Initially it was a boarding school, with boys and girls separated, and until 1987 it was an oral school. However, part of its hidden curriculum was the transmission of LSU and Deaf culture. LSU, despite being prohibited in the school until 1987, was, paradoxically, the "central character" during those years, in all those spaces that escaped the eyes of censorship, and made the school one of the principal socializing spaces in LSU for Deaf people. Therefore, this school has always been, despite some of the authorities who have run it, one of the main contexts in which Deaf people established themselves as a speech or linguistic community (Peluso, 2010).

In 1987, the school began the process of a formal transition to bilingualism that is still in progress. The schools in Maldonado, Salto, and Rivera also offer a bilingual curriculum and have similar problems concerning the implementation of bilingualism as the school in Montevideo. These other schools are also important socialization contexts for Deaf children and adolescents who otherwise would not have early access to the LSU and Deaf culture.

In smaller cities throughout the country, classes for Deaf children within regular public schools do not follow the integration model. In these schools, Deaf students are in separate classrooms, only sharing some activities with hearing students in the school such as recess, physical education and/or educational field trips. There may be some instances of integration in academic classes depending on the individual characteristics of the students, and the teachers, principally involving collaboration between teachers.

The difference between the bilingual schools and the classes for Deaf students in regular public schools is the presence or absence of a local Deaf community. Bilingual schools have a strong relationship with the local Deaf community, which does not occur in most regular public schools. As discussed later in this chapter, this is a significant difference because bilingual schools specialize in deaf education. In bilingual schools, there is greater development of language, identity, and sense of belonging when the presence of the Deaf community is strong, which provides a situational context to the school and makes its existence viable.

In all cases, the common principles for bilingual deaf education at the elementary level are as follows:

- LSU is considered the natural language of Deaf people and therefore the curriculum is approached in this language.
- Written Spanish is considered a second language and the one through which Deaf students will have access to the globalized majority culture.
- The Deaf community is understood as a key element in the development of bilingual/bicultural Deaf schools.
- The use of information and communication technologies is considered a key element in the deaf education.

Secondary Schools

Secondary school consists of three years of Basic and three years of Higher (e.g., secondary) school. Basic Secondary No. 32, a small school centrally located in Montevideo, was the first public secondary in Uruguay to incorporate LSU in its education program in 1996 owing to pressure from parents and members of the Deaf associations. Deaf students work with hearing teachers who speak Spanish and have a full-time LSU–Spanish interpreter. Some hearing teachers over time have begun directly teaching classes using LSU (e.g., Spanish as a second language, physics, and literature). A Deaf biology teacher teaches her class in LSU, her native language.

From the beginning, a Deaf teacher was in charge of teaching LSU and providing pedagogical advice on teaching Deaf students. In 2000, a course on LSU as mother tongue and taught by Deaf teachers was approved. This course is similar to courses in Spanish grammar for hearing students. It allows students to engage in deeper study of LSU in a formal context. The course has two objectives. The first objective is to equalize the knowledge of LSU by Deaf students, who are very heterogeneous and differ in competence in LSU. Some secondary school Deaf students are highly competent because LSU is used at home or because they have had a prior bilingual education. Other Deaf students come from oral backgrounds and were not educated in state institutions specializing in bilingual deaf education. Their first contact with LSU is when they enter secondary school. The second objective is based on the view that the formal teaching of LSU will generate a space for discussion, study, and research of aspects of LSU as a mother tongue, including vocabulary, morphology, and syntax, discussions of which have often been reduced to non-formal settings.

The curriculum of this secondary school established for the first time that Deaf students would have Spanish formally taught as a second language, only in its written form, as well as English as a foreign language (also only in its written form). Additionally, in 2004, extracurricular classes in LSU for hearing students in this secondary school were approved.

For the Secondary Higher level (the fourth to sixth years of secondary school), the Secondary Higher n° 35 (IAVA) began three years after that of Secondary Basic n°32. The type of work in the fourth year is similar to that which was implemented in Secondary Basic n° 32, but in the fifth and sixth year, there are no longer any classes exclusively for Deaf students, and Deaf students have to be integrated in classes of hearing students, with an interpreter.

These schools are currently one of the main socializing areas for young Deaf community members. For young Deaf people, the place to be with others is in the secondary school and adjacent contexts (the corners near schools, cybercafé in the area, etc.) and not the historical Deaf associations. Also, there are new social practices where young people gather: getting together at someone's house to study, going out with classmates to other social venues (e.g., dancing), public dining halls (used by low-income students), gyms and exercise clubs, and so forth. Moreover, the corners near schools have become not only an important point of contact among Deaf students, but, indirectly, an area of visibility of LSU for the neighborhood, passersby, and onlookers.

In departments (states) of Uruguay other than Montevideo, there are also Deaf students attending secondary schools with interpreters in classes with hearing students. These departments are: Maldonado, Paysandú, Rivera, Salto, and Tacuarembó. It is worth noting the importance of bilingual education in primary school and the provision of various bilingual spaces in secondary schools and universities. These bilingual programs communicate to the Deaf community and Deaf students that the bilingual system not only enables, promotes, and encourages the continuation of Deaf students in the education system but also creates an expectation for this to happen.

In 2006, another bilingual option with LSU interpreters for Deaf students in classes with hearing students began in the Council of Technical Education (CETP), historically called Labour University of Uruguay (UTU). The UTU has always been a place that accepted Deaf students, before bilingual education was even considered, because it is an institution for training in trades. Students could attend despite limited schooling and literacy skills, and it didn't *require* interpreters. Deaf students were concentrated in trade courses and couldn't take advantage of the academic courses the UTU offered, such as technical-professional courses. With the shift in perspective that involves interpreters in the system and a focus on bilingualism, five years ago Deaf students began to participate in academic courses at UTU and its various schools in Montevideo: IEC (School of Construction), Brazo Oriental (School of Commerce), Malvín Norte, Julio Cesar, Palermo, ITI, National School of Graphic Arts, and Arroyo Seco.

The interpreter service is provided by the Office of Educational Management of the institution (Alvarez, 2012). The situation in the capital has not been completely replicated in the other Departments of Uruguay, although there is a significant demand. The major problem is the shortage of interpreters in other parts of the country. In 2010, the program started in San Jose, Tacarembó, Pando, and Canelones City. Pando and Canelones City are located in the Department of Canelones that borders Montevideo, and Pando is a part of the capital's Metropolitan Area. In 2013, the program was replicated in the cities of Las Piedras (also belonging to the Metropolitan Area of Montevideo) and Maldonado (Alvarez, 2012).

Tertiary Level Education

At the Tertiary level, the University of the Republic (UDELAR) has had Deaf students and LSU interpreters since 2003. When Deaf students started to graduate from high school and entered the University of the Republic, the need for an interpreter service emerged for the first time. The various Schools of the University solved the issue of providing sign language interpreters in different ways. The School of Psychology hired an interpreter as early as 2003 when its Teaching Support Unit noted the need. Later, the University placed the Central University Welfare Service (SCBU) in charge of sign language interpreting services to provide interpreters to all Deaf students entering the University.

According to Alvarez (2012), this centralized interpreter service started in the second half of 2006, when a Deaf student attended the second half of the basic cycle of the School of Social Sciences, UDELAR. The following year there were four Deaf students enrolled, and by 2012, the University had 14 Deaf students in various schools of Montevideo: Science, Law, Architecture, Fine Arts, Economics, Administration, Chemistry and Medicine, and the Welfare Service had 20 interpreters working on a rotating basis. Thus, the University has, at present, a permanent team of interpreters that meets the linguistic and communicational needs that arise in intercultural spaces where Deaf and hearing people interact within the institution.

This is a significant change. In the 1980s, it was not expected that Deaf students would enter tertiary education, and neither was it conceivable that they could have their classes taught directly via sign language. Recently, the University entered a new stage in options for Deaf students in higher education. In 2009, School of Humanities and Education of UDELAR opened the Tecnicatura Universitaria en Interpretación LSU–Español–LSU interpreting school (TUILSU). This places LSU within the University, both as a subject of study and as a language of instruction and use, conveying Deaf culture into the university. This makes this School special. In the other Schools within the University, LSU is simply a vehicle of transmission of curricular content.

It is not just that Deaf students have become students whose linguistic rights are respected in the three levels of education. From the beginning of bilingual education, Deaf people have also been involved in primary school as teachers in these spaces. This began in the 1980s when Deaf instructors were hired to take over the teaching of LSU and Deaf culture in bilingual Deaf schools. Later, Deaf teachers were hired by secondary schools to be responsible for teaching classes in LSU and Deaf culture. With the formation of TUILSU, the University hired Deaf teachers to be in charge of teaching, research, and community-related activities, which has given a major boost to the development of linguistics of the LSU in our country. In 2009, one Deaf teacher started working at TUILSU and the number rose to three in 2010. In 2015, the TUILSU has 13 Deaf teachers. The headquarters of TUILSU in Montevideo has seven Deaf professors; there are two in the Salto branch, and one in Tacuarembó.

This entrance of Deaf people and their language into the University of the Republic, via students and teachers, has high relevance for the Deaf community. On the one hand, it is important and indeed "revolutionary" for the Deaf community in aspects regarding LSU and its processes of intellectualization (lexical expiation of the language, as it was pointed out by Garvin and Mathiot, 1976), to be generated naturally in certain scientific fields, as well as in aspects regarding the expansion of the Deaf community into new social spaces. On the other hand, the entrance of the Deaf community into the University also has political value, both for its effect on society at large, as LSU gains exposure in socially valued new areas, and for the Deaf community, by the concomitant change in the prestige and the possibility of occupying spaces to which, previously, the Deaf community had no access.

Bilingual Education of Deaf Students and Functional Distribution of Languages

Bilingual and bicultural education is a modality that incorporates a way to observe and characterize deafness in terms that take into account sign language as the natural language of Deaf people, the language that forms patterns of social and cultural identity and is spoken in the context of the Deaf community (Behares, Monteghirfo, & Davis, 1987; Erting, 1982; Parasnis, 1998; Peluso, 2010; Stokoe, 1960). For this reason the bilingual and bicultural educational model would be the most appropriate one for deaf education.

This type of bilingual and bicultural education highlights the place of sign language in the development of Deaf children and appears as a *culturally sensitive pedagogy* for students in a minority situation, that is, a pedagogy that takes into account and respects the cultural and linguistic needs of its students without defining them as deficit. This conception of culturally sensitive pedagogy was introduced by Erickson (1996) for intercultural and minority schools, and it is in line with studies that address intercultural communication (Samowar, Porter, & Richard, 1994; Zimmermann and Bierbach, 1997).

Thus, bilingual and bicultural education involves a shift in the view of deafness from the perspective that views it as a disability to a minority group issue, that is, of speakers of a language of low social prestige. It becomes, then, an education in a cultural and linguistic borderland (ANEP, 2008, 2009, 2010, 2011, 2012, 2013; ANEP/CEP/National Inspection of Special Education, 1987).

Bilingual and bicultural deaf education also takes into account their right, which is a right of all human beings, to acquire both the language of their community (sign language) and the national language (the language spoken by the hearing majority). In addition, it takes into account the right of Deaf people to be educated in a kind of language that suits their psychophysical characteristics, as stated in Law No. 17.378 (Uruguay, 2001) and Law 18.437 (Uruguay, 2008/2009).

We can argue that bilingual deaf education, when it is really bi- or multicultural, is the only educational model aimed at social and educational inclusion of Deaf students. It is the only model that aims at social and educational inclusion because it does not intend to integrate Deaf students into classes of hearing students, speaking oral language. The integration model, in opposition to the bilingual model, eliminates schools for the Deaf, which form the genuine place of sign language transmission due to the fact that parental transmission is very low. Integration exterminates sign languages, while believing at the same time that integration is inclusive education. However, the bilingual and bicultural model, through its transmission within a community, promotes cognitive and affective instruments and socio-cultural and historical awareness, under the recognition and respect of their distinctiveness, and enables Deaf students to carry forward the process of social inclusion they feel they need for their own development and that of their community.

In the case of bilingual and bicultural deaf education, it is necessary to clarify the particular functional distribution between Spanish and LSU. Typically, bilingualism involves eight psycholinguistic skills. In Uruguay they would be:

1. comprehension of spoken Spanish;
2. production of spoken Spanish;
3. comprehension of written Spanish;
4. production of written Spanish;
5. comprehension of spoken LSU;
6. production of spoken LSU;
7. comprehension of written LSU; and
8. production of written LSU.

But in the case of Deaf people, Spanish and LSU have different relationships. Orality in Spanish is limited because most Deaf children and adults do not have full (and for some, any) auditory access to spoken language. Sign languages are not written, though there have been some efforts to do so. Thus, in Uruguay, bilingual deaf education tries to fit the needs of that community's particular bilingualism, that is, take into account that the languages involved—Spanish and LSU. It maintains a functional distribution in which LSU specializes in orality (in the face-to-face interaction) and Spanish in writing. This occurs primarily in Montevideo and some provincial capitals. In these educational contexts, the classes are taught in LSU (directly by the teachers who are bilingual or through an interpreter), but the texts used in classrooms are in Spanish (Larrinaga, 2013, 2014; Larrinaga & Peluso, 2004, 2007, 2009).

This particular specialization of Deaf bilingualism is embedded in the syllabi and obviously strongly challenges models of teaching writing, as the relationship between mother tongue and second language come into play.

Language Technologies and LSU

Throughout history, primarily of Western culture and its languages, various technologies have been applied to languages that, in turn, as they spread and were used massively, have generated significant changes to those languages and how their speakers relate to them and to the linguistic environment. As discussed in Peluso (2011), these technologies are: representation instruments (writing systems in different material supports), grammatization (grammars and dictionaries), reproducing instruments (video and audio recordings), and computing systems.

Nowadays, these technologies have different levels of application for the Spanish language than they do for LSU, and that is why we can say that these languages do not have the same degree of technologization. We believe that such a situation deeply affects the possibilities of really achieving a bilingual and bicultural deaf education, and we will discuss this in the last part of this chapter.

Representation Instruments: The Writing Systems

As Sampson indicates (1997), writing systems are sets of marks representing units of language. There are writing systems that represent phonological units, as for example, the one used in Spanish. These phonographic systems are absolutely useless in writing sign languages. There are other writing systems that represent morphological units, called logographic writing systems. These would have more proximity with certain characteristics of sign languages. However, these systems have remained remote from the Western world, and as a result, they have not been applied to sign languages.

Writing systems are composed of units that represent units of language and amplify metalinguistic function and therefore metacognitive functions (Olson, 1998). These systems require their users (literate subjects) to reflect constantly on the units represented. Those who use a phonographic writing system would be conditioned to think in the units their system represents—phonemes.

Another property of writing that transforms languages is the possibility of separating the text from the moment of enunciation: *Verba volant, scripta manent* (Spoken words fly away; written words remain). This possibility of transforming the text into a permanent object makes it a deferred text, independent from the sender and the context of utterance. Also, it makes the text a manageable object by the writer and readers. Those who become literate subjects not only learn the writing system but also learn that the text must be read and understood apart from the moment of enunciation. This separation between the subject producing the text and the text itself forces language to expand certain syntactic, morphological, and lexical structures so as to replace what orality would transmit at a pragmatic level, and of course, requires literate individuals learn this. We have to take into account that a written text must be readable without the presence of a writer to clarify doubts. The text must be *self-sufficient* and therefore the writer has to maintain certain standards of construction of the text so it can be understood on its own. As we said before, this property brings the expansion of the syntactic, morphological, and lexical structures of the language.

Unlike Spanish, LSU has no writing system. While, internationally, there is a writing system for sign languages, Signwriting (Sutton, 2015), it has not been adopted by the

Uruguayan Deaf community nor has it been widely adopted anywhere in the world. Thus, bilingual Uruguayan Deaf people face the incongruity of accessing Spanish as their second language through writing when their own language has no written form.

Grammatization: Grammars and Dictionaries

Another form of technologies related to languages are grammatization technologies, which are made up of descriptive or prescriptive grammars and dictionaries (Auroux, 1992). These technologies were used in Ancient Rome and Greece and reappeared in Europe between 1100 and 1500 CE when most European languages were being grammatized. These technologies are not intended to represent the language, as is the case with writing systems, but to describe levels other than the phonological: dictionaries point to the lexical level and grammar points to the morphological and syntactic levels.

For Auroux (1992) there are two different types of grammatization processes, which produce different types of instruments: the exo-grammatization and the endo-grammatization. The exo-grammatization technologies provide us with dictionaries and grammars that are made from outside the language that is described. For example, when the first grammars of Guarani and Quechua were made, these languages were described in Spanish or Latin; or when the first Spanish *Lexicon* was made, it was a translator between Spanish and Latin. However, the endo-grammatization implies another step in the evolution of the grammatization process applied to a language, because it involves the construction of instruments of description in the same language that is described. Thus, with this technology, monolingual dictionaries and grammars are made.

Appling these technologies of grammatization (and writing) to a language leads to the generation of a standard variety of that language. Since the grammar and the lexicon (and the phonemics) appear explicitly described, these levels are elaborated and expanded. For example, through the dictionary the limits of the lexical items are set, while the grammars establish an explicit model of grammatical rules that become the norms to be followed.

The process of grammatization in LSU is very recent and limited, beginning in the late eighties. The degree of LSU grammatization is so limited that we are still far from having a fully grammmatized language. Regarding the processes of grammatization that took place in LSU, we must say that now we have only two LSU–Spanish dictionaries and one descriptive grammar. These dictionaries are: *Lengua de Señas Uruguaya: Su componente léxico básico* (*Uruguayan Sign Language: Its Basic Lexicon Component*) (Behares, Monteghirfo & Davis, 1987) and *Diccionario bilingüe de Lengua de Señas Uruguaya/Español* (*Bilingual dictionary of Uruguayan Sign Language/Spanish* (ASUR/CINDE, 2007). Both texts are instruments of exo-grammatization, as they are presented in written Spanish and illustrations. In 2012, a descriptive grammar of LSU was published (Fojo & Massone, 2012). This grammar is also a tool of exo-grammatization, due to the fact that it analyzes LSU elements of morphology and syntax using written Spanish and the methodology of glossing.

We are in the process of endo-grammatization, which involves the development of a linguistic methodology of phonological analysis of LSU, in LSU and without using written Spanish (Bonilla & Peluso, 2010). This phonological model is the basis for developing the first LSU monolingual dictionary. In this dictionary, videos of the signs are matched with videos with their definitions and a phonological clue put with each lexical item is used to search for the various signs in the dictionary. Thus, the signs are organized through the phonological analyzer described earlier, and not by alphabetical order, as in other dictionaries. This is the first instrument of endo-grammatization for LSU, and an instrument made entirely without using Spanish as the language of description (de Leon, Muslera, Peluso, & Val, 2013; Peluso & Val, 2012). Thus, in the making of this dictionary (*Lexicon TRELSU*) we had to combine a linguistic technology (the specific monolingual description of the sign language we referred to before), the video recording technologies (video recordings of the signs and their definitions), and computer technology (the videos must be hosted in a program, developed by us, that allows searching for the signs).

All this work aims to achieve the grammatization of LSU. The development of these instruments tends to hinder natural variation of LSU. Dictionaries and grammatical descriptions of a language tend to slow down the amount of language variation that commonly occurs with any unwritten and ungrammatized language. This process leads to a national form of the language. As a result, the grammatization of any variety of LSU leads to its standardization. During this process, LSU is taking on new forms, functions, and status, which leads to many conflicts within the community of speakers who had a strong sense of belonging to an homogenous linguistic minority, without linguistic differences and without language authority.

Reproducing Instruments: Video and Audio Recordings

Unlike the writing systems that represent language units, video and audio recordings merely reproduce the language in use. Reproducing technologies are of very recent origin. These technologies allow us, among other things, to record audio and video texts. This introduces a textuality that has certain similarities to written textuality but is not the same. It has properties similar to writing because it allows the production of deferred texts (separate from the moment of enunciation) and because they objectify the text. Upon making the texts an object, subjects are allowed to manage them, going backward or forward, which amplifies the metalinguistic function (as occurs with writing systems). However, as it is a reproducing technology and not a technology to represent units of language, it produces lower degrees of metalinguistic and metacognitive effects.

As video and audio recordings are technologies that reproduces a language but do not represent it, these recordings produce different relationships between the speaker and the text and with language itself, than occur with the use of a written text. Facing a written text, a reader must perform certain cognitive processes to decode it, and as it is represented and not actually present, this processing will occur at the highest metalinguistic level. However, having audio or video recorded texts implies a type of processing that is similar to what occurs in a conversational context, so the metalinguistic and metacognitive levels used are lower.

In the case of the Deaf community, the use of videotapes as writing (deferred texts) and the technologies of information and communication is widespread. This new way of constructing deferred textuality, as it occurs with the writing of oral language, can be divided into two types: unplanned (spontaneous) videos and planned ones.

The mostly unplanned videos are, for example, chats via web or phone cameras, or the recording and uploading of videos onto the web (YouTube, Facebook) of short informative texts (e.g., sharing of news) in LSU. This type of video production is minimally planned, and the narrator has little control of the production process and the product itself. Occasionally short LSU videos are published on the web featuring political issues or fictional stories that show a higher level of development. These videos show planning and control. However, videos are always short, although longer than the unplanned ones. Long LSU videos with academic or fictional content have not appeared to date. Longer videos require specialized skills, as they must be recorded in short segments with subsequent editing in order to create a unique text with a planned internal structure. Those videos are planned and controlled, in all textual aspects, which is obligatory in the case of long and formal texts.

LSU videos could serve as deferred textuality in a different way than written Spanish. The development of deferred textuality is essential in the consolidation of a truly literate Deaf culture in LSU, which has no writing system or writing tradition. This is the goal of the *TRELSU* Project when it videotapes planned LSU texts. This project aims to consolidate a registered (or recorded) textuality in LSU through video recordings of texts originally created in LSU as well as texts translated from written Spanish. This project aims to create a text tradition made up of LSU video texts. These video texts will fill the gap creating a collection in which aspects of Deaf culture (literature, geography, history) will be *written*, as well as other universal texts about art, literature, science, and technology.

Computing Systems

Computer and digital technologies are the latest to be applied to languages. These technologies, which integrate image, audio, and writing in novel ways, bring language processing and communication routes to new levels. With these technologies, new functions of written language appear, for example, the use of SMS and chat, to pursue new ways of introducing orality into writing.

   With these new technologies, a departure from the *obligatory* use of standard variety in written text takes place. The function of hypertext (via the almost infinite links that the Internet offers) is consolidated, and we have almost unlimited access to information. The use of the Internet imposes new search strategies using written language. The revolutionary possibilities of rewriting text (e.g., cut and paste) in an easy and instantaneous way, changes the linguistic and cognitive strategies used to approach a written text. Boundaries between your own texts and those of others are blurred, which could increase the possibility of plagiarism.

Information and communication technologies are required in the production of planned LSU videos. The particular organization of these texts (recorded in segments and edited afterwards) demands the use of information technology in order to organize the whole text. In the global world, these technologies allow communication between people who do not share the same physical context. The ability to write SMS and chats in Spanish has completely revolutionized the ecology of communication in the Deaf community with the hearing world. Although TTYs and relay services have existed for Deaf people for decades, their use in Uruguay was limited.

The new technologies widely disseminated a new way of communicating. Cell phone video cameras allow Deaf people to communicate directly in LSU, without written Spanish, which is more comfortable for them.

Rethinking Deaf Education: The Technological Context and Plurilingual

We believe that bilingual and bicultural deaf education should consider the new technological context and the different degrees of technologization of LSU. LSU must be the target language in education. However much of the time, LSU is used merely as a didactic device to more effectively teach the Spanish language school curriculum. Spanish should be considered as a second language (L2). By incorporating the concept of plurilingualism (Larrinaga, 2014), we are able to break with the concept of native speaker as a model and of whole language as "listening, speaking, reading, and writing." In order to have genuine bilingual and bicultural education with LSU at the center, it is important to foster LSU monolingual tools (endo-grammatization) that allow the metalinguistic reflection about LSU in LSU and to create a significant amount of textuality in LSU so that Deaf students can "read" (and also mediate in) a curriculum content that connects them with the national and global context and with their own roots.

Regarding the teaching of writing to Deaf students, and taking into account everything mentioned in this chapter, we must introduce two premises—one theoretical and the other theoretical and methodological—that restate a different relationship between orality and literacy (Larrinaga & Peluso, 2009). LSU video registered texts function as "written" LSU, and learning the writing system of Spanish itself, for Deaf people, involves learning a second language (Spanish) and new forms of representation concomitantly.

First, LSU video texts function as "written" LSU. While currently there are not writing systems, at least in Uruguay, that Deaf people have adopted to write their language, there have emerged technologies to document, archive, and record texts in LSU. Thus, through these technologies, the Deaf community can produce deferred texts. They can reproduce forms and functions that are characteristic of writing, in their recorded LSU texts, even when they do not have a writing system for LSU but rather a visual recording technology. Through texts videotaped in LSU, speakers of this language, who can manage this technology, will have access to some cultural and psychological practices that are the realm of literate subjects only. We refer to practices such as: (a) access or produce an LSU text that is deferred in relation to the moment of utterance; (b) deal with LSU texts that, as registered/recorded, become permanent and visible objects, potentially archived and interpreted; and (c) incorporate strategies to think and talk about LSU deferred texts which stimulates the metalinguistic and metacognitive strategies and functions. We think that those practices, learned by using LSU deferred textuality (i.e., using deferred textuality in their own language) could comfortably be transferred into practices with written Spanish (the second language).

Second, for Deaf people, learning the writing system of Spanish involves learning a second language (Spanish) and new forms of representation at the same time. Thus, as the writing system is necessarily linked to the management of a second language, in its learning, the metalinguistic and metacognitive levels of processing involved are much higher. As noted above, for Deaf people, Spanish is a L2, in which they cannot achieve native fluency, and LSU is their first or native language, which has no writing system. Thus, the teaching of writing is not merely the teaching of a system that can represent the units of a language and transcribe statements in that language. Rather, teaching writing is teaching another language that depends on a different channel, for example, hearing (audition) and speech, and Deaf people cannot access the orality of that language.

According to the particular bilingualism of Deaf people, the teaching of written Spanish should be undertaken in what the tradition of applied linguistics has called teaching of a L2 (second language). But as we have seen, the case of the Deaf community is very unique. On the one hand, unlike, Spanish-speaking (hearing) university students, who are taught to read in English as a L2, Deaf people have not already learned to write in their own language and are not already "literate subjects" (Larrinaga, 2000; 2013). On the contrary, the languages at play in the case of the Deaf community have a different structural support for the signifier, which does not occur in the case of the university students with Spanish and English. The writing system they use as a technology is based on phono-articulatory structural support, which is completely at variance with that of sign languages (visual-spatial). Additionally, Spanish and LSU do not have the same degree of intellectualization, and so, at the formal level, there will be lexical and syntactic divergences.

These two premises—that LSU video texts could function as *written* LSU and that learning the writing system of Spanish involves learning an L2—would entirely change the methodological approaches for teaching written Spanish to Deaf students. It had always been claimed that teaching written Spanish exclusively from the point of orality in LSU was methodologically challenging. These new technologies open possibilities as they allow the production of LSU deferred texts and introduce new intermediate links in the chain.

With this LSU deferred textuality, Deaf students can be taught the forms and functions of writing in their own language. That is, with the proposal of thinking of videotapes as writing, we should consider a form of teaching writing that starts from orality in LSU, going towards *writing* in LSU (through production and understanding of LSU video-taped texts), regardless of the learning of written Spanish. We believe that the acquisition of functions related to deferred texts (the essence of writing) is key to the education of literate individuals and not just the learning of the mechanics of writing itself. It is also key that these functions be culturally situated, as this is what gives a meaning to the learning process and propels it. The new LSU deferred textuality is completely culturally situated as it has a special social role that makes it valuable for Deaf people to learn.

On the other hand, it appears that the teaching of written Spanish can then be sustained more clearly, not as a transcription of the language but as a second language and a system of representation of its units. This makes it easier to break with the methodological principle that the relationship between orality and literacy is one of transcription, as it allows trainees to sustain the idea of representation from the LSU consistently, to the extent that a meta reflection is already introduced with the use of LSU deferred texts.

Also, in this technological concert, and taking into account that the Deaf community still tends to function, in Uruguay, as an "oral" community due to the fact that there is no writing system for its own language, Spanish can be taught through orality and from contexts that are functionally meaningful for Deaf students. As pointed out by Massone, Buscaglia, and Bogado (2005) and our own research (Larrinaga & Peluso, 2009; Perez, 2014), Deaf people spontaneously learn and use the messages written in Spanish from cell phones, chats, social networking, and Internet searches. These usages of written Spanish are clearly linked to orality and have a strong functional value for speakers. As such, we believe that the methodology of teaching written Spanish should come from these oral uses of writing and talk towards more decontextualized uses and functions of written Spanish textuality, such as scientific or literary texts or, even popular online sources such as Wikipedia.

With this proposal, we think that the teaching of writing (in this case Spanish) for Deaf people in a bilingual and a bicultural context should migrate to the teaching of deferred textuality that includes not only representation technologies but also reproducing ones (videos). Thus, in this proposal we should combine: (a) notions of deferred textuality that include LSU videotapes and not simply written Spanish; (b) the development of metalinguistic and metacognitive skills that come from the use of and reflection on such textuality; and (c) the oral uses of written Spanish (such as SMS and chat) functionally meaningful for Deaf students. So, the use and metalinguistic reflection on LSU recorded texts and on written Spanish in oral functions, such as SMS and chat, could be the links between LSU and Spanish that we have been looking for since the beginnings of bilingual and bicultural deaf education.

We seem to be facing new ways of being literate subjects. These Deaf students could promptly establish multiple and creative relationships between the various registration forms of the languages and oral forms, which would enable the use of texts in both languages and various technologies. They could be literate subjects, plurilingual and pluridialectal, who could choose freely from a broad linguistic and technological repertoire.

References

Álvarez, C. (2013). Acerca de los servicios de interpretación en la Universidad de la Repúblic y en la Universidad del Trabajo del Uruguay [About interpreting services en the University of the Republic and the University of Labor of Uruguay]. En ANEP, *Quinto Foro Nacional de Lenguas de la ANEP*. Montevideo, Uruguay: Author, 73–74.

ANEP. (2008). *Documentos de la Comisión de Políticas Lingüísticas en la Educación Pública* [Documents of the Commission of Linguistic Policies in Public Education]. Montevideo, Uruguay: Author.

ANEP. (2009). *Primer Foro Nacional de Lenguas de la ANEP* [First National Forum on Languages in the ANEP]. Montevideo, Uruguay: Author.

ANEP. (2010). *Segundo Foro Nacional de Lenguas de la ANEP* [Second National Forum on Languages in the ANEP]. Montevideo, Uruguay: Author.

ANEP. (2011). *Tercer Foro Nacional de Lenguas de la ANEP* [Third National Forum on Languages in the ANEP]. Montevideo, Uruguay: Author.

ANEP. (2012). *Cuarto Foro Nacional de Lenguas de la ANEP* [Fourth National Forum on Languages in the ANEP]. Montevideo, Uruguay: Author.

ANEP. (2013). *Quinto Foro Nacional de Lenguas de la ANEP* [Fifth National Forum on Languages in the ANEP]. Montevideo, Uruguay: Author.

ANEP/CEP/Inspección Nacional de Educación Especial. (1987). *Propuesta para la implementación de la Educación Bilingüe en el Uruguay* [Proposal for the implementation of bilingual education in Uruguay]. Official document. Montevideo, Uruguay: Author.

ASUR/CINDE. (2007). *Diccionario Bilingüe de Lengua de Señas Uruguaya/Español* [Bilingual dictionary of Uruguayan Sign Language and Spanish]. Montevideo, Uruguay: Author.

Auroux, S. (1992). *A revolução tecnológica da gramatização* [A technological revolution of grammaticization]. Campinas, Brazil: Editora da Unicamp.

Behares, L. E. (1989). Diglosia escolar: Aspectos descriptivos y sociopedagógicos [Scholarly diglossia: Descriptive aspects and socio-pedagogies]. *Trabalhosem Lingüística Aplicada, 14*, 147–154.

Behares, L. E., Brovetto, C., & Peluso, L. (2012). Language policies in Uruguay and Uruguayan Sign Language (LSU). *Sign Language Studies, 12*(4), 519–542.

Behares, L. E., Monteghirfo, N., & Davis, D. (1987). *Lengua de Señas Uruguaya. Su componente léxico básico* [Uruguayan Sign Language: The basic lexical component]. Montevideo, Uruguay: Instituto Interamericano del Niño.

Bonilla, F., & Peluso, L. (2010). Hacia un descriptor del nivel fonológico de la LSU [Toward a descriptor of the phonological level of LSU]. *Lengua de señas e interpretación, 1*, 2–56.

Catach, N. (Ed.) (1996). *Hacia una teoría de la lengua escrita* [Toward a theory of written language]. Barcelona, Spain: Gedisa.

Council of Europe/Language Policy Division. (2001). *Common European framework for languages: Learning, teaching, and assessment*. Strasbourg, France: Author.

de León, A., Muslera, S., Peluso, L., & Val, S. (2013). *Programa Léxico TRELSU [Lexical program TRELSU]* (Beta version). Montevideo, Uruguay: Ediciones TUILSU-imagen.

de Saussure, F. (1916/1993) *Curso de lingüística general* [Course of general linguistics]. Madrid, Spain: Alianza.

Erickson, F. (1996). Transformation and school success: The politics and culture of educational achievement. In E. Jacob and C. Jordan (Eds.), *Minority education: Anthropological perspectives* (pp. 27–51). Norwood, NJ: Ablex.

Erting, C. (1982). *Deafness, communication and social identity: An antropological analysis of interaction among parents, teachers, and deaf children in a preschool.* Doctoral dissertation. American University: Washington, DC.

Gallardo, A. (1978). Hacia una teoría del idioma estándar [Toward a theory of the standard language]. *Revista de Lingüística Teórica y Aplicada, 16*, 85–119.

Garvin, P. L., & Mathiot, M. (1974). La urbanización del idioma Guaraní. Problema de lengua y cultural [The urbanization of the Guarani language: Problem of language and culture]. In P. L. Garvin and Y. Lastra (Eds.), *Antología de estudios de etnolingüística y sociolingüística* (pp. 303–313). México City, México: UNAM.

Goody, J., & Watt, I. (1996). Las consecuencias de la cultura escrita [The consequences of the written culture]. In J. Goody (Ed.), *Cultura escrita en sociedades tradicionales* (pp. 39–82). Barcelona, Spain: Gedisa.

Gumperz, J. (1968). Types of linguistic communities. In J. Fishman (Ed.), *Readings in the sociology of language* (pp. 460–472). The Hague, The Netherlands: Mouton.

Larrinaga, J. A. (2000). *La transparencia en el desarrollo de comprensión lectora en inglés (L2) por hispanohablantes* [Transparency in the development of reading comprehension in English by Spanish-speakers]. Anales del vigésimo Congreso de la Federación Internacional de Profesores de Lenguas Vivas. Paris, France. Retrieved from http://lettres.univ-lemans.fr/fiplv

Larrinaga, J. A. (2013). Enseñanza de una asignatura y enseñanza de lengua: Dos caras de una misma moneda [Teaching of a course and teaching of language: Two sides of the same coin]. In ANEP (Ed.), *Quinto Foro Nacional de Lenguas de la ANEP* (pp. 75–78). Montevideo, Uruguay: Author.

Larrinaga, J. A. (2014). Reading process and language education. Linguistic, educational and political aspects regarding two groups in Uruguay: Deaf students and university students. *Psicología, Conocimiento y Sociedad, 4*(2), 62–88.

Larrinaga, J. A. & Peluso, L. (2004). Alumnos sordos en la enseñanza media: Los profesores de asignaturas humanísticas y científicas como profesores de lengua [Deaf students insecondary school: Teachers of humanities and science courses as language courses]. In *Anais do FILE III.* Pelotas, Brasil (CD-ROM).

Larrinaga, J. A., & Peluso, L. (2007). Educación bilingüe de los sordos: Consideraciones acerca de la escritura, procesamiento del conocimiento y rol docente [Bilingual education for the deaf: Considerations of the writing, procedural and knowledge of the teaching role]. In *Memorias de las XIV Jornadas de Investigación y Tercer Encuentro de Investigadores de Psicología del Mercosur*, 3, (464–466). Buenos Aires. Argentina: Ediciones de la Fac. de Psicología de la Universidad de Buenos Aires.

Larrinaga, J. A., & Peluso, L. (2009). Sordera, escritura y enseñanza de lengua [Deafness, writing and teaching language]. *Memorias del I Congreso Internacional de investigación y práctica profesional en Psicología, XVI Jornadas de Investigación, Quinto Encuentro de Investigadores en Psicología del MERCOSUR* (pp. 529–531). Buenos Aires, Argentina: Ediciones de la Fac. de Psicología de la Universidad de Buenos Aires. Retrieved from: http://www.aacademica.org/000-020/38

Massone, M. I., Buscaglia, V., & Bogado, A. (2005). Los sordos aprenden a escribir sobre la marcha [The Deaf learning and writing on the move]. *Lectura y Vida, 26*(4), 6–17.

McLuhan, M. (1964/1996). *Comprender los medios de comunicación. Las extensiones del ser humano I* [Understanding the means of communication: Extensions of the human being]. Barcelona, Spain: Paidós.

Olson, D. (1998). *El mundo sobre papel* [The world on paper]. Barcelona, Spain: Gedisa.

Ong, W. (1982) *Oralidad y escritura. Tecnologías de la palabra* [Orality and writing: Technologies of the word]. Buenos Aires, Argentina: Fondo de Cultura Económica.

Parasnis, I. (Ed.) (1998). *Cultural and language diversity and the Deaf experience*. Cambridge, UK: Cambridge University Press.

Peluso, L. (2010). *Sordos y oyentes en un liceo común: Investigación e intervención en un contexto intercultural* [Deaf and hearing in a common school: Research and intervention in an intercultural context]. Montevideo, Uruguay: Udelar/Psicolibros.

Peluso, L. (2011). Entre la lengua oral escrita y la oralidad de la lengua de señas: Buscando los eslabones perdidos [Between spoken written language and orality in sign language: Seeking the lost connections]. In *Anales del III Congreso Internacional de Investigación y Práctica Profesional en Psicología*. Buenos Aires, Argentina: Universidad de Buenos Aires.

Peluso, L., & Val, S. (2012). Léxico TRELSU. Primer léxico de la LSU en LSU. Caracterización, aspectos teórico-metodológicos y manual de uso [First lexicon of LSU in LSU: Characterization of theoretical metholological aspects and manual of use]. *Lengua de señas e interpretación, 3*, 31–49.

Perez, C. (2014). Relaciones de estudiantes sordos con la escritura: Lo ficcional escrito en clase de literature [Relationships of deaf students to writing: Fiction writing in a literature class]. Tesis de Maestría. Universidad de la Republica de Uruguay. Montevideo, Uruguay.

Samowar, L., Porter, A., & Richard, E. (Eds.) (1994). *Intercultural communication. A reader*. Belmont, CA: Wadsworth.

Sampson, G. (1997). *Sistemas de escritura* [Writing systems]. Barcelona, Spain: Gedisa.

Stokoe, W. (1960). Sign Language structure: An outline of the visual communication system of the American Deaf. *Studies in Linguistics, Occasional Papers*, No. 8.

Sutton, V. (2015). Sign Writing Site. Retrieved from http://signwriting.org/

Uruguay. (2001). Ley No. 17.378. Ley de reconocimiento de la Lenguas de Señas Uruguaya - LSU. Retrieved from: http://www.discapacidaduruguay.org/index.php/servicios/legislacion/176

Uruguay. (2008/2009). Ley 18.437. Ley General de Educación. Retrieved from http://www2.ohchr.org/english/bodies/cat/docs/AnexoXIV_Ley18437.pdf

Vygotsky, L. (1931/1995). Historia del desarrollo de las funciones psíquicas superiors [History of the development of superior psychiatric functions]. In L. S. Vygotsky (Ed.), *Obras escogidas*. Vol. III (pp. 183–206). Madrid, Spain: Visor.

Vygotsky, L. (1934/2001). Pensamiento y lenguaje [Thinking and language]. In L. S. Vygotsky (Ed.), *Obras escogidas*. Vol. II (pp. 9–348). Madrid, Spain: Visor.

Wertsch, J. (1988). *Vygotsky y la formación social de la mente* [Vygotsky and the social formation of the mind]. Barcelona, Spain: Paidós.

Wertsch, J. (1993). *Voces de la mente. Un enfoque sociocultural para el estudio de la acción medida* [Voices of the mind: A sociocultural focus for the study of mediated action]. Madrid, Spain: Visor.

Zimmermann, K., & Bierbach, C. (Eds.) (1997). *Lenguaje y comunicación intercultural en el mundo hispánico* [Language and intercultural communication in the Hispanic world]. Madrid, Spain: Biblioteca Ibero-Americana.

12

Bicultural Bilingual Deaf Education in Venezuela: Approaching a Necessary Debate

Ana María Morales García and Yolanda Mercedes Pérez Hernández

Bicultural bilingual deaf education has gained increased relevance in the last 20 years as the Deaf population claims educational, linguistic, cultural, and above all, human rights (Pérez, 2006). Many experts in deaf education have thought, pessimistically, that such education has been a failure, even identifying it as a chimera, or mythical creature. Others, with an optimistic perspective, consider that important steps have been taken in order to make bilingual bicultural deaf education a reality.

To evaluate the history of the development of bilingual bicultural deaf education in Venezuela, we must recap the beginnings of deaf educational programs in the country. In 1935, the first Deaf boarding school opened (Hoffmann, 1965; Luque and Pérez, 2012; Morales and Pérez, 2010; Pérez 2006, 2008), and it is here that *Lengua de Señas Venezolano* (LSV, Venezuelan Sign Language) emerged (Oviedo, 2003). However, for the next 50 years, deaf education in Venezuela was marked by oralism. In the mid-eighties, a radical change emerged, as our country became a pioneer for bicultural bilingual deaf education. Between 1985 and 1986, the Ministry of Education implemented the *Propuesta de Atención Integral al Niño Sordo* (Proposal for Comprehensive Attention to the Deaf Child; hereinafter, PAINS, its acronym in Spanish), which was in place until 1995. In 1997, an in-depth assessment by the governmental department responsible for *Deficiencias Auditivas* (Hearing Impairment) reported weaknesses and successes in PAINS. This report led to the suspension of PAINS and the creation of the *Conceptualización y Política de Atención Integral al Deficiente Auditivo en Venezuela* (Conceptualization and Comprehensive Attention Policy for the Hearing Impaired in Venezuela) in 1997. This policy is still in force but being reviewed. In the new document the bilingual character of deaf education was established. As a result, since 1985, it is possible to identify actions undertaken by the government that attempt to respond to the psycho- and sociolinguistic characteristics of Deaf students nationwide.

By examining these policies, it is possible to identify the emergence, progress, and setbacks in deaf education policies in Venezuela (Luque & Pérez, 2012). This chapter provides a thorough and critical examination of the development and implementation of bilingual bicultural education in Venezuela and proposes a plan that will lead to improved methods of delivering effective education to all Deaf children.

PAINS: The Beginning of Bicultural Bilingual Deaf Education in Venezuela

The bicultural bilingual model of deaf education is linked to the emergence of the socio-anthropological conception of Deafness. This perspective is the foundation for a radical change in representations of Deafness and Deaf people. It rejects a prejudiced vision, anchored in the idea of deficiency for which the goal is the recognition of difference. Skliar, Massone, and Veinberg (1995) point out two events that marked this shift:

> On the one hand, the fact [is that the] Deaf make communities, where the glue is sign language, despite repression by society and by the school. On the other hand, (you have) the confirmation that Deaf children of Deaf parents achieve higher academic standards, acquire better skills for learning spoken and written language, (achieving) levels of reading similar to those of hearing (children), a balanced identity, and do not develop any of the social-emotional problems the Deaf children of hearing parents have. (p. 8)

These observations and the contribution of scientific disciplines, such as anthropology, linguistics, and psychology, have led to a new conception of Deaf people as a diverse sociolinguistic community, and resulted in new philosophical and educational views with pedagogical alternatives for the education of Deaf children. A social representation of Deaf people, radically opposed to the pathological vision rooted in the traditional model and oralism, was born.

The emphasis shifted to regarding sign languages as the greatest assurance for normal development of language by Deaf individuals. With this frame of reference, in 1985, PAINS—an innovative pedagogical model, oriented towards bilingual education— emerged in our country. The proposal was framed in bilingual and bicultural pedagogical principles that acknowledged LSV as a natural language and as the first language of Deaf Venezuelans (Morales & Pérez, 2010).

PAINS reinforced the value of sign language in shaping the local Deaf culture and the unique role that language and culture have on the comprehensive development of Deaf individuals. It follows that it is the right of Deaf people to be educated in their language and culture. However, PAINS was implemented only in the public education sector, because it was an educational policy issued by the Ministry of Education. Private schools for the Deaf maintained an oral approach.

The first PAINS document included five key points: (a) establishing a language environment in LSV, (b) early intervention, (c) the importance of the written language, (d) changing the school curriculum, and (e) teaching the oral language (see Pérez & Sanchez, n.d.). The first key point was the urgent need for schools to become an environment in which Deaf children could acquire LSV as their first language through language interactions with Deaf teaching assistants and Deaf peers of mixed ages, and varied language and communication skills. The second point concerned early intervention with an LSV environment with fluent signers. The third point addressed the constructive acquisition of written language as a second language, crucial for communication and the development of thought, without the interposition of spoken language.

The fourth point emphasized necessary changes in the organization of the school and the curriculum. These included the creation of *activity areas* such as games, sports, theater, literacy, science, and fine arts, among others. The first PAINS document did not explicitly describe these as part of the curriculum. Some traditionalists argued that these subjects would replace the customary structure of classrooms for Deaf students that focused on the development of spoken language. These new subjects for Deaf students taught in their own language offered rich opportunities for meaningful linguistic exchanges in LSV. This would occur in genuine contexts among Deaf peers of different ages, providing rich interchanges in their natural language.

The final and fifth point is that the bilingual status of Deaf students is demonstrated by their mastery of LSV and written Spanish, which addresses the role of spoken language. However, this aspect was not thoroughly explained, from either a methodological or theoretical point of view needed to facilitate implementation.

PAINS never achieved widespread acceptance among stakeholders in deaf education, including teachers, specialists, Deaf teaching assistants, and the Deaf community. Rather, it was seen as a set of guidelines or directives issued by the Ministry through the Directorate of Special Education. The introduction of PAINS throughout the country included two stages aimed at administrators, educators, and technical and auxiliary staff, including parents and guardians (Pérez and Morales, 2010). The first stage was to build awareness and the second was training.

PAINS emphasized the right of Deaf individuals to be educated in LSV. This involved the creation of LSV language environments, understanding that these spaces fostered the development of communication skills in schools for the Deaf through genuine linguistic situations. As mentioned earlier, PAINS called for grouping Deaf students of different ages and different levels of competencies in LSV to allow for linguistic enrichment.

However, the classroom teachers (who were hearing) were not fluent in LSV and instead used a kind of "signed Spanish" (signs with Spanish syntax). Educational activities were planned with a Deaf assistant, who along with the teacher designed teaching strategies to facilitate linguistic exchanges. Actually, it was the Deaf assistants who ultimately taught the classes for Deaf students, although in most cases, the teacher would explain unfamiliar content to the Deaf assistant.

Another key aspect in this educational change was school curriculum. Before the implementation of PAINS, deaf education had been based on language rehabilitation rather than a bilingual approach. Notably, this resulted in a lack of educational support and the disorganization found in schools for the Deaf. There was a lack of curricular planning for preschool and elementary education and no support from curriculum specialists for teachers.

Implementation of these changes were further limited by negative attitudes of teachers and specialists, as well as oral Deaf adults who opposed the recognition of the fundamental value of sign language in deaf education. This was the result of the pervasiveness of the oralist ideology. Additionally, there was a shortage of Deaf adults to serve as linguistic models of LSV in schools working to implement bilingual and bicultural deaf education. There was also a lack of timely and quality supervision of the new model by the Directorate of Special Education. As a result, each school interpreted the pedagogical guidelines of PAINS according to their own theoretical approach and methodology. The result was the dilution of many of the positive achievements that PAINS brought to deaf education due to the lack of attention to its implementation, monitoring, and evaluation. Additionally, there were legal complications. The Constitution of Venezuela (1960) and the Organic Law of Education (1980) predated the recognition of LSV, which meant there was a lack of crucial legal support for bilingual bicultural education.

Our review of the launching of PAINS and implementation of a bilingual deaf education model led to the following four categories of analysis: (a) education policies, (b) laws, (c) training and teaching, and (d) participation of the Deaf community.

Tensions and Paradoxes: From 1995 to 2014

In 1995, the Directorate of Special Education of the Ministry of Education (now known as the Ministerio del Poder Popular para la Educación, the Ministry of Popular Power for Education) was taken over by new adminstration. This administration designed an action plan for a national evaluation of each of the areas related to "impairments," including hearing impairment. They provided information on: (a) range of services and functioning units available, (b) number of trained professionals in the field, (c) school enrollment, (d) number of school graduates, (e) criteria for entry, placement and endorsement of students, and (f) supervision procedures (Ministry of Education, 1997a).

These evaluations revealed strengths and weaknesses and were key to the formation of the action plan. The plan called for the creation of the document *Paradigmas que Orientan la Política de la Modalidad de Educación Especial en Venezuela* (Paradigms to Guide Policies Related to Special Education in Venezuela; Ministry of Education, 1997a), which updated the philosophical, axiological, and political principles set out in the *Conceptualización y Política de la Educación Especial en Venezuela* (Conceptualization and Special Education Policy in Venezuela) in 1976. They updated the wording for each area of focus in policy documents, which led to the document *La Conceptualización y Política de Atención Integral del Deficiente Auditivo* (Conceptualization and Policies of Integrated Attention to the Hearing Impaired) and the end of PAINS.

Various administrative teams in charge of the Directorate of Special Education from 1997 to November 2011 took the lead in the conceptualizations of each area. The Constitution of 1961 and the Education Act of 1980 were repealed and replaced with the Constitution of the Bolivarian Republic of Venezuela (1999) and the Education Act (2009). After considerable delay, *Transformación de la Modalidad de Educación Especial en el Marco de una Educación sin Barreras*—(Transformation of Special Education in the Context of Education without Barriers) was implemented from November 2011 to January 2014. Therefore, we consider this official action as marking the second period, which we address in this chapter, to be from the conceptualization in 1997 to January 2014, the finalization of the transformation.

We will next present what happened in that period, using the categories that emerged from our analysis of the historical moment, between 1985 and 1997, discussed in the preceding section.

Education Policies

In this section we analyze the *La Conceptualización y Política de Atención Integral del Deficiente Auditivo* (The Conceptualization and Policies for Comprehensive Attention to the Hearing Impaired; Ministry of Education, 1997b). This document is organized into the following parts: (a) historical synthesis, (b) current situation, (c) service model, and (d) administration model. Undoubtedly, having an official statement that clarifies the educational context and clearly expresses the policy of the state, as well as intra and inter-sectoral connections, was an important step.

The criticisms we present relate mainly to the service model it contains. Although it explicitly states it is based on a model of bilingual deaf education, when read critically, it is possible to detect implicit ideas that are not in line with a genuine socio-anthropological conception of Deafness and a true bicultural bilingual education.

Pérez (2006, 2008) points out evidence of this in the document:

- The Deaf are viewed in terms of audiological data, which leads to reverting to the term "hearing impaired." It devotes an entire section to the issue referred to the categories of hearing loss and lacks any references to the Deaf in terms of linguistic and cultural differences.
- It reduces the LSV to a simple educational tool to achieve academic goals, ignoring: (a) the linguistic status of the language; (b) the central importance a sign language has in the development of the Deaf; and (c) the value of LSV as a cohesive factor of Deaf culture in Venezuela.
- It considers Deaf adults working in schools simply as supports for school and extra-curricular activities rather than acknowledging their participation in the educational context as cultural-linguistic models for students.
- It uses the terms of the bilingual bicultural orientation to represent a therapeutic orientation. (Pérez, 2006, p. 173)

Pérez (personal communication, 2014) elaborated on actions of obvious therapeutic nature, promoted by the Directorate of Special Education between 1998 and 2006, some of which were:

- courses for advanced techniques in speech therapy
- meetings with staff to come to agreement on services for Deaf and hard of hearing people
- technical seminars in all federal institutions with emphasis on detection of hearing loss
- audiological evaluations of Deaf students
- delivery of hearing aids
- efforts to support the use of cochlear implants
- design and implementation of a diploma in audiory-verbal therapy
- processes for integrating Deaf students with interpreters in regular education education settings, instead of attending secondary schools for the Deaf, which was consistent with the State's refusal to create new Deaf institutions (Pérez, 2006, p. 175)

Pérez (2006) warned of an oralist repositioning in which the "flags of integration" were unfurled as a leitmotif, or recurrent theme.

As previously noted, actions by the State remained in place until November 2011, without modification to the conceptualization and policy of 1999. In the 1999 document, despite some contradictions relative to bilingual bicultural deaf education, we recognize two positive outcomes. The first was the management model, which focused attention on Deaf people in all schools and public services in the country. The second was the connection to the guiding principles set out in the *Paradigmas que Orientan la*

Política de la Modalidad de Educación Especial en Venezuela (Paradigms that Guide the Policies of Special Education in Venezuela; Ministry of Education, 1997a).

We highlight these points in order to address what happened during the transformation of special education in Venezuela. This occurred in early 2012 when the Ministerio del Poder Popular para la Educación (Ministry of Popular Power for Education; MPPE) implemented *La Modalidad de Educación Especial en el Marco de la Educación Bolivariana "Educación sin Barreras"* (Special Education in the Context of Bolivarian Education "Education without Barriers") conceived in Novemeber 2011. This document contained the following sections: (a) current status of special education, (b) proposal to transform the state of special education, (c) aspects evaluated leading to decisions for transformation, and (d) action plan for the transformation of the state of special education (Ministerio del Poder Popular para la Educación, 2011).

We focus on the section that the MPPE identified as a *proposal,* which we see as developed within a normative framework. This is indicated by the following. A change of terminology was made in the *Disability Act* (2007). People with disabilities or special educational needs were to be known from then on as *people with functional diversity*. Additionally, there was a change in the organizational structure of special education at national and municipal levels, which would impact all schools and services in the country. New structures and reconfigurations of human resources were established as well as redefining the spaces where they would work. This with the consequent establishment of the functions of each of the new structural elements, the respective configuration of the human resources teams that should take part, as well as the spaces where they should operate.

Regarding terminology, we note that the proposal aligns with the approach of Romanach and Lobato (2005) who describe *functional diversity* as one that "fits a situation in which a person works differently or is different from most society members" (p. 4) and "considers the difference of the individual and the disrespect of the majority" (p. 5). The analysis of those who subscribe to this terminology points to a discriminatory, oppressive, and disrespectful majority. However, this thinking seems to remain superficial. In this regard, the Department of Special Education of the Pedagogical Institute of Caracas (2012) notes that the term:

> does not go beyond the term *people with disabilities*, as it maintains the idea of normality as the qualifying parameter, and doesn't go beyong the medical view. It must be emphasized that there within this medical representation is an ideal of organic and cognitive functioning of human beings which is not resolved with this new concept. (Departmento de Educación Especial, 2012, p. 3, emphasis added)

Furthermore it warns that:

> The new currency only makes explicit that the term "disability" does not seem to be adequate. It neither solves the educational problems present in these groups nor does it generate increased participation. In short, it doesn't matter what we name the "other," but instead, how we understand *difference,* difference that is inherent in human beings and should be considered from an ethical position. (Departmento de Educación Especial, 2012, p. 3)

Regarding changes in organizational structure, there are a number of such changes. However, we will refer only to those most directly related to services for Deaf people. The first of these follows:

> The services attached to special education, such as: Equipos de Integración Social (Teams for Social Integration), Centros de Desarrollo Infantil (Child Development Centers) and Centros de Rehabilitación del Lenguaje (Centers for Language Rehabilitation) (CRL) will be redirected to elementary schools where students with "functional diversity" are integrated. (Ministerio del Poder Popular para la Educación, 2012, p. 1)

There was no explanation given for what was meant by "redirecting" or clarification of what would happen to the functions traditionally fulfilled by these services. Principally, the future of the Child Development Centers (CDI) was in jeopardy because early prevention and comprehensive care, important guiding philosophical principles of special education were overlooked.

The Child Development Centers (CDI) were designed to provide an appropriate environment for acquisition of LSV in close liaison with preschool classrooms in schools for the Deaf. Early acquisition of LSV for the majority of Deaf children who were from hearing families was imperative and central to bicultural bilingual deaf education. Since the beginning of bilingual bicultural education in 1985, many CDI centers found it challenging to provide the necessary linguistic context and to work directly with schools for the Deaf.

All decisions shaping the new organizational structure of special education were flawed. But perhaps the most serious was the closure of many schools for the Deaf in the country and the resulting inclusion (mainstreaming) of Deaf students in regular primary and secondary education. The argument made to support this move was for the sake of "inclusion." However, inclusion neuters the integral development of the Deaf child and linguistically and culturally annihilates these Deaf children and adolescents. The result is to exclude, marginalize, and ignore.

Fortunately, a change in the leadership in the Ministry in early 2014 stopped these changes and undertook a new effort, the *Consulta Nacional por la Calidad Educativa* (National Consultation for Educational Quality). Thus, 2014 is the beginning of the final period to be discussed, one we call *Complex Challenges: 2014 to the Future.*

Legal Platform

Against the background just described, we found contradictions when reviewing the legal context of the same period, from 1997 to January 2014. The Constitution of the Bolivarian Republic of Venezuela 1999 acknowledges the rights of Deaf people in the country, particularly sociolinguistic and educational rights. New legal instruments are enshrined in the new Constitution. We will present a chronological account of the most important legal instruments in support of bilingual and bicultural deaf education. The Table 1 illustrates these laws and their implications for the rights of Deaf people in Venezuela.

Bicultural Bilingual Training of Teachers of Deaf Students and Related Professionals

Luque and Pérez (2012) report that the impact of PAINS, among other things, resulted in changes in teacher training in the Hearing Impaired Program at the Universidad Pedagógica Experimental Libertador/Instituto Pedagógico de Caracas (Pedagogical Institute of Caracas/Experimental Pedagogical University Libertador) (IPC-UPEL). Such changes were possible due to the process of curricular innovation carried out in this case study. This process, completed in 1996, resulted in new curricula.

The National Curriculum Committee of IPC-UPEL established guidelines for the process to ensure consistency of approach in all specializations offered. Such guidelines included four components of training: (a) general, (b) teaching, (c) specialization, and (d) professional practice. Only the specific programs could make changes to the specialization component, with the exception of those assigned to the Department of Special Education, which could also modify the contents of professional practice, as historically they had been directly responsible for the administration of this area.

Within this context, the changes to the Hearing Impaired Program were: (a) theoretical foundations, (b) content of programs of coursework and professional practices, and (c) the substitution of other courses. It was necessary to continue special education and neuroanatomy courses as they formed a common thread with the other programs in the Department of Special Education. Changes made included:

- establishing a socio-anthropological concept of Deafness as part of the fundamental theoretical framework;
- designing teacher training within the context of bicultural bilingual education;
- changing programs and subjects to respond to the new knowledge matrix; and
- replacing courses of therapeutic nature by others with a new vision, such as:
- teaching LSV as a second language. (It was only possible to create 3 levels); and
- utilizing a pedagogical approach to the language of Deaf children based on a nativist and psycho-social-linguistic conception.

These modifications were a qualitative leap, but they did not represent curricular transformation and were likely insufficient for producing bicultural bilingual teachers fluent in LSV.

The professors in the Hearing Impaired Program designed a specialization in Sociocultural Studies in Deafness, which opened in 2009. The program aimed to deepen the social and cultural knowledge of the Deaf population in order to promote the quality of life of the Deaf community within innovative educational praxis.

PARTICIPATION OF THE DEAF COMMUNITY

During this period, in a progressive manner, Deaf Venezuelan leaders, and groups they led, built greater awareness of themselves as people whose sociolinguistic difference is demonstrated through LSV and local Deaf culture. This awareness led to actions claiming linguistic and cultural rights.

Over the years, these claims for rights have been intensified, particularly in education. Defending the core principal of bilingual bicultural education, LSV as a first language, and Spanish as a second language allowed for more radical proposals with a strong community identity.

We believe that changes in special education that violated the educational rights of Deaf children at unacceptable levels triggered radical statements. One example is found in the November 2012 presentation *¿Reflexiones sobre la Educación del sordo? Propuestas sordas* (Thoughts on the Education of the Deaf? Deaf proposals) by Yuliana Carreño Pérez, coordinator of the *Comisión de Educación de la Federación Venezolana de Sordos* (Education Commission of the Venezuelan Federation of the Deaf; FEVEN-SOR). In that speech, occurring 11 months into changes in special education, the Deaf community demanded that education should respond to what had already been established in Venezuelan law. To conform with existing laws, key elements of deaf education must include: (a) early intervention to ensure the acquisition of LSV, (b) establishment of LSV linguistic environments, (c) adaptation of school curricula to include subjects that address the study of LSV, written Spanish, and Deaf culture, (d) bilingual growth, (e) linking families, schools, and the Deaf community, (f) promoting families learning LSV and Deaf culture, (g) and assuring well-prepared teachers and bilingual bicultural directors. However the most radical proposal was put forward in the closing statement which called for: "intercultural bilingual education separate from the Directorate of Special Education, as we are not special, nor have disabilities. We are Deaf, members of a linguistic and cultural minority,users of Venezuelan Sign Language" (Pérez, 2012).

Expectations: From 2014 to the Present

Education Policies Emanating from the Governing Body

In early 2014, the new administration at the MPPE undertook the *Consulta Nacional por la Calidad Educativa* (National Consultation for Quality Education,) unprecedented in the country, whose objective was:

> To provide guidelines for the formulation of the curriculum, for the design of national education policies and to transform the education system towards a model of more efficient, transparent, committed and participatory development in harmony with the objectives and the constitutional value of institutional management education. (Ministerio del Poder Popular para la Educación, 2015)

The process was conducted over five months and involved the participation of over seven million people. The results mandated the formulation of public policies at all levels and kinds of education, expressed in 10 major guidelines:

1. ensuring quality education for everyone
2. developing a pedagogy of love, example, and curiosity
3. strengthening the role of teachers as key players in the quality of education
4. promoting a school climate characterized by harmony
5. ensuring a system of student safety
6. ensuring a close relationship between families, school, and community
7. developing a national integrated and updated curriculum
8. ensuring modest, welcoming, and safe school buildings
9. developing a system for evaluating educational quality
10. reconfiguring the organization and operation of MPPE

In this context, the question of the structure of special education was also addressed. A process, unprecedented in the country, was developed from workshops in the 24 states of the country with the participation of over 11,000 people. Workshops were conducted within four sectors: (a) students, (b) families, (c) teachers, and (d) co-responsible agents. In all 24 states, Deaf students, Deaf adults, and Deaf associations participated, and LSV interpreters were provided.

The MPPE (2015) brochure *Opiniones y miradas de la educación especial* (Opinions and Views of Special Education) highlighted aspects related to:

(a) the need for the continuation of specific schools for populations with special educational needs or disabilities,

(b) the gradual recovery of services necessary for quality care of students with special educational needs,

(c) a review of congruence between training and staff functions,

(d) provision of educational materials and adaptive technologies, such as the development of educational content and learning materials in sign language for Deaf students,

(e) reestablishment of interdisciplinary teams,

(f) attention to employment needs of the adult population,

(g) evaluation, renewal, and adaptation of the infrastructure,

(h) establishment of networks with the families,

(i) selection and development of consistent pedagogical processes,

(j) resume pedagogical meetings,

(k) establish measures to ensure the right to education of students with special educational needs and their retention in the education system,

(l) incorporate special education staff in the Sistema Nacional de Investigación y Formación Permanente del Magisterio (National System of Research and Continuing Education of Teachers),

(m) interdisciplinary theoretical and methodological procedures,

(n) reactivation of the Consejos Técnicos de Áreas (Technical Consultants),

(o) the creation of a training plan that allows the strengthening of the school–family–community triad,

(p) promoting a culture of respect and tolerance towards people with special educational needs or disabilities,

(q) an improved dietary program to meet the nutritional requirements of the population according to the type of disability,

(r) development of a policy of continuing training to prepare regular education teachers for the integration of special needs students,

(s) the establishment of a training and information policy for all print and audiovisual media, public and private, that promotes respect for and dignity of people with disabiities, and

(t) the allocation of school transportation for every child or person in a wheelchair in each municipality and parish.

Professor Moraima Cazola, current General Director of Special Education explained in an interview (Personal communication, August 2015) that this national discussion generated other democratic review processes, among which was the updating of the conceptualizations and policies in all areas and support programs related to special education. Repeatedly, she emphasized attention to the educational needs of Deaf students, guaranteeing bicultural bilingual education. These reassurances altered our uncertainties into positive hopes.

Legal Platform

As previously noted, until 2014, the laws guaranteeing the educational and linguistic rights of Deaf people in the country remained unchanged. Currently, the *Ley para Personas con Discapacidad* (Law for Persons with Disabilities) is undergoing modification through democratic participation of stakeholders. The expectation is that changes in relation to Deaf people will lead to a deepening of these guaranteed rights.

Bilingual Bicultural Training

There have been three major efforts in the area of bilingual bicultural training for teachers of Deaf students and other professionals. The first is a new curriculum that the Programa de Deficiencias Auditivas (Hearing Impaired Program) at IPC-UPEL expects to complete for teacher training for deaf education by the end of 2015. It is designed to ensure the production of bicultural bilingual teachers.

The second effort is undertaken by the Universidad Politécnica Territorial del Estado Mérida (UPTM) Kléber Ramírez (Territorial State Polytechnic University Merida Kleber Ramirez), created in April 2012. UPTM's social mission is training those closely connected with various communities with a view of eradicating all forms of discrimination. In April 2014, this institution began the Estudios Abiertos (Open Studies) Program. This program includes various areas, including Pedagogías Alternativas (Alternative Pedagogies), which aims to bring innovative educational processes to excluded populations. This non-traditional context has been very important in providing undergraduate and graduate university education in various communities across the country, including the Deaf community and LSV interpreters.

There are 422 Deaf students enrolled. To date, five Deaf students have graduated in Caracas and six in Barinas. Before the Open Studies Program started, UPTM Kleber Ramirez did not provide educational opportunities for the Deaf community. There were some Deaf individuals who attended classes (made up of hearing students) with LSV interpreters.

The Open Studies Program has been a breakthrough for LSV interpreters, particularly those with greater skills and competencies. For the first time in the country, interpreting professionals have the possibility of university training. UPTM Kleber Ramirez currently has 365 of these students enrolled and two have graduated.

Related to the third effort, the Ministerio del Poder Popular para Educación Universitaria Ciencia y Tecnología (Ministry of Popular Power for Higher Education Science and Technology; MPPEUCT) has set up discussion groups for universities training special education teachers in order to reach important consensus on the subject. It is expected that IPC-UPEL to take the lead in guiding the efforts related to training teachers of Deaf students.

Participation of the Deaf Community

The radical pronouncement of Deaf people cited earlier has remained as a guiding principle and draws on the expression of popular power by Deaf people to defend their right of participation, a right our Constitution gives every citizen. The Deaf community demonstrates growing awareness of their rights and demands them vehemently.

Challenges in the Complexity: From 2015 to the Future

The analysis in this chapter presented is not intended to be exhaustive. There are still areas we haven't addressed. However, reflection on the distance traveled seems useful because it explains the complexity that we face in addressing bicultural bilingual deaf education. Complexity is inherent in every educational act. Additionally, our analysis provides objective data that highlight the need to look across categories to detect paradoxes and obstacles. This will deepen the strengths and overcome the weaknesses found in both the implementation and the achievement of the goals of bicultural bilingual deaf education in the country.

From our perspective, the critical element is participation of Deaf people, as this community is essential to lead these efforts. The empowerment of the Deaf community is evident in the global movement that advocates a socio-anthropological conception of Deafness and requires an emancipating education. Bilingual bicultural deaf education, in the context of interculturalism, creates a bridge of harmony between various groups, including Deaf people and hearing people. Opting for this type of education includes claiming the right to: (a) acquire the local sign language and Deaf culture as early as possible, in the school context, (b) access all curriculum, via sign language, (c) learn the written language (in this case Spanish), and (d) be assured of having effective teachers fluent in LSV and knowledgeable of Deaf culture.

Deaf leadership through the principle of *Participation of Deaf people* is of unquestioned legitimacy, as they are the protagonists of the cause they defend. Furthermore, our analysis demonstrated that the social, linguistic, and educational rights of the Deaf community are supported and recognized in Venezuelan law. So it follows that national educational policies and training of teachers and other professionals must also align with these legal and ethical mandates.

In the case of education policies, there should be recognition of the significance of the national consultation undertaken by the Ministry of Popular Power for Education. For the first time, teachers, students, and Deaf leaders were consulted to create a new conceptualization and policy in the area of Deafness in our country. Additionally, the process of triangulation of the information collected should be legally guaranteed. The socio-anthropological conception of Deafness must be emphasized in the new document, and important ideas in the original PAINS document should be reclaimed, as they were the first to generate ideas regarding bicultural bilingual deaf education in the country. These include the proposals for the creation of linguistic environments in sign language, as spaces that fostered the development of language in Deaf students, in authentic contexts.

Training of teachers and related professionals requires finalizing the new curriculum, from IPC-UPEL, in the training of bilingual bicultural teachers for Deaf students, and the new specialty LSV–Spanish interpreters. IPC-UPEL, supported by the demands of the Deaf community, must offer solutions to meet the demands of the entire country, not just the capital city, by means of new technological options for distance education.

We stand as defenders of the leadership that the Deaf community must assume as the foundation of this urgent process to move towards a true bicultural bilingual education. It is Deaf people, in this national context that allows their participation, who will take charge of their education. This is the greatest challenge for the future and to which we pledge ourselves in solidarity with the ongoing work.

References

Constitución de la República Bolivariana de Venezuela. (1999, March). Gaceta Oficial 5453.

Departamento de Educación Especial. (2012, May). *Posición del Departamento de Educación Especial sobre la Transformación de la Modalidad de Educación Especial propuesta por el Ministerio Poder Popular para la Educación* [Position of the Department of Special Education Transformation Mode of Special Education proposed by the People's Power Ministry for Education]. Presentation at Educación Especial hoy: Retos desde una mirada colectiva. Instituto Pedagógico de Caracas. Venezuela.

Hoffman, M. (1965). *La educación del niño sordo en Venezuela* [Bilingual deaf education: School stage. Learning Paths]. Ministerio de Educación. Dirección de Educación Primaria y Normal. Caracas, Venezuela.

Instituto Nacional para Sordos. (INSOR, 2006). *Educación bilingüe para sordos: Etapa escolar. Orientaciones pedagógica*s [Bilingual education for the deaf: School stage. Pedagogical orientations]. Bogota, Colombia: Ministerio de Educación Nacional.

Ley Orgánica de Educación. (2009, Agosto). Gaceta Oficial de la República Bolivariana de Venezuela, número 5.929 (Extraordinaria).

Ley para las Personas con Discapacidad [Law for people with disabilities]. (2007, Jan. 2005). Gaceta Oficial de la República Bolivariana de Venezuela, 38, 598.

Luque, B., & Pérez, Y. (2011). La historia de la educación del Sordo en Venezuela [The history of deaf education in Venezuela]. In G. Luque (Ed.), *Venezuela medio siglo de historia educativa 1951–2001* (pp. 289–314). Caracas, Venezuela: Ministerio del Poder Popular para la Educación Universitaria.

Ministerio de Educación. (1997a). *Paradigmas que orientan la política de la modalidad de educación especial en Venezuela* [Paradigms that orient the policies of the modality of special education in Venezuela]. Caracas, Venezuela.

Ministerio de Educación. (1997b). *Conceptualización y política de la atención integral del deficiente auditivo en Venezuela.* [Conceptualization and policies for integral attention to hearing loss in Venezuela]. Caracas, Venezuela.

Ministerio del Poder Popular para la Educación. (noviembre de 2011). *Transformación de la modalidad de educación especial en el marco de una Educación sin Barreras.* [Transformation of the modality of special education in the context of Education without Barriers]. Caracus, Venezuela.

Ministerio del Poder Popular para la Educación. (2012). *Lineamientos para la transformación de la modalidad de educación especial en el marco de una Educación sin Barreras.* [Guidelines for the transformation of the modality of special education in the context of Education without Barriers]. Caracus, Venezuela.

Ministerio del Poder Popular para la Educación. (2015). *Opiniones y miradas desde la educación especial* [Opinions and Views of Special Education]. Caracus, Venezuela: Ministerio del Poder Popular para la Educación.

Morales, A. M. (2008). *La comunidad sorda de Caracas: una narrativa sobre su mundo.* [The Deaf community of Caracus: A narrative of their world]. Doctoral Thesis, Universidad Pedagógica Experimental Libertador, Instituto Pedagógico de Caracas. Caracus, Venezuela.

Morales, A., & Pérez Y. (2010). *La educación del sordo en Venezuela: Una visión critica* [Education of the Deaf in Venezuela: A critical vision]. Retrieved from http://www .cultura-sorda.eu/resources/Morales-y- Pérez -La_educacion_del_sordo_Venezuela_ 2010.pdf

Oviedo, A. (2003). La comunidad sorda venezolana y su lengua de señas [The Venezuelan Deaf community and its sign language]. *Venezuela. Editorial Edumedia.* Retrieved from http://www.cultura-sorda.eu

Pérez, C., & Sánchez, C. (n.d.). *La propuesta de atención integral del niño sordo: el modelo bilingüe en Venezuela* [The proposal for integrated attention to the Deaf child: The bilingual model in Venezuela]. Caracas, Venezuela: Ministerio de Educación.

Pérez, Y. (2006, September). *La educación del sordo en Venezuela: hacia una visión de la situación en Latinoamérica* [Deaf education in Venezuela: Towards a vision of the situation in Latin America]. Presentation at: Anais do Congreso. Surdez: familia, linguagem, educação. INES. Brazil.

Pérez, Y. (2008). *Marcadores en conversaciones en Lengua de Señas Venezolana entre Sordos* [Markers in conversations among the Deaf in Venezuelan Sign Language]. Doctoral Thesis. Universidad de los Andes. Mérida, Venezuela.

Romañach, J., & Lobato, M. (2005). Diversidad funcional, nuevo término para la lucha por la dignidad en la diversidad del ser humano [Functional diversity, new term for the struggle for dignity in diversity of human beings]. *Foro de vida independiente, 8,* pp. 1–8. Retrieved from http://www.atelfar.com/images/Diversidad_funcional.pdf

Sánchez, C. (2010). *Las escuelas de sordos entre la espada y la pared* [Las escuelas de sordos entre la espada y la pared]. Retrieved from http://www.cultura-sorda.eu/

Skliar, C., Massone, M., & Veinberg, S. (1995). *El acceso de los niños sordos al bilingüismo y al biculturalismo* [The acccss of Dcaf childrcn to bilingualism and biculturalism]. Retrieved from http://www.cultura-sorda.eu/resources/Skliar_Massone_Veinberg_acceso_ninos_sordos_al_bilinguismo_1995.pdf

13

Bilingual Education: Repeated Deaf Resistance to the Imperatives of the Brazilian Government

Gladis Perlin and Patrícia Luiza Ferreira Rezende

In Brazil, many researchers develop studies in different theoretical fields, such as Cultural Studies, Linguistic Studies, Foucauldian Studies, and Deaf Studies. Such studies break the previously established paradigms that consider the Deaf individual as being disabled or incapable.

Such cultural and linguistic directions are already acknowledged and ensured by legal mechanisms in our country as well as international conventions. Nonetheless, the government and other social powers remain ambivalent by not granting Deaf linguistic policies; instead, they propose egalitarian, inclusive education policies.

We seek to question the governmental policies surrounding Deaf people and present the driving forces behind the resistance and presence of the Deaf community in negotiating spaces. At the request of the organizers of this book, we sought to write this chapter on the policies necessary for our survival. Thus, the proposed question is: why does the Brazilian government not accept our demands for change in policies regarding cultural and linguistic difference of Deaf people? This chapter will, for the most part, consist of citations of documents given to the government and of events in the negotiating spaces. It also presents research data and stories of resistance by Deaf leaders. Finally, we list some of the victories against these policies achieved by our leaders. Facing these governmental policies, FENEIS, the Federação Nacional de Educação e Integração dos Surdos (National Federation of Deaf Education and Integration, the institute that represents Deaf people in Brazil and is affiliated with the World Federation of the Deaf) organized a security request and created negotiating spaces with the government and the parliament, drawing attention to human rights issues and the political needs of Deaf people. There were demonstrations and great resistance in the negotiating spaces. Lastly, we hope that this chapter will act as a space where new, strong consciences arise, strengthening the struggle of the Deaf cause for human rights and against policies based on the conception of a single and universal identity.

Productivity in Research regarding Deaf People

Research in Deaf Studies has grown in importance within Brazilian universities. Here we limit ourselves to cultural, postcolonial, Foucauldian, post-structuralist studies. These studies differ from, but intermediate and complement, one another. Thus, they discourse over cultural and linguistic difference, policies in the negotiating spaces, and the productive and constructive character of Deaf people. In this theoretical context, it is possible to rewrite and understand the needs for policies regarding development and bilingual education, among others. This conceptualization is based on Foucault (2006) and sees Deaf people as a fragmented individual, devoid of a fixed, essential, or permanent identity.

These studies go against the concept of Deaf people as disabled, as defined by the Organization of American States (OAS): "a physical, mental, or sensory impairment, whether permanent or temporary, that limits the capacity to perform one or more essential activities of daily life" (Declaration of Guatemala, 1999, p. 3). We reject the view that regards Deaf people as disabled, because it constitutes a reason for controversy. This happens because it creates contradictory practices regarding Deaf people, which in turn originates erroneous governmental policies. We defend that there must be a difference and a shift in the language used to refer to Deaf subjects because "history does not cease to teach us—speech is not simply that which translates struggles or systems of domination, but that for which one fights, the very power one wishes to hold" (Foucault, 2008, pp. 9–10).

Research in Deaf Studies points to a new solution in which sign language is the sovereign language of Deaf people, deaf education is bilingual, and Portuguese is taught in the written modality, as their second language. Dallan explains the dream of Deaf teachers:

> They show their concern with the learning of their Deaf students, they show an intention to provide quality education so that Deaf children may have better educational opportunities. (2013, p. 133)

One of the most significant studies in defense of the use of sign language and bilingual deaf education was developed by Fernando Capovilla, a professor at the University of São Paulo, funded by the government. This wide-reaching study was conducted in the five regions of Brazil (north, northeast, midwest, southeast, and south) and represents one of the largest amounts of data on the linguistic and scholarly development of Brazilian Deaf students. Between 2001 and 2011, the study, named *Programa de Avaliação Nacional do Desenvolvimento da Linguagem do Surdo Brasileiro* (Pandesb, National Program of Evaluation of Language Development of the Brazilian Deaf), examined 9,200 Brazilian Deaf students from first grade to higher education.

Each student was evaluated during a total of 26 hours of testing in different competences, such as alphabetical and lip reading, reading comprehension, writing vocabulary, orthography, Brazilian Sign Language (Libras) and Portuguese vocabulary, and working memory, among others. Capovilla concludes:

> *Deaf students learn more and much better in bilingual schools* (special schools that teach in Libras and Portuguese) than in monolingual schools (common schools that teach in Portuguese only). . . . [C]ompetences such as word decoding and recognition, reading comprehension, Libras vocabulary, among others, *were significantly superior in bilingual schools than in common schools.* (2011, pp. 86–87, emphasis added)

Studies like this provide scientific support for our demands for policies that tend to the linguistic and educational needs of Deaf people.

Legislative Landmarks regarding Linguistic Rights

Due to the imperatives of the government, FENEIS has, across several meetings with the government, fought to create a Work Group within the Ministry of Education. This Work Group, of which the two authors were members, aimed to give FENEIS a larger representation in the discussions regarding goals and recommendations when it came to creating linguistic policies for bilingual education. Appointed by the Decrees 1060/2013 and 91/2013, the Work Group produced a document titled "Final Report of Linguistic Policy—Bilingual Education—Brazilian Sign Language and Portuguese Language."

The report cites from other documents, including Article 24 of the Universal Declaration of Linguistic Rights, promoted by UNESCO in Barcelona in 1996. Linguistic rights, one of the most notable rights, do not refer only to the uses of Deaf people.

> All language communities have the right to decide to what extent their language is to be present, as a vehicular language and as an object of study, at all levels of education within their territory: preschool, primary, secondary, technical and vocational, university, and adult education. (UNESCO, 1996)

The report also refers to Decree 7387 of 2010, which allowed the government to do the first national inventory of Brazilian languages. The government then committed to realize some measures:

> Art. 2 The language on this inventory shall be relevant for the memory, the history and the identity of the groups that compose the Brazilian society.

Art. 3 Any language included in the National Inventory of Linguistic Diversity shall receive the title of "Brazilian Cultural Reference," issued by the Ministry of Culture.

Art. 4 The National Inventory of Linguistic Diversity shall map, characterize and diagnose the different situations related to linguistic plurality in Brazil, categorizing this data in a specialized form. (BRASIL, Decree 7387/2010)

Additionally, the National Institute of Historical and Artistic Heritage of the Ministry of Culture cites indigenous languages, regional varieties of the Portuguese language, immigration languages, language of the African-Brazilian community, Libras, and creole languages as languages of the National Inventory. Thus, it is the responsibility of the Deaf community to preserve their language, remembering their right to schools, libraries, and bilingual teachers and interpreters.

In the case of Deaf people as a community of users of sign language, Article 24 of the Convention on the Rights of Persons with Disability establishes:

Facilitating the learning of sign language and the promotion of the linguistic identity of the Deaf community; and

Ensuring that the education of persons, and in particular children, who are blind, Deaf or Deafblind, is delivered in the most appropriate languages and modes and means of communication for the individual, and in environments which maximize academic and social development.

And Article 30, paragraph 4:

Persons with disabilities shall be entitled, on an equal basis with others, to recognition and support of their specific cultural and linguistic identity, including sign languages and Deaf culture.

The Work Group refers then to a series of legal achievements, which support our recurring struggles for linguistic policies and bilingual education. The Law 10436/2002 regulated by Decree 5626/2005 establishes the right for Deaf individuals and their family to choose their modality of schooling, the right to sign languages, the right to a school with bilingual professors, and the right to quality education that considers cultural difference. These achievements range from elementary to higher education. It is the responsibility of universities to introduce a Libras discipline in their courses, as well as supporting the development of bilingual educators for Basic Education and interpreters and translators.

Therefore, as Deaf people, we have the legal right to decide how our language should be included in every level of education, and these documents form the basis in which the government finds support to provide linguistic and educational policies for all the different Brazilian peoples. This is why we are in constant struggle in the negotiating spaces.

Matters of Our Bilingual Education

Education in Brazil, as proposed by the Ministry of Education, is inclusive education. Deaf students must be in regular classes and learn alongside so-called normal students. The Deaf community stands with a perspective of respect to the cultural and linguistic identity, as assured by the Declarations of Human Rights.

According to Thompson, cultural studies motivate educational programs:

> Educational programs such as those of Cultural Studies and media studies may help educators and educational institutions to develop an awareness of different motivations and values, as well as providing research data that evaluate the effects of their policies and practices. (2005, p. 35)

The space of bilingual education is understood as the space that allows for the interaction between Deaf individuals, which is essential to the constitution of our subjectivities. If this process does not occur at school, it will happen during contact with other Deaf individuals outside school, as with many of us. This aspect is related to the perception of our difference; hence, we resist the imperatives of the government, why it is far from the ways we experience our otherness? The International Disability Alliance (IDA) recommends that:

> Deaf children need first to be included by their most appropriate language and their culture before they could be included in different areas of life at later stages, for instance in secondary and tertiary education as well as working life. Peer support is needed. (IDA,[1] 2011)

In the Report on Linguistic Policy of Bilingual Education the Work Group defines bilingual education as follows:

> Bilingual education for the Deaf involves the creation of linguistic environments for the acquisition by Deaf children of Libras as a first language (L1), in the expected linguistic development age, similar to hearing children, and the acquisition of Portuguese as a second language (L2). Bilingual Education

---

1. Promulgated in Brazil as a Constitutional Amendment by the Decree 6.949/2009 (based on Legislative Decree 186 on July 9, 2008, in accordance to § 3 of art. 5 of the Federal Constitution).

is done regularly in Libras, encompassing all languages in its curriculum and is not part of specialized educational assistance. The goal is to guarantee the acquisition and learning of the languages involved as a necessary condition of education for the Deaf individual, constituting his or her linguistic and cultural identity in Libras and leading to the conclusion of basic educational in parity with hearing and Portuguese-speaking children. (BRASIL, 2014, p. 6)

In this document, bilingual education in Libras–Portuguese is understood as the schooling that respects the condition of the Deaf individual and his visual experience as formative of a unique culture, without, however, considering the scholarly acquisition of Portuguese unnecessary. This definition demands that linguistic policy is designed in such a way that defines that two languages will be present throughout schooling, thereby allowing legitimacy and prestige to Libras as a curricular language and as a formative language for the Deaf individual (Brasil, 2014).

The members of this Work Group emphasize that bilingual education must take place since birth, with a view of providing guidance for the families of Deaf individuals to look for sign language education from the first months of life onwards. This guidance also applies to subsequent stages of education, from elementary to higher.

Considering the terms of Article 24 of the Convention on the Rights of Persons with Disability and the right guaranteed to the Deaf, FENEIS (2013) defines bilingual schools as follows:

Bilingual schools are those where the language of instruction is Brazilian Sign Language and Portuguese is taught as a second language, after the acquisition of the first language; these schools are installed in their own architectural spaces and in them bilingual teachers must work, without interpreters in the teacher-student relationship and without the use of signed Portuguese.

Bilingual schools for the Deaf must provide full-time education. Municipalities that are not able to provide bilingual schools for Deaf students must guarantee bilingual education in bilingual classes at regular schools.

Deaf Resistance in the Negotiating Spaces

In the last 25 years we have been assaulted by a form of imperative knowledge with which we, as a Deaf people, continuously negotiate for policies of linguistic identity and bilingual education. The struggle of countless Deaf leaders takes place both in the negotiating spaces as well as behind the scenes.

Here we mention the many negotiating spaces that have arisen and the fierce clashes that have been fought against the imperative proposals of a single language and an inclusive school in a way that holds Deaf individuals as inferior and in need of correction, as a result of the supremacy of the hearing and the sovereignty of Portuguese holding sign language as an inferior, incapacitating language.

When working on our document "The education that we the Deaf want," proposed since 1999, we registered our demands, that is, our values, linguistic and cultural views. The document was originated by a group of leaders from the southern Brazilian state of Rio Grande do Sul who led the Deaf community to demand proposals for linguistic, cultural, and identity-related policies. The two different discursive constructions regarding Deaf people were already confronted in this document. On the one hand, the Deaf individual as dependent on hearing people due to his disability, in need of a cure to be found in medicine and special education; on the other, the Deaf individual as a cultural subject, a participant in power relations, carrying his own culture and sign language. The document deals with themes such as linguistic identity, educational practices, Deaf policies, identity and culture, and professional Deaf development. It provides important clues by showing paths that are always potentially present as a way to tell the Deaf story, to rewrite our culture: language, identity, and pedagogy.

Before requesting the inclusion of bilingual education to the Plano Nacional de Educação (National Education Plan), which at the time was being examined by the National Conference of Education (CONAE, 2010), we had a long record of struggles in the negotiating spaces, since it was first written until it was sent to the National Congress (the Brazilian parliament) and approved by the president of the Republic. The Deaf delegates present at CONAE 2010 presented the summary: "Assurance to the Deaf and their families of their right to choose the schooling modality most appropriate to the full linguistic, cognitive, emotional, psychic, social and cultural development of Deaf children, youth and adults by ensuring their access to bilingual education in Brazilian Sign Language and Portuguese" (Report by the Deaf delegates).

However, what the delegates found was that the team of what was then the Secretary of Special Education (SEESP/MEC[2]) handed to the hearing delegates of CONAE a pamphlet explaining that they rejected the Deaf amendment delegated under the claim that it "promotes the organization of segregated schools based on differentiation, contrary to the concepts of inclusive education."

This daring act of flagrant disregard for the demands of Deaf people revolted the leaders of the movement. Deaf actor and researcher Cláudio Mourão wrote:

> We are saddened to see our proposals rejected, to go home defeated, as we try to come to grips with the "discrimination" we suffered. There is a feeling of pain, or sorrow inside me, as I feel like a slave with my hands tied, unable to "speak."

---

2. SEESP/MEC had been merged into SECADI/MEC, Department of Continuing Education, Literacy, Diversity, and Indusion, the Ministry of Education.

They have condemned the future of Deaf children. We are reliving the same pain caused by the Milan Conference; CONAE 2010 in Brasília and especially the leaders of the Ministry of Education are leaving their mark on Deaf history, to be remembered by those alive today and those whose will speak in Brazil and all over the world about a minority crushed by audism. (2010, p.11)

Afterwards, an issue of *FENEIS* Magazine reported on the resistance in the negotiating spaces:

The opinion of the Deaf who are users of sign language is that, in the conference, majority vote did not lead to a democratic outcome. Of the eleven proposals defended by the representatives of the Deaf community, only three were approved. . . . In general, these proposals related to the continuity and creation of bilingual schools for the Deaf. According to delegate Neivaldo Zovico, there was strong lobbying by parties favorable to inclusive education, a position also held by the government. The conference was divided in six subthemes, and proposals regarding the Deaf were under number six: "Social justice, education and work: inclusion, diversity and equality." "During the internal discussion phase we agreed that different groups would vote in favor of proposals made by other groups—blacks, quilombolas, the Landless Movement, among others. We agreed that no one would understand the reality of a group better than that group," explains the delegate, who is also a professor. At the time of voting, seven proposals were completely rejected, three were approved at 50% and one obtained 30%. Neivaldo states that leaders from the government manipulated the group. "After we left the plenary meeting, the participants of group six were called, behind our backs, to a meeting with representatives from the Federal Governmental and NGOs associated with the Ministry of Education. They convinced them to vote against the proposals of the Deaf community, claiming our ideas were segregationist. The only movements that supported us until the end were the Brazilian Lesbian League (LBL) and Education in the Countryside (Educação do Campo)," says Neivaldo. (Lucas, 2010, pp. 22–23)

After the proposal of the Deaf delegates present at CONAE 2010 was rejected, FENEIS takes over the negotiating spaces. The leaders at FENEIS understand that negotiating spaces regarding education are the most difficult, as put by Lane: "Education is the battlefield where linguistic minorities win or lose their rights" (1992, p. 103). After this point, there was an increase in awareness within the Deaf community and the use of social media and press, such as the headlines of *FENEIS* Magazine: "What is the best school for Deaf children?" "Is there such as thing as Deaf culture?" "Are bilingual schools segregationist?" In this issue, researchers grapple with these questions and conclude that bilingual education is the best for Deaf people.

FIGURE 1: Cover of *FENEIS* Magazine, issue 41,
September to November 2010.

Nonetheless, the Ministry of Culture pushes forward and presents the proposal of the National Plan of Education to the National Congress on November 15, 2010. This includes a conceptual error regarding bilingual deaf education. It is this:

> To continue and deepen the national accessibility program in public school to include architectural adaptations, availability of accessible transportation, availability of accessible didactic material and assistive technology resources, and *availability of bilingual education in Portuguese and Brazilian Sign Language— Libras.* (BRASIL, MEC, 2010, emphasis added).

Another revolting event took place after CONAE 2010. On March 17, 2011, the Director of Special Education Policies, Martinha Claret, visited the Instituto Nacional de Educação de Surdos (INES,[3] National Institute of Deaf Education), to inform the Board of Directors—before students, professors, and parents—that the Institute would be closed by the end of 2011 and that Deaf students would be moved to regular schools. This revolting news sparked a series of reactions. A video[4] by Deaf leader Nelson Pimenta, today a professor and researcher at INES, shows his reaction to the closure of the Institute by the Ministry of Education, translated below.[5]

> Outrageous! OUTRAGEOUS! O-U-T-R-A-G-E-O-U-S! Truly outrageous. What? The INES will close?! Hold on a minute. I can't stand this. I can't. No, please! Please, I beg you. For all that is most sacred. Stop it! Wake up! Spread the word. NO to closing the INES. I want you the Deaf to think hard about this. Look at it, defend the Deaf! The Deaf will cease to interact with other Deaf in sign language, they will lose their culture, their identity. And so we can be oppressed by the hearing inclusive mentality? NO! Open your eyes! Please! I ask you: do not let this brutality happen. The Deaf will lose their culture. I'm crying on the inside, my heart is aching. Please! We the Deaf must discuss this. The Ministry of Education cannot change the INES. This is the INES! We cannot take this lying down. Stand up! Fight! I'm counting on you and stay alert. (2011)

The parallels between the Milan Conference and the closure of the INES are illustrated in Figure 2.

FENEIS fought the closing of the school. It took a great deal of negotiation with government representatives to keep INES open.

At one point, then Minister of Education Aloízio Mercadante issued a press release denying that goal 4 of the National Plan of Education had been approved. The apprehension this news caused led Deaf PhDs to write an open letter to the Ministry of Education, the most prominent parts of which follow:

> We, the Deaf, militants for the causes of our Deaf compatriots, appeal to Your Excellency for the right of choice of education that best suits the Brazilian Deaf who have Libras as a first language. We agree that "Brazil must have

---

3. INES is the first school for the Deaf in Brazil, built 150 years ago during the Empire. It is a linguistic cornerstone for the Deaf people, part of our cultural heritage. It currently provides classes from elementary to higher education. It is equipped to be a national reference in education for the Deaf. Some of its teachers are leading bilingual educators. INES is a landmark for the consolidation of theories of policies related to linguistics and bilingual education, as well as for the achievement of new material, political, social, and legislative spaces.
4. https://www.youtube.com/watch?v=yl6cfWmUrtU
5. Translation of Libras to Portuguese was realized by students of UFSC—Universidade Federal de Santa Catarina—Course: Letras/Libras.

FIGURE 2: Illustration by Fabio Selani, deaf cartoonist (*FENEIS* Magazine, issue 44, 2011).

100% of disabled children and youth in school," but we do not agree that regular, inclusive school is the only or even the best space where all these people can receive quality education. To claim that "the policy of inclusive education allows for spectacular growth, and disabled students and non-disabled students interact with one another" causes us great distress, because as much as we want to interact with all Brazilian citizens, we want, above all else, quality education. Inclusive education generally allows for students to interact, but has not guaranteed effective learning for Deaf students. Classes are not taught in our first language and the second language is taught in school in a modality to which we do not have full access. Therefore, to say that "the special needs school is indeed a right, but one that is to be exercised in a complementary and not excluding way" oppresses the potential of many students, undeveloped by the current guidelines of the Ministry of Education of opening inclusive schools to Deaf students.

We are, so far, the only 7 (seven) Brazilian Deaf Doctors, active in the fields of Education and Linguistics. We are all professors at federal universities, namely, five of us at the Federal University of Santa Catarina, one at the Federal University of Rio de Janeiro and one at the Federal University of Santa Maria. We teach and develop research in the fields of Portuguese Linguistics, Libras Linguistics and Deaf Education. We jointly write the present letter to respectfully—but with seriousness adequate for the gravity of the matter—inform that your statements on the matter have no scientific or empirical grounds, as our own (and countless other Brazilian researchers') studies show. Several studies show that the Deaf are better integrated into society if they have attended a bilingual school that used Libras as their first language for interaction and instruction, allowing for the acquisition of written Portuguese language competences, as a second language for reading, social interaction and learning. We are not alone in this defense. Indeed, there is a relatively large number of masters and doctors, researchers of different fields of knowledge, as well as elementary and higher education teachers who identify this reality and join us in our fight. All serious researchers proclaim that BILINGUAL SCHOOL FOR THE DEAF, where the languages of instruction and interactions are Libras (L1) and written Portuguese (L2) are the best academic spaces for learning and educational inclusion for the Brazilian Deaf youth. It pains us to see that these spaces of linguistic acquisition and mutual interaction between peers, speakers of sign language, have been labeled as "segregationist." This is not true! A segregationist and segregating school is that which imposes that Deaf and hearing students be in the same space without having the same opportunities to learn. Deaf students learning in Bilingual Schools, where they are considered and accepted as a linguistic minority is not segregation. Libras is the first language of the majority of the Brazilian Deaf and not just a language spoken by "disabled" persons. From the point of view of human nature, we need nothing else to live as the hearing do, but to have our sign language as a main path for communication and learning. A segregating posture is not a part of us, but of those who do not understand our specificities and needs. This posture is as unacceptable linguistically, anthropologically and philosophically as saying that languages depend on race or climate. We insist, therefore, that schools that offer bilingual education for Deaf children and youth be based not on disability, but on sign language, a wholly accessible language for all who have vision as their main pathway for communication, information and instruction.

This open letter was accompanied by references on Deaf language and education and caused a great impact throughout Brazil, being constantly referenced among academics and parliamentarians alike, as well as in public spaces where educational policies were discussed.

The Brazilian parliament (House of Representatives and Senate), due to resistance by the Deaf movement during the four long years in which the law project of the National Plan of Education was processed, finally acknowledged the strength of FENEIS and accepted the proposal for inclusion of goal 4 in the National Plan of Education, as follows:

> To ensure the availability of bilingual education in Brazilian Sign Language—
> LIBRAS—as a first language and written Portuguese as a second language, to
> Deaf students and students with hearing impairment from 0 (zero) to 17 (seventeen) years of age, *in bilingual schools and classrooms and in inclusive schools*
> in the terms of article 22 of Decree number 5626 of December 22, 2005 and
> articles 24 and 30 of the Convention on the Rights of Persons with Disabilities,
> as well as the adoption of the Braille system of reading for the blind and Deaf-
> blind. (BRASIL, law 13005/2014, emphasis added)

The law was finally sanctioned by President Dilma Rousseff under number 13005/2014. This achievement by the Deaf community for bilingual education underscored the importance of resistance in the parliamentary construction of the Brazilian Deaf community.

Struggle for Untying

Another discussion in the Work Group related to the untying of deaf education from special education. Tying deaf education to special education leads to ambiguous resolutions. A starting point was the Convention on the Rights of Persons with Disabilities whose article 24 draws attention to differentiated education:

> Ensuring that the education of persons, and in particular children, who are
> blind, Deaf or Deafblind, is delivered in the most appropriate languages and
> modes and means of communication for the individual, and in environments
> which maximize academic and social development.

The UN Convention does not tie deaf education to special education. The Convention allows for linguistic education for the Deaf, and the target languages for this education are sign language and written Portuguese. We had troubled times in this Work Group, but we managed to settle on one demand:

> The untying from the field of Special Education is fundamental so that a new formal and public educational architecture may arise consistent with the perspective of Bilingual Deaf Education. For that, it is necessary that the Department of Continued Education, Literacy, Diversity and Inclusion restructures its conception of bilingual deaf education.

The Secretaria de Educação Continuada, Alfabetização, Diversidade e Inclusão (SECADI, Department of Continued Education, Literacy, Diversity and Inclusion) of the Ministry of Education manages several educational questions, such as literacy of youth and adults, environmental education, human rights education, special education, countryside education, indigenous and quilombola education, and education for ethnic-racial relations. The Special Education section is not able to meet the demands of bilingual deaf education, as it is intended to tend to other disabilities with a more clinical perspective. Therefore, the untying of deaf education from special education would lead to the former being grouped with differentiated education, such as indigenous education, bilingual education at the borders, bilingual education for immigrants, quilombola education, and so forth. The report of the Work Group requests this untying as follows:

> Creating a board of directors for bilingual education, in collaboration with the other boards that compose SECADI/MEC, under which the following General Offices will be created, according to demand: the General Office of Bilingual Libras–Portuguese Education for the Deaf, the General Office of Bilingual Education for Indigenous Peoples, the General Office of Bilingual education for Immigrant and Border Populations, the General Office of Bilingual Education in Portuguese and Foreign Languages.

We are a linguistic minority in the struggle for Libras as a language of instruction, for the preservation, listing, and dissemination of sign language, and the training of interpreters. We do not want inclusive education as it is proposed, let alone special education; we want linguistic education and a national linguistic policy that includes our language alongside others, and that is idealized by our Deafhood. As the GT states:

> The National Institute of Historical and Artistic Heritage of the Ministry of Culture performed a categorization of minority Brazilian languages which included indigenous languages, regional varieties of the Portuguese language, immigrant languages, language of the African-Brazilian community, Brazilian sign language and creole languages. As a result of this inventory, there was,

once again, the recognition of Libras a national language, and, consequently, the recognition of the rights of the Deaf communities to have their language—Libras—and culture preserved, which in turn grants the right of these communities to have adequate schools and training of specialized educators who can meet the specific linguistic and cultural demands of these people.

Based on the conception stated in the previous paragraph, a proposal is made to remove bilingual deaf education from special education, moving it to a board or sector of the Ministry of Education that handles national bilingual and multicultural educational policies.

Bilingual schools for the Deaf are specific differentiated spaces for Deaf students. The criterion for selecting students is not a disability but rather their linguistic and cultural characteristics recognized by the Convention on the Rights of Persons with Disabilities (CRPD). The CRPD seeks to promote *the linguistic identity of the Deaf community,* as well as their social development.

Thus, we emphasize that bilingual deaf education be separated from special education, since it does not make sense to us that we Deaf be placed under the Board of Policies of Special Education. This historical connection has left our education subject to the imposition of inclusive education policies that place Deaf students in regular schools with Specialized Educational Service, which are not meeting the linguistic identity needs of the Deaf community.

Right now, this untying and the creation of a new General Office of Bilingual Education are our focus. Nevertheless, the Ministry of Education did not go forward with the recommendations of the Final Report. Some positions continue to be fought. While private initiatives open bilingual schools, allies of MEC/SECADI continue to close schools for the Deaf.

Conception of Linguistic Policies for Deaf People in the Report of the Work Group

Below are listed some of the linguistic goals of bilingual education, as written by the Work Group:

1. Creating a bilingual linguistic environment (Libras and Portuguese) in the educational space.
2. Creating early immersion programs for the acquisition of Libras in child education, with fluent Libras speakers, preferably adults.
3. Ensuring the access to programs of early linguistic stimulation in Libras for the acquisition of the language, based on the diagnosis of Deafness by means of the identification of Deaf babies, in a collaboration between education and health professionals.

4. Providing for the families of Deaf children courses of Libras as an L2, as well as access to the Deaf community through social programs that include house visits for guidance on interaction with the Deaf children.

5. Creating Center of Bilingual Assistance to parents and Deaf babies in bilingual schools for the Deaf.

6. Providing to Deaf school children contact with Libras and written Libras and Portuguese in a playful and creative manner, preferably with Deaf teachers.

7. Ensuring the teaching of reading and written Portuguese using L2 and M2 (second modality) methodologies.

8. Ensuring that Libras is the language of instruction of Deaf children through bilingual, fluent Libras teachers, preferably Deaf.

9. Ensuring the presence of Libras and Portuguese translators to translate literary, teaching and supplementary teaching materials to Libras throughout the education of Deaf persons.

10. Providing the presence of the Deaf community in the education of the Deaf.

11. Ensuring that evaluations be performed in Libras (signed and/or written modalities).

12. Ensuring that evaluations be made available in written Portuguese.

13. Ensuring that evaluations of Portuguese as an L2 and M2 be performed.

14. Build a corpus of Libras that is representative of the uses of Libras across the national territory.

Lastly, some recommendations made by the Work Group, in the last part of the document:

1. Creating a board of directors for bilingual education, in collaboration with the other boards that compose SECADI/MEC, under which the following General Offices will be created, according to demand: the General Office of Bilingual Libras-Portuguese Education for the Deaf, the General Office of Bilingual Education for Indigenous Peoples, the General Office of Bilingual education for Immigrant and Border Populations, the General Office of Bilingual Education in Portuguese and Foreign Languages.

2. Ensuring bilingual deaf education in bilingual classrooms at regular schools in municipalities with small Deaf communities, where there are no specific schools for the Deaf in the greater metropolitan area.

3. Ensuring the teaching of Libras and Portuguese language as L2 and M2 in the education of Deaf students enrolled in regular schools, with the presence of Libras-Portuguese interpreters, preferably Deaf Libras teachers and teachers of Portuguese as an L2 where there is no possibility for Deaf groups.

4. Ensuring that, in addition to what is stated in Law 9394/96, the Basic Education Curriculum for Bilingual Education for the Deaf be elaborated with an

intercultural, visual, and digital perspective, built with the values and interests of the Deaf communities.

5. Regular schools shall include in their Political Pedagogical Project a curricular component of Libras as a second language.

6. Prohibiting that the Portuguese language becomes a factor in excluding Deaf students.

Conclusion

For a quarter century, the Deaf community has manifested their needs for policies that take into account Deaf difference, Deaf identities, sign language, and Deaf interests within daycare centers, schools, and universities, particularly with regards to the availability of an appropriate linguistic, architectural, and pedagogical environment. There was no shortage of resistance and struggle, though very little was actually achieved.

When we reminisce over the resistance, we feel that things were left unsettled. There is still much to do. The Report of the Work Group is filed away at the Ministry of Education, without any real progress. We continue to fight for our demands.

There are only legislative landmarks in Brazil. We lack protection and incentive to implementing these policies. Deaf children are still far from forming a true linguistic identity with the Deaf community, as established by the Convention of the Rights of Persons with Disabilities.

It is worth noting that, among the policy-makers, there are no Deaf members to represent the interests of the Brazilian Deaf people. The risks are too great, since, as hearing members, most do not defend the educational and linguistic policies that are necessary for the survival of Deaf people as citizens.

In the documents containing inclusive policies, one finds the proposal for a bilingual education based around the interests of audist inclusion. The document "National Policy of Special Education in the perspective of Inclusive Education" (BRASIL, 2008) did not take into consideration the document "The Education that We the Deaf Want" of 1999.

References

Brasil. (2010). Decreto 7.387. [Decree 7387]. Institui o Inventário Nacional da Diversidade Linguística [Establishing of the National Inventory of Linguistic Diversity]. Retrieved from: http://www.planalto.gov.br/ccivil_03/_Ato2007 -2010/2010/Decreto/D7387.htm

Brasil. (2009). Decreto n. 6.949, de 25 de agosto de 2009. *Diário Oficial da União,* Brasília, DF [Decree 6949 of August 25, 2009]. Retrieved from: http://www .planalto.gov.br/ccivil_03/_ato2007-2010/2009/decreto/d6949.htm

Brasil. (2014). Ministério da Educação. Secretaria de Alfabetização e Diversidade. *Relatório sobre a política linguística de educação bilíngüe: Língua Brasileira de Sinais e língua Portuguesa do Grupo de Trabalho, designado pelas Portarias nº 1.060/2013 e nº 91/2013 do MEC/SECADI.* [Ministry of Education. Department of Literacy and Diversity. Report on the Linguistic Policy of Bilingual Education – Brazilian Sign language and Portuguese Language made by the Work Group, appointed by decrees number 1060/2013 and 91/2013 by the MEC/SECADI]. Brasília. Retrieved from http://www. bibliotecadigital.unicamp.br/document/?code=56513

Capovilla, F. C. (2011). Sobre a falácia de tratar as crianças ouvintes como se fossem surdas, e as surdas, como se fossem ouvintes ou deficientes auditivas [On the fallacy of treating hearing children as if they were Deaf, and the Deaf as if they were hearing disabled]. In N. R. L. de Sá (Ed.), *Surdos: qual escola?* [The deaf: What school?] Manaus, Brazil: Valer.

Carta aberta ao Ministro da Educação [Open letter to the Ministry of Education]. (2012, June 8). Retrieved from https://docs.google.com/file/d/0B8A54snAq1jAQnBYdVRPYmg1VUk/edit?pli%3D1&pli=1

Dallan, M. S. (2013). Analise discursiva dos estudos surdos em educação [Discourse analysis of Deaf Studies in education]. Campinas, Brazil: Mercado de Letras.

Declaração de Guatemala. (1999). Convenção interamericana para a eliminação de todas as formas de discriminação contra as pessoas portadoras de deficiência. [Inter-American Convention on the Elimination of All Forms of Discrimination Against Persons with Disabilities]. Retrieved from https://www.oas.org/pt/cidh/mandato/Basicos/discapacidad.pdf

FENEIS. (1999). *A educação que nós surdos queremos* [The education we Deaf want]. Document developed in the Pre-Congress of the V Congresso Latino Americano de Educação Bilíngüe para Surdos. Porto Alegre, RS, UFRGS, 1999. Digital text.

FENEIS. (2013, July). A Luta da Comunidade Surda Brasileira pelas Escolas Bilíngües para Surdos no Plano Nacional da Educação-PNE. [The struggle of the Brazilian Deaf community for bilingual schools for the Deaf in the National Plan of Education]. Rio de Janeiro, pp. 10–14.

FENEIS. (2010, September–November). Revista da Feneis. Publicação trimestral da Federação Nacional de Educação e Integração dos Surdos. [*FENEIS* Magazine. Trimonthly publication of the National Federation of Deaf Education and Integration.] p. 41.

FENEIS. (2011, September). Nota sobre a International Disability Alliance (IDA). [Notes on the International Disability Alliance(IDA)]. Rio de Janeiro.

Foucault, M. (2006). Microfísica do poder [Microphysics of power]. (22nd ed.) Rio de Janeiro, Brazil: Graal.

Foucault, M. (2008). A ordem do discurso [The discourse on language]. (16th ed.). São Paulo, Brazil: Loyola.

Lane, H. (1992). A máscara da benevolência: a comunidade surda amordaçada [The mask of benevolence: Disabling the Deaf community]. Lisboa, Portugal: Instituto Piaget.

Lucas, R. (2010, June–August). Conferência Nacional de Educação rejeita a proposta que apoia a escola de surdos [National Education Conference rejects proposal supporting Deaf school]. Revista FENEIS, 40.

Mourão, C. H. N. (2011). Educação de Surdos: Retrocedendo para Milão. Será? [Deaf education: Retreating to Milan?] 4º Seminário Brasileiro de Estudos Culturais e Educação / 1º Seminário Internacional de Estudos Culturais e Educação (pp. 1–12). Canoas, Brazil: Editora da ULBRA.

Perlin, G., & Souza, R. (In press). Política inclusiva e acesso ao ensino público: Resistência e espaços de negociação [Inclusive policy and access to public education: Resistance and negotiating space].

Thompson, K. (2005). Estudos culturais e educação no mundo contemporâneo [Cultural studies and education in the contemporary world]. In R. M. H. Silvereira (Ed.), *Cultura, poder e educação: Um debate sobre estudos culturais em educação* [Education in the contemporary world : A debate on cultural studies in education] (pp. 15–58). Canoas, Brazil: Ed. ULBRA.

UNESCO. (1996). 24.ª Declaração universal dos direitos linguísticos. [Article 24 of the Universal Declaration of Linguistic Rights]. Retrieved from <http://www .dhnet.org.br/direitos/deconu/a_pdf/dec_universal_direitos_linguisticos.pdf>

United Nations. (2011, July). Summit meeting between the Economic and Social Council and members of the International Disability Alliance (IDA. Annual Ministerial Review. New York.

Index

Figures and tables are indicated by "f" and "t" following page numbers.